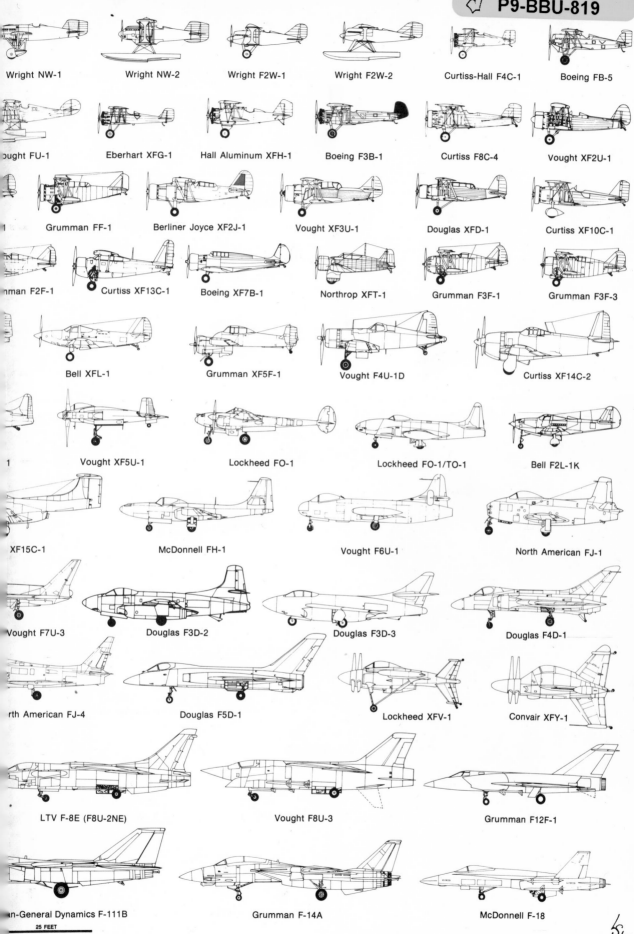

Wright NW-1   Wright NW-2   Wright F2W-1   Wright F2W-2   Curtiss-Hall F4C-1   Boeing FB-5

ought FU-1   Eberhart XFG-1   Hall Aluminum XFH-1   Boeing F3B-1   Curtiss F8C-4   Vought XF2U-1

Grumman FF-1   Berliner Joyce XF2J-1   Vought XF3U-1   Douglas XFD-1   Curtiss XF10C-1

man F2F-1   Curtiss XF13C-1   Boeing XF7B-1   Northrop XFT-1   Grumman F3F-1   Grumman F3F-3

Bell XFL-1   Grumman XF5F-1   Vought F4U-1D   Curtiss XF14C-2

Vought XF5U-1   Lockheed FO-1   Lockheed FO-1/TO-1   Bell F2L-1K

XF15C-1   McDonnell FH-1   Vought F6U-1   North American FJ-1

Vought F7U-3   Douglas F3D-2   Douglas F3D-3   Douglas F4D-1

rth American FJ-4   Douglas F5D-1   Lockheed XFV-1   Convair XFY-1

LTV F-8E (F8U-2NE)   Vought F8U-3   Grumman F12F-1

an-General Dynamics F-111B   Grumman F-14A   McDonnell F-18

25 FEET

U.S. NAVAL FIGHTERS

DEDICATION

To Trendle-San, who opened the door to the future; to Gordy, who opened up the past.

U.S. NAVAL FIGHTERS

By

LLOYD S. JONES

1977

AERO PUBLISHERS, INC.
329 West Aviation Road, Fallbrook, CA 92028

Library of Congress No. 77-20693
ISBN 0-8168-9254-7

Library of Congress Cataloging in Publication Data
Jones, Lloyd S   1931-
   U.S. naval fighters.

   Includes index.
   1. Fighter planes.   2. United States. Navy—
Aviation—History.   3. United States. Marine
Corps—Aviation—History.   I. Title.
VG93.J65   358.4'3   77-20693
ISBN 0-8168-9254-7

Printed and Published in the United States by Aero Publishers, Inc.

TABLE OF CONTENTS

Cross Reference by Manufacturer

INTRODUCTION

The involvement of the United States Navy with the airplane as a potential weapon began some five years before such a machine had actually flown. In March, 1898, Assistant Secretary of the Navy Theodore Roosevelt suggested that Professor Samuel P. Langley's flying machine might have some value as a military weapon. Of course, at this time it was mainly hypothetical since the subject aircraft was only a scale model with a twelve foot wingspan. However, a month later, a joint Army-Navy board encouraged continued development of the project.

By 1909, Navy visionaries were perceiving the use of catapults to launch flying machines from battleship decks; and in November of that year, Lt. George C. Sweet became the first Navy officer to actually be flown in an airplane.

The year 1910 was a significant date in the history of naval aviation for this marked the initial flight of an airplane from a naval ship when on November 14, Eugene Ely flew his Curtiss from the bow of the USS Birmingham. On January 18, 1911, Ely landed on the USS Pennsylvania anchored in San Francisco Bay; then took off and returned to Selfridge Field, San Francisco, thus completing the cycle that proved the airplane could be compatible with naval ships.

The early flying machines were designed for one purpose—to fly. Therefore, there was little to differentiate between the performance characteristics of one type or the other, although some could operate off the water instead of land. It was one of these water-based types which became the first naval airplane, but a set of wheels which could be raised or lowered in flight gave it remarkable versatility allowing operation from both land and sea. Beyond this, the Navy's first airplane could do little more than fly.

During the First World War, the British experimented with towed barges from which scout planes could take off and the first rudimentary aircraft carrier was born. In March 1922, a converted collier, christened USS Langley, was commissioned into the Navy as its first aircraft carrier. The initial U.S. Navy carrier takeoff occurred on October 17, 1922, when a VE-7SF was flown from the USS Langley. The first Navy carrier landing took place a few days later in an Aeromarine 39-B.

In the meantime, naval aircraft were beginning to develop into specific classes. The Navy's first "fighter" types were being refined as racing planes. Several of the renowned Curtiss and Wright racers of the 1920's were not only classed as racing types, but also carried "F" designations on paper; no doubt to justify the expenditure of government funds in such a frivolous manner. However, much technical knowledge was acquired during the Navy's participation in the air racing programs.

With speed and maneuverability an available commodity in aircraft, the Navy fighter quickly took shape and kept pace with similar Army types. Several Army and Navy fighters were developed from the same prototype, each service modifying the basic design for its specific requirements. But the need for short takeoff and landing runs, as well as physical size restrictions for carrier-based planes, finally led to a distinctly different aircraft for the role of naval fighter.

The fighting plane which evolved as a result of the specific requirements of the Navy was strengthened to withstand the shock of slamming onto a carrier deck and jolting to a stop within a few feet. It could surge forward and quickly become airborne with a combat load within the confining length of the carrier deck. As the planes became larger, folding wings were introduced to allow the compacting of several planes in a restricted area. Even the cockpit was tailormade for the Naval aviator to enable him to view the carrier deck during critical landing approaches. With many hours of flying done over water, provisions were made to carry flotation bags which would inflate with compressed gas in the event a ditching was forced upon the pilot. These bags were either strapped to the fuselage sides or built into compartments in the wings or fuselage and were intended to keep the plane afloat until a rescue could be effected, or at least until the pilot could extricate himself from the aircraft.

The air-cooled radial engine found favor with the Navy who preferred it to the heavier liquid-cooled inline types with their complicated, and sometimes vulnerable, radiator systems. Among the advantages of the radial engine were smaller proportions coupled with greater range and climb rate, besides the obvious simplicity of maintenance—an important factor in the confines of a carrier hangar. At the Navy's urging, such engineering masterpieces as the Wright J-5 Whirlwind and Pratt & Whitney's Hornet and Wasp were developed, benefitting also the Army and commercial aviation.

On March 27, 1914, an attempt was made to serialize all the planes in the budding air fleet for identification, using a combination of two letters and a number, but no continuous series was established. The first true serialization began on February 10, 1916, when the designator A-51 was assigned as the beginning of a continuous numerical sequence with a maximum of four digits. The A- was dropped at #9207, and when 9999 was reached a new series of four digits was begun at 0001. In January of 1941, when this list reached 7303, a completely new range was adopted beginning at 00001. In 1945, a six-digit sequence came into use, and since it will take one-million airframes to run through these numbers, it is likely to be some time before another series is begun. Marine Corps aircraft are included in this serial, or Bureau Number (BuNo) sequence.

In March of 1922, a precise identification system was adopted to classify the airframe by manufacturer, mission, and model through a group of letters and numbers. Each manufacturer was assigned a letter to be used as a part of this designation. Every military mission also received a letter. A sequential number was added to these letters to identify the type if more than one of a given type had been built by a company. For example, the Vought F7U-3P: F= Fighter (mission), 7= seventh fighter design by manufacturer, U= Vought (airframe manufacturer), -3= third subtype of the F7U, P= airframe modified for photo-reconnaissance role. This system of identification was used by the Navy until September 18, 1962, when the Defense Department made a move to simplify classifications and eliminate conflicting designations by the Navy and Air Force when referring to the same airplane. Several Navy aircraft found roles with the Air Force and received new designations when operated by that service. For example, the McDonnell F4H Phantom II was called F-110 by the Air Force, yet it was basically the same plane as used by the Navy. The new DoD order made both versions of the Phantom the F-4 with a letter denoting subtype. Thus, the F-4B was originally the Navy's F4H-1 and the F-4C was the new designator of the Air Force's F-110. The entire military designation program began again at "-1" for every aircraft type and all subsequent aircraft now receive successive numbers regardless of the branch of service using them.

This history of the U. S. Navy/Marine fighters is presented in chronological sequence to illustrate the technical development of the type. The specifications for these fighters and the basis for the three-view drawings were obtained from official Navy documents or direct from the manufacturer's records and files whenever possible. In some cases where official documentation was not available, data was compiled from sources considered factual by historical authorities. The reader must bear in mind, however, that even official weights and performance specifications are average, or were actually achieved under strictly-controlled conditions.

Like the Army, the Navy conformed to the standard of one or two .30 or .50 cal. machine guns in their fighters. The folly of such light weaponry became apparent only when World War II began and banks of .50 cal. guns capable of shattering enemy fighters, were installed. Today, the rotary cannon and air-to-air missiles form the basic fighter armament, and these are aided by radar direction.

America's naval fighting force is made up of the most advanced weapons in aviation technology, but the most perfect system in the aircraft is still the human crew making the final judgment in the hottest combat situation. As highly refined and technically advanced as a machine can be made, it is only as good as the man under the canopy. This book, then, is a tribute to the American Naval aviator, yesterday, today, and into the future.

ACKNOWLEDGEMENTS

There are many individuals whose cooperation and assistance are greatly responsible for this book. To them I give my most sincere appreciation:

Gordon S. Williams, Boeing; Harry Gann, Douglas; Eldon Corkhill, LTV; William Wagner, Ryan; Dustin W. Carter, AAHS; Gene Boswell, Rockwell International; Rick DeMeis and Andre Hubbard, Grumman; John McGrath, McDonnell; Bill Larkins; Fred Jache; Roy Dwyer; Al Lloyd; Ray Wagner; Warren Bodie; the United States Navy and Marine Corps; and the many others whose efforts have touched this book.

A special note of thanks for three people whose assistance far exceeds any means of expressing adequate thanks: Gordy Williams, who so generously shares his vast collection of photos with the readers of this book; Jack Leynnwood for his beautiful rendering which adorns the jacket; and especially my wife, Peggy, for her untiring help in completing this project.

LSJ

PHOTO CREDITS

Photo credits are noted on every photo in this volume. To conserve space in the captions, the following Corporate names were abbreviated:

ABBREVIATIONS	COMPLETE NAMES
(1) Bell	Textron Bell Aerospace Division
(2) Boeing	Boeing Company
(3) Convair	Convair Division, General Dynamics Corp.
(4) Douglas	McDonnell Douglas
(5) General Dynamics	General Dynamics Corp.
(6) Grumman	Grumman Aerospace Corp.
(7) Hughes	Hughes Aircraft Co.
(8) Lockheed	Lockheed Aircraft Co.
(9) LTV	Ling-Temco-Vought
(10) North American (Rockwell)	North American (Rockwell International)
(11) Republic	Fairchild Republic Co.
(12) Ryan	Teledyne Ryan Aeronautics Co.

Vought's VE-7 was originally built as a trainer, but became the Navy's first fighter.   *Vought*

In the midst of World War I, America's lagging aviation industry valiantly set about to re-establish itself as a major influence in aircraft design. Caught short by the war, American industry had few original combat designs, and even these were considered below the standard displayed by the European combatants.

The Lewis & Vought Company, formed in 1917, constructed a two-place trainer which bore a strong resemblance to several noted European designs. Power was provided by a Wright-built Hispano Suiza engine similar to that used by the French Spad fighter. Pilots who flew the VE-7 soon learned that, while it was intended to serve as a trainer, its performance compared well with the latest European fighters. Realizing its possible value in the fighting role, the U. S. Army placed two orders totalling 1,000 planes for an improved model to be designated VE-8. Conclusion of the war brought a cancellation of these contracts before the VE-8 was built, but by this time the Navy could see a great potential use for the VE-7 in a wide range of operations.

The Navy received its first VE-7 in May 1920, and soon ordered it into production.

The small Lewis & Vought organization was unable to handle a large production order and arrangements were made for the Naval Aircraft Factory to assist in the construction of the planes. Between the two plants, the Navy was supplied with 128 of the Vought-designed biplanes.

The fighter model of the VE-7 was modified for single-seat operation and designated VE-7S. The forward cockpit was faired over and a single Vickers .30 cal. machine gun was mounted to the left side of the cowl, synchronized to fire through the propeller arc. In case of an emergency in which the plane might be forced to land at sea, some of the single-seaters were fitted with flotation gear and identified as VE-7SF. This equipment, which was to become standard on Navy fighters for many years, consisted of inflatable bags tucked away inside or strapped to the side of the airplane. In the event of an emergency landing at sea, the bags would be inflated and support the crippled plane until a rescue could be effected.

The Navy's first two fighter squadrons, VF-1 and VF-2 were provided with Vought VE-7's. The U. S. Navy's first carrier takeoff

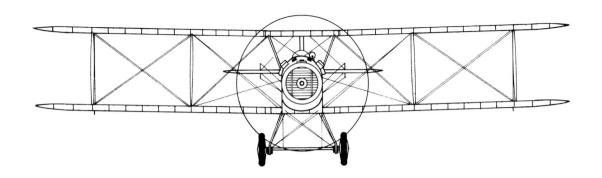

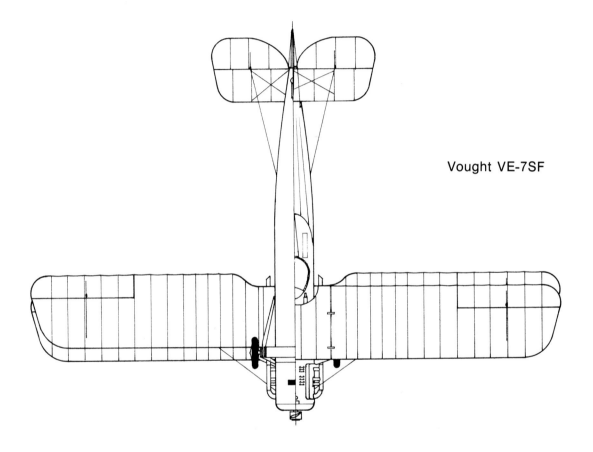

Vought VE-7SF

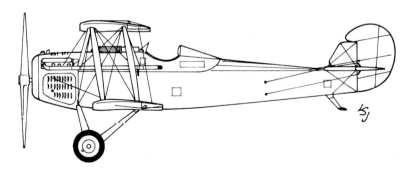

25 FEET

A VE-7 squadron in flight. The VE-7 was the first Navy plane to take off from a carrier, and was issued to the Navy's first two fighter squadrons, VF-1 and VF-2. *Navy*

was made on October 17, 1922, when Lt. V. C. Griffin flew his VE-7SF from the USS Langley anchored in the York River. Although Vought's plane was intended as a trainer in World War I, it more than proved that American designers were capable of engineering a first-rate machine matching the best European fighters. For six years, the VE-7's were used as first-line equipment in the Navy; and three of the planes were still assigned to the Langley in 1927. The last VE-7 was retired from a combat unit in 1928.

The VE-7SF single-seat fighter was a double-bay biplane with a wingspan of 34 feet 1 inch. Area of the two wings was 284½ square feet. Overall length was 24 feet 5 inches; height was 8 feet 7 inches. Empty weight was 1,505 pounds; loaded the VE-7SF weighed 2,100 pounds. The Wright-built Hispano Suiza E-2 inline engine was capable of providing 180 h.p. with which the fighter could achieve a maximum speed of 121 m.p.h. at sea level. Service ceiling was 15,000 feet and enough fuel was carried to provide a range of 291 miles.

The TS-1 was designed by the Naval Aircraft Factory and built by Curtiss. It was the first Navy plane specifically designed as a fighter.
Gordon S. Williams

With the VE-7's in service, the Navy's fledgling fighter squadrons were at least in the air. But as a fighter, the operational capabilities of the modified VE-7 trainers were severely limited and the need for a true shipboard fighter was clear. Engineers at the Naval Aircraft Factory evolved a simple biplane design which would be powered by a new 200 h.p. Lawrance J-1 air-cooled radial engine. Curtiss received a contract to construct the original example, which was identified as the TS-1, BuNo A-6248.

The TS-1 arrived at the Navy's flight test center at Anacostia on May 9, 1922. Of straight forward design, its most notable feature was the location of the boxy fuselage suspended between the two untapered wings. The center section of the lower wing was fattened to accommodate a 50 gallon fuel tank which could be jettisoned if necessary. When delivered, the TS-1 mounted wheels; but testing of the little fighter was also done with a pair of wooden floats designed by the NAF. Though the TS-1 was the first fighter specifically designed for carrier operations, the added versatility of the floats allowed its use on other types of naval vessels. Catapults were not required

for launching the TS-1's as they were simply lowered over the side by a crane, and recovered in the same manner.

The successful evaluation of the TS-1 led the Navy to order thirty-four of the fighters from Curtiss in late 1922, with the first of these arriving on the Langley in December. Five more of the fighters were built by the Naval Aircraft Factory for cost comparison. Four additional airframes were constructed by the NAF in order to evaluate performance with two types of water-cooled inline engines. Two of these planes, labeled TS-2's, were each fitted with a 240 h.p. Aeromarine U-8-D engine; the other two were classed as TS-3's and mounted the 180 hp Wright-Hispano E-2 engine. The TS-2 weighed 207 pounds more than the radial-powered TS-1, but despite this it was 8 mph faster.

Nevertheless, the radial engine had proven its capabilities and the Navy was more than satisfied with its performance. With the Navy's encouragement, the Pratt & Whitney Company was formed to develop and refine the Lawrance J-1 engine used on the TS-1. If the Navy was to have a first-rate fighter, it must also have a reliable engine

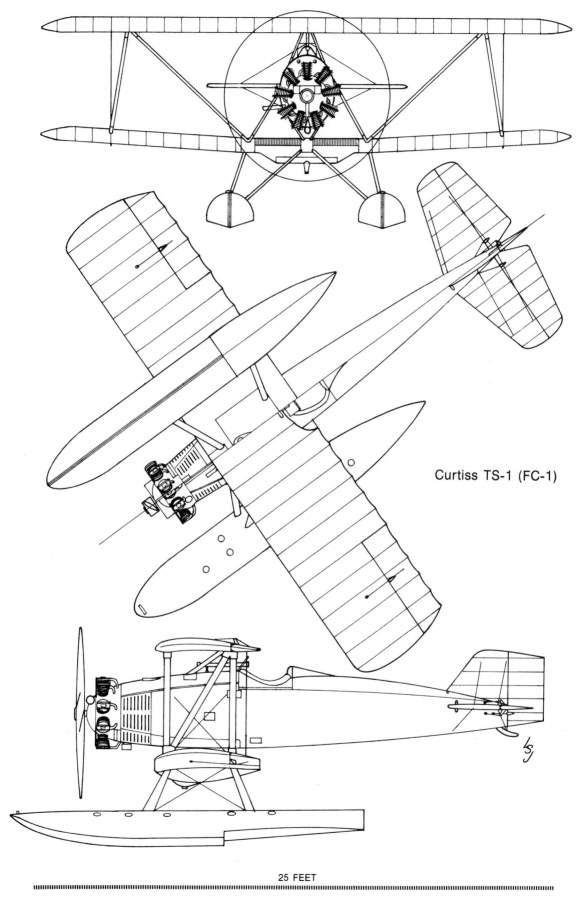

Curtiss TS-1 (FC-1)

25 FEET

Floats and wheels were interchangeable on the TS-1. This is the first Curtiss-built example. Gordon S. Williams

Navy fighter squadron VF-1 shows off its TS-1's. These planes based on the USS Langley. Gordon S. Williams

comparable in performance to the more complex liquid-cooled powerplants favored by the Army and many of the European manufacturers. Navy designers were convinced that the radial engine could be made to deliver enough power to compensate for the increase in frontal drag area over the slimmer inline machines. The result of this dedication was embodied in the splendid Wright J-5 Whirlwind and the renowned Pratt & Whitney Wasp and Hornet, all descendants of the Lawrance J-1.

During the operational life of the TS-1's a new designating system was adopted and they were classed as FC-1's.

The first Navy carrier fighter had a wingspan of 25 feet with an area of 228 square feet. From propeller to rudder, it measured 22 feet 1 inch. Height was 9 feet. With the Lawrance J-1, or later the Wright J-5, the TS-1 landplane had a speed of 125 mph and a service ceiling of 16,250 feet. Range on its fifty gallons of fuel was 482 miles. With floats, the range was reduced to 339 miles; ceiling was 14,450 feet; and top speed was 123 mph. Armament for both models consisted of one .30 cal. machine gun on the cowl.

Curtiss/NAF TS-1's served in the Navy's fighting and reserve squadrons until 1929.

Note the bulge in the center section of the lower wing. This housed the fuel tank. VF-1 operated float-equipped TS-1's from battleships for a while.
Gordon S. Williams

CURTISS
R2C, R3C (F2C, F3C)

The Curtiss R2C-2. Although it was officially a racer, it was also assigned the F2C designation to justify its expense.
Gordon S. Williams

Racing planes and fighting planes have several parallels within their design parameter. Indeed, if you were to mount offensive weapons on a speedy racer you would have a fairly presentable fighter. Bearing this in mind, it is easy to understand why the military often entered their most advanced fighters in the National Air Races. It did not take long before the fighters were being altered for better racing performance; and finally, entirely new aircraft configured expressly for competition were found on the starting lines.

Race promoters, realizing that the flashy military racers thrilled the spectators, encouraged their appearance and there were no restrictions in the armed forces rules which prevented their participation. The result was a generation of military aircraft conceived expressly for competitive racing on an international scale. Through the twenties and thirties, the hero of the day was the daring young race pilot.

The Navy's first entries in this exciting new field were the two inline-powered NAF TS- modifications, the TS-2 and TS-3. Reclassed TR-2 and -3, the converted fighters were not notably successful. On the

other hand, Curtiss, who already had some racing experience with a triplane-fighter prototype and two privately financed racers, undertook the construction of two competition machines intended expressly for the Navy as racers.

Departing from the Navy's favored radial engine for its racing, Curtiss mounted a 450 hp Curtiss D-12 to the firewall of the sleek biplanes. Designated simply Curtiss Racers, they promptly set a series of world's records and won the 1921 Pulitzer Race at 176.7 mph. When the Navy accepted the two planes, they were designated variously as CR-1 through -4 depending on modifications. At the hands of the Navy's pilots, the CR's continued to collect trophies and records, reaching a maximum speed of 194 mph.

With the outstanding success of Curtiss CR's, the Navy was encouraged to refine the design and two R2C-1's were ordered for the 1923 National Air Races. Now the fame of the Navy's racers was widespread and such remarkable contrivances clearly cost money. Perhaps there were some misgivings about the expenditure of large sums of military funds for sporting events; or the

18

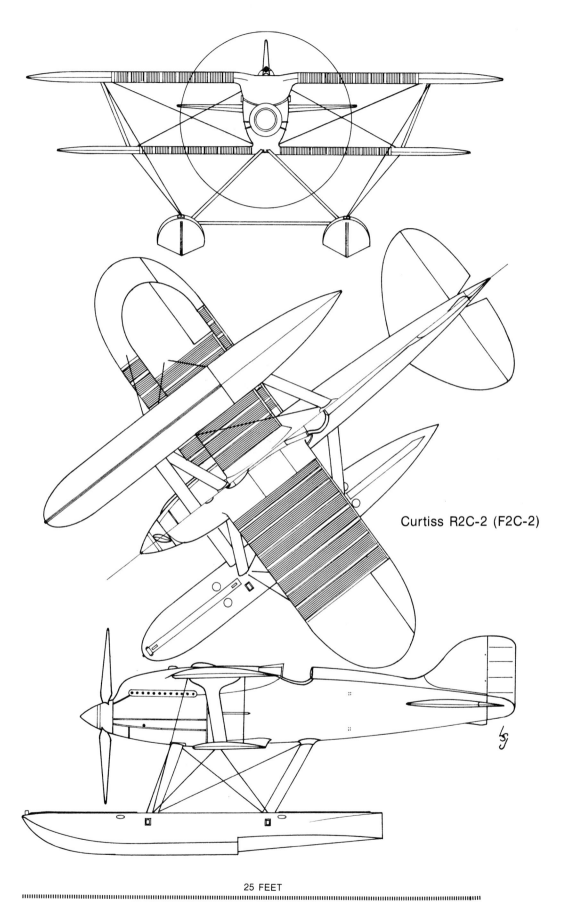

Curtiss R2C-2 (F2C-2)

25 FEET

The parallel lines on the wings of the R2C-2 are the flush radiators.   *Gordon S. Williams*

Navy may have recognized the militaristic value of such fine craft, but in any case, the new R2C-1's and their sisters, R3C-1's, were designated on paper as F2C-1 and F3C-1 fighters.

In appearance, the R2C-1 was similar to the CR's. A big Curtiss D-12A provided 488 hp to fling the trim racer along at 266 mph. All four wing surfaces were used to cool the water flowing through the engine to keep its temperature within the operating range. Living up to expectations, the R2C-1's took first and second in the 1923 Pulitzer, with speeds of 243.68 mph and 241.77 mph. In 1924, the second R2C-1 was sold to the Army and redesignated R-8, but it crashed before it could repeat its feat at the 1924 races.

For the 1925 races, the Army joined the Navy in ordering three more of the speedsters, these being the R3C-1's. Externally, the new racer was virtually identical to the R2C, but concealed beneath the carefully contoured metal of the cowling was a 610 hp version of the big Curtiss D-12 engine.

By the time the 1924 Pulitzer event was run, the Curtiss racers were competing against themselves. It became an Army versus Navy show with the two planes flying separately for elapsed time. In this case, the Army was victor.

The R3C's could be fitted with floats for water racing. Thus equipped, they were classed R3C-2's. They continued racing and compiling speed records until the 1926 Schneider Trophy Race when the R3C-3, a 700 hp Packard-powered modification, capsized and the R3C-4, with a 700 hp Curtiss, failed to finish. The R3C-2 which had captured the 1925 Pulitzer finished second and thus ended the Curtiss Navy Racer saga. This R3C-2 was retired to the Smithsonian Institution and has been displayed both at the National Air and Space Museum and the Air Force Museum.

The R2C and R3C racers were single-seat biplanes with liquid-cooled inline engines. Cooling was achieved by forcing water through a series of brass channels wrapped completely around the wings. The air flowing past the wings cooled the water which circulated between the engine and the wings. This method was efficient and the radiators created virtually no drag, but they would certainly be a problem on a plane subject to gunfire. It is interesting to note, though, that despite the Navy's avowed preference for air-cooled engines, the in-line engines actually produced superior performance and were notably trouble-free in their racing service.

The dimensions of the R2C and R3C were nearly the same, differing in height and

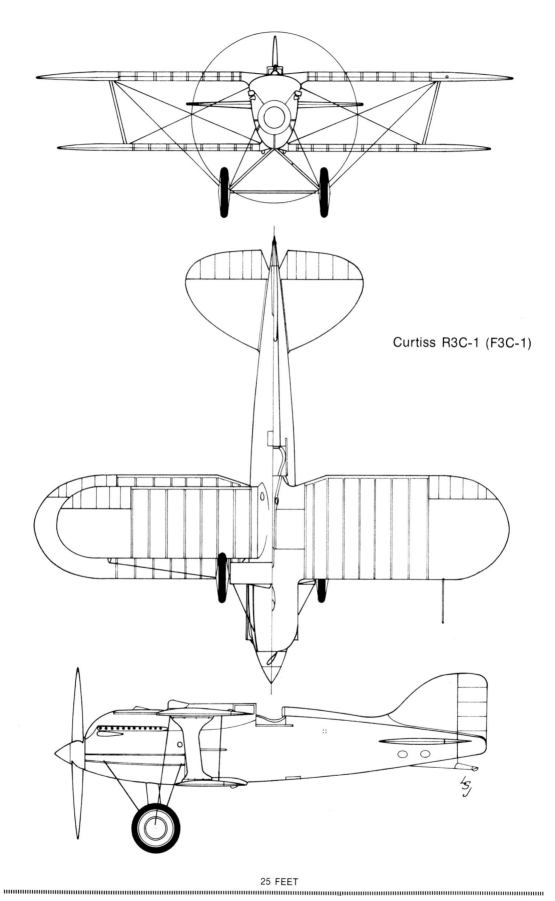

Curtiss R3C-1 (F3C-1)

25 FEET

wing area. Wingspan was 22 feet, the R2C area was 144 square feet to the R3C's area of 149 square feet. Length of the planes was 19 feet 8½ inches. Height of the R2C, at 8 feet 1 inch, was 7 inches lower than the R3C.

The maximum speed reached by the R2C was 266 mph at sea level, while the R3C only registered 265 mph. Of the several engines which were used in the two types, the Curtiss D12A in the R2C-1/-2 was rated at 488 hp; the V-1400 used by the R3C-1/-2 had 610 hp. The R3C-3's Packard 2A-1500 developed 700 hp; and as the R3C-4, a 700 hp Curtiss V-1550 was used. With the different engines, the weight would vary, but the original figure for the two types show an empty weight of 1,677 pounds with a gross of 2,150 pounds.

Due to engine and landing gear changes altering designations, it appears that a whole fleet of Curtiss racers was constructed. In fact, only two R2C's (BuNo A-6691 and 6692) and three R3C's (BuNo A-6978, 6979 and 7054) were built.

The R3C-2 shown here was more powerful than the R2C's. R3C's won both the 1925 Pulitzer and Schneider Cup races.
Gordon S. Williams

With wheels, this became the R3C-1. Note the twisted tire cover as the plane moves for takeoff.
Gordon S. Williams

A 700 hp Curtiss V-1550 engine was installed for the 1926 Schneider Cup Race and this ship was designated R3C-4.   *Gordon S. Williams*

The R3C-4 poses on its alternate alighting gear. The Curtiss racers dominated the competition from 1921 to 1925.   *Gordon S. Williams*

The Navy-Wright "Mystery Racer" looked powerful but suffered a serious heating problem during its only race.   *Gordon S. Williams*

At the same time the Navy ordered the Curtiss Racers in June of 1921, a request was submitted to the Wright Aeronautical Corp. to draw up an engine which could produce 500 hp on straight gasoline. It was to be simple to service and fit interchangeably on the same mounts as the famous Liberty engine then in use. Designated Wright T-2, the first engine was completed and bench tested by May 1922, and delivered 525 hp. Enthused by this success, the Navy then decided to enter the engine in the 1922 Pulitzer race to be held in October. Of course, they would need an airplane in order to do this, so on July 5, 1922, the Airplane Department of Wright Aeronautical Corporation was formed.

Within three months, the Navy-Wright NW-1 "Mystery Racer" was prepared—the result of round-the-clock effort by Wright's designers and engineers. Even without considering the unusually short development time, the NW-1 was a remarkable piece of equipment. By contemporary standards it was monstrous, both in size and appearance. It was by far the largest racer entered in competition and featured a sesquiplane format with the fuselage perched on the upper

wing in such a manner as to appear as though it were already airborne.

The first flight of the Navy-Wright racer took place just three days before the Pulitzer race. The upper engine cowling was not completed before the initial flight and the cylinder heads were exposed, but no problems were encountered during the test.

The day of the race, October 14, 1922, found the NW-1 assigned to the second of three heats. Its competitors were four Curtiss racers. Taking off, the Navy's "Mystery Racer" responded well and the big Wright engine performed as planned. However, the rising oil temperature soon began to give concern. The close-fitting cowling, finally installed, retained the engine heat and the oil exceeded its operating temperature. It was not long before a thick trail of smoke traced the NW-1's path around the race course and it became necessary for the pilot to consider a premature landing. Part of the course extended over Lake St. Clair, near Detroit, and it was here that the pilot found himself when the red-hot engine ceased functioning. The extreme low position of the lower wing was not conducive to ditching and the "Mystery Racer" flipped

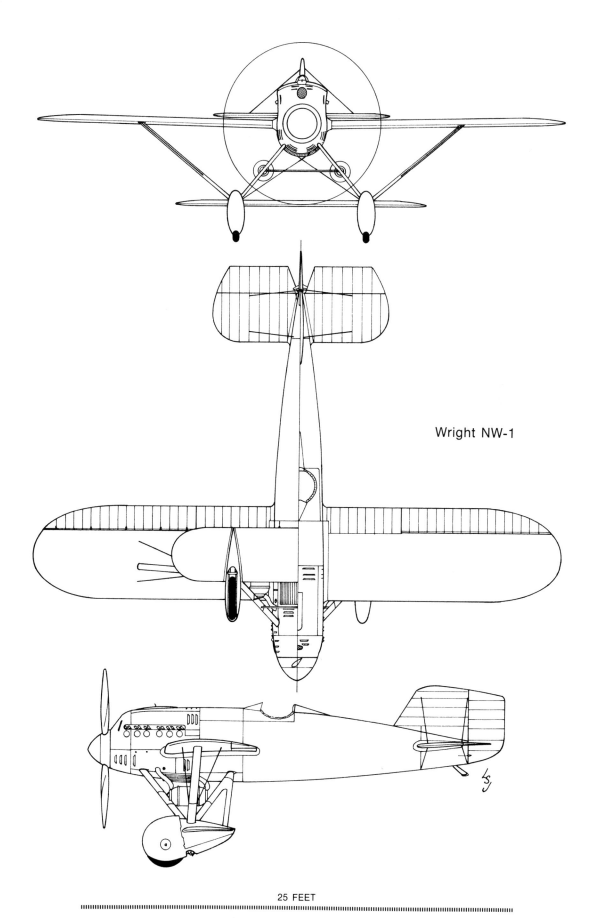

Wright NW-1

25 FEET

After the crash of the NW-1, a second example of the Wright racer was built. It was converted into a conventional biplane and had floats for the 1923 Schneider Cup Race, but the engine blew apart during pre-race tests.

over and sank in the mud. The plane was written-off but the pilot emerged unscathed.

The performance of the NW-1 was encouraging enough to justify completion of a second example, and the NW-2 was ready for testing in January 1923. The most noticeable differences between it and its predecessor were the unfaired wheels and exposed cylinder heads. In this form, the NW-2 made a few test flights before it was sent back to the shops for conversion to a float plane for the 1923 Schneider Cup race in England. The revisions created a new airplane of standard biplane form. The barrel-like Lamblin radiators used on the NW-1 were replaced with flush wing units. The engine was another Wright T-2 capable of 650 hp. Before the race, an adjustable three-bladed propeller was mounted. The pitch was set to enable the powerful T-2 engine to

develop its greatest revolutions for the race; but during a practice run over the Schneider course, the big engine disintegrated, plunging the NW-2 into the water. Once again, the pilot escaped unharmed, but the Navy-Wright "Mystery Racer" passed into oblivion without completing a contest.

The NW-1 wing spanned 30 feet 6 inches and had a total of 180 square feet including the half wing between the wheels. Length was 24 feet; height was 11 feet. Fuel capacity was 56 gallons. Unloaded, the NW-1 weighed 2,480 pounds, and gross weight was 3,000 pounds. During the Pulitzer race, the NW-1 reached 209 mph.

As prepared for the Schneider Cup race, the NW-2 had a 27 foot 11 inch wingspan with an area of 266 square feet. Length over the floats was 28 feet 4½ inches. Maximum speed achieved was 204 mph.

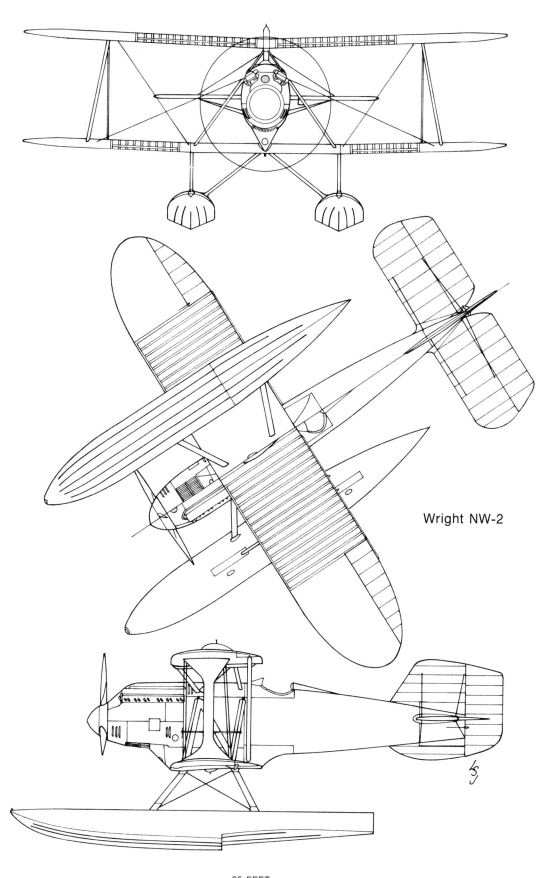

Wright NW-2

25 FEET

The bright-red F2W-1 was actually intended for racing but was given a fighter designation.

Gordon S. Williams

In spite of the misfortunes which plagued the Wright NW-1 and -2 racers, Wright Aeronautical Corp. was determined to create an airplane capable of besting the champion Curtiss planes. The NW's had proven the theories of both airframe and engine, and the accidents were no indication of a lack of engineering prowess by the Wright team.

A new liquid-cooled engine, called Tornado, was constructed which could put out as much as 780 hp and safely turn up to 2,-300 rpm during a race. To absorb this great power, Wright built a compact wooden biplane with flush wing-mounted radiators and just enough fuel to complete the race in which it was to compete. Even the cooling system was designed so carefully that it was effective only for one-half hour at full power. The original designation of this craft was TX, for Tornado Experimental. With it, Wright hoped to prove they could build an airplane with performance exceeding that of the fastest racers then flying. Surely, such an airplane would be a candidate for adaptation into a fighter; and with the second TX, the planes were officially designated F2W-1. Obviously, no

fighter could be effective with a fuel capacity limiting it to a half-hour so the second F2W-1 was provided with twice as much fuel. Nevertheless, in spite of the fighter designation, the F2W's were racers, plain and simple.

The first F2W-1 began flight testing on August 27, 1923. No doubt, the little racer had all the earmarks of a champion as it responded well and was easy to fly. In measured dashes the F2W-1 averaged 238 mph, and then bettered this later with a sizzling 247.7 mph. The two F2W-1's were prepared for the 1923 Pulitzer Race. On the rudders appeared the Bureau Numbers of each plane plus the legend "Navy Wright Fighter," just in case anyone wanted to know.

The first F2W-1 began the race and streaked around the course four times, its fastest lap indicating 240.3 mph, ultimately winning third place in the race. The first heat had taken just under 33 minutes and the bright red and white racer zoomed upward to clear the course for the next heat. At 1,500 feet, the powerful Tornado engine became silent—the thirty minute fuel supply had been exhausted! Nosing downward, the

28

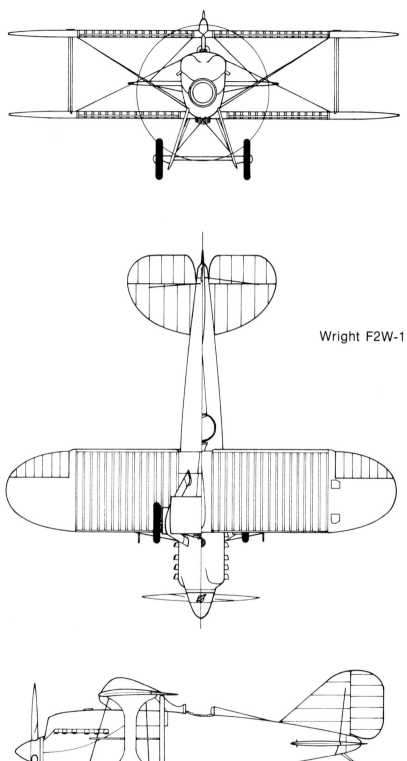

Wright F2W-1

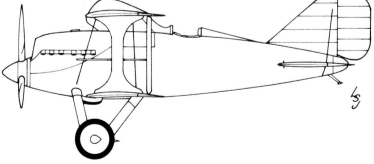

25 FEET

Wright F2W-2

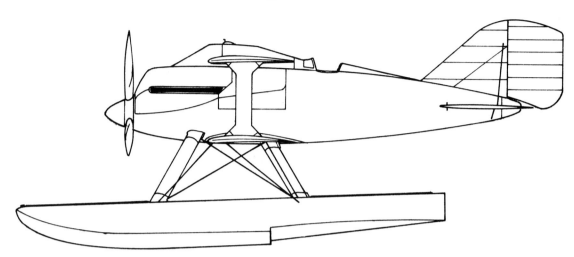

pilot aimed for a convenient haystack to cushion the anticipated impact. The pilot was thrown clear, suffering little more than bruised pride; but the little red racer was a total loss.

The remaining F2W-1 with its greater fuel load finished the race just .06 mph slower than the first Wright racer for fourth place. Returned to the Wright plant, the surviving racer was groomed for the 1924 Schneider Trophy Race which was to be held at Bay Shore Park, Maryland. As in the case of the NW before it, the F2W-1 was ex-tensively altered and a pair of large floats reposed where the wheels had previously been attached.

From the beginning, the F2W-2, as the racer was now known, was dogged with problems. The original rudder was too small for a water takeoff, the stalling speed was dangerously high, and it was unstable when it finally became airborne. On its sole flight, the tremendous torque of the huge Tornado engine flipped the racer onto its back during landing. The last of the four Wright racers had completed its bizarre cycle.

The second F2W-1 was modified into the F2W-2 floatplane for the 1924 Schneider Trophy Race. Because of its poor flying qualities it made only one flight and was wrecked on landing.

While the Wright-designed racers had good performance, they suffered technical flaws that led to their demise.
Gordon S. Williams

The plywood-covered wings of the F2W-1 had a span of 22 feet 6 inches. Most of the surface was covered with the brass tubing making up the radiator. Area was 174 square feet. Overall length was 19 feet 9 inches. Height was 9 feet 4 inches. Empty weight was 2,468 pounds and gross, with the large 60 gallon capacity fuel tank, was 3,086 pounds. When modified to the Schneider Cup configuration, the wingspan was increased to 23 feet, but area was reduced to 170 square feet. Overall length, including floats, was 26 feet 1½ inches and

height was 10 feet 10½ inches.

FOOTNOTE:

Although it is not the purpose of this history to delve into air racing, these planes had a direct bearing on the development of Navy fighters and actually filled a designation gap in the classification of this combat type. For additional material on these planes, we recommend the articles in Historical Aviation Album, Vols. IV and V by Thomas G. Foxworth, and the series of Racing Planes and Air Races by Reed Kinert, Aero Publishers.

The Curtiss-Hall F4C-1 was an exercise in all-metal frame construction.   *Gordon S. Williams*

Charles W. Hall was an aircraft engineer who's interest in the use of aluminum for airframe structure led to the eventual forming of the Hall Aluminum Aircraft Company in 1927. Prior to this time, Hall was an engineer for Curtiss. In 1923, the Navy drew up a proposal for an experimental model of the TS-1 using lightweight aluminum for its framework instead of wood. With Hall's experience working with the metal, he was selected to develop the revised airframe.

Two metal-structured TS-1's were ordered (BuNo A-6689 and 90) and designated F4C-1. Since the object was to make a direct comparison between the wooden and metal planes, the F4C-1's were kept as close to the original design as possible. The most obvious difference was the location of the lower wing, which was attached directly to the fuselage on the metal plane. The wings were constructed of tubular spars with stamped dural ribs, and aluminum tubing forming a Warren truss made up the fuselage. Like the TS-1 the entire structure was covered with fabric but the powerplant was a 200 hp Wright J-3.

Flight testing of the first F4C-1 began on September 4, 1924; the second airframe was destined for static testing. Much interest was generated in the metal structure, and the testing was followed closely by both civil and military builders. The F4C's weighed 214 pounds less than the TS-1, but were considerably stronger. This resulted in an increase in maneuverability and a maximum speed of 132 mph. This was an improvement of 7 mph, or 5.6% better than the TS-1. Test pilots were in agreement that the F4C performed quite well and was a definite improvement over the TS, but the TS-1's design was already nearing obsolescence and the metal airframe was not sufficiently advanced to merit production. The F4C presented one other major drawback to full-scale production: manufacturing costs for the all-metal structure were prohibitive at this point in time.

The F4C was delivered to VF-1 for service evaluation and it was absorbed into the squadron, remaining with them into 1927. The wingspan of 25 feet was the same as the TS-1, but the area of 185 square feet was considerably less. Overall length was 18 feet 4 inches; height was 8 feet 9 inches. Maximum speed achieved during tests was 132

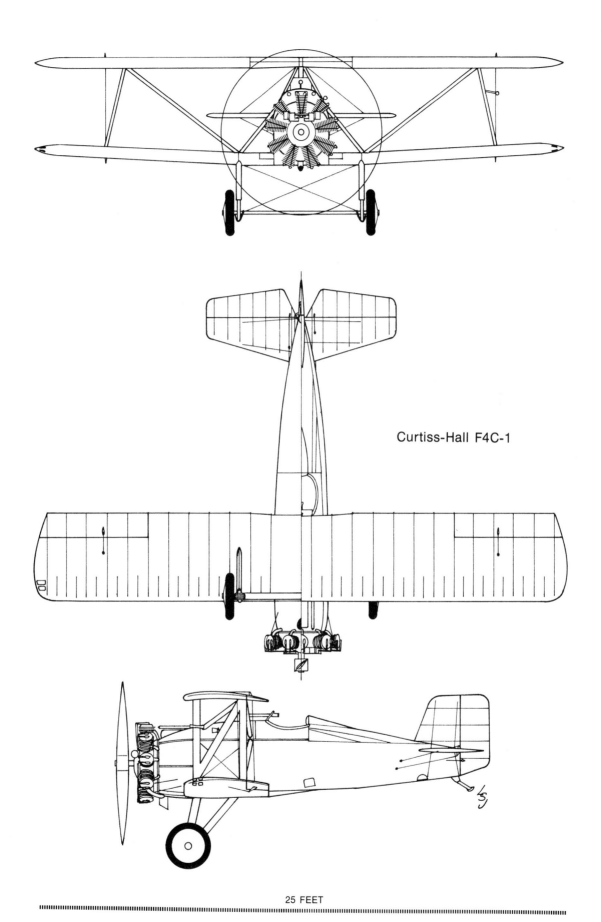

Curtiss-Hall F4C-1

25 FEET

mph. Fifty gallons of fuel gave the F4C-1 a range of 525 miles. Service ceiling was 17,400 feet with the first 5,000 feet reached in 3.9 minutes. Two .30 cal. machine guns with 250 rpg were installed in the cowling ahead of the cockpit.

Even without a production contract, the aluminum-framed Curtiss fighter paved the way for the next generation of combat planes by proving the attributes of the lightweight metal.

The F4C-1 was lighter and stronger than the TS-1 from which it was developed but production costs were prohibitive.   *Gordon S. Williams*

The lines of the TS-1 are apparent in this view. The main difference was the location of the lower wing to the fuselage.   *Gordon S. Williams*

The hooks on the spreader bar of this FB-5 were intended to guide the plane between rows of cables on the carrier deck.

Boeing

Boeing's entry into the naval fighting arena came in December 1924, when an order for fourteen Boeing Model 15's was accepted. Based on a privately funded original design, Boeing's fighter had already been ordered by the Army as the PW-9 and the first 10 of the Navy's planes, called FB-1, were virtually identical to the Army machines. These ten fighters were assigned to the Marine Corps Squadrons VF-1M, VF-2M and VF-3M.

The FB-1's were constructed with fabric-covered wooden wings, but the fuselage frame was made of welded steel tubing. A 435 hp Curtiss D-12 liquid-cooled engine provided speeds up to 167 mph at sea level. Since they were intended only for operation from airfields, no provision was made for arresting gear.

The next two examples of the Boeing fighter were structually altered to withstand the stress of operations on the carrier Langley. These were designated FB-2. A straight-across axle, as opposed to the in-verted Vee (or split) axle, identified these planes as well as the installation of arresting gear. VF-2 received these planes on Christmas Day, 1925, and subsequent flights indicated only minor changes would be necessary to make them acceptable for fleet operations. These changes were incor-

porated into the production FB-5's.

Twenty-seven FB-5's were ordered and became the first Navy fighters intended from the outset for carrier operations. The FB-5 mounted a 525 hp Packard 2A-1500, a powerplant which had been evaluated on two FB-3's (a third FB-3 was lost before delivery). The production version FB-5 also differed from the rest of the series with the enlargement of the rudder by addition of an aerodynamic balance and an increase in the wing stagger. The first FB-5 flew on Oc-tober 7, 1926, and deliveries were com-pleted on January 21, 1927. The planes were barged from the Boeing plant in Seat-tle directly to the Langley, anchored in Seat-tle Harbor. They were then hoisted aboard ship and made their first official flights from the deck of the carrier itself.

The FB-5 wings were identical to their Army cousins with a span of 32 feet and area of 241 square feet. Length was 23 feet 9 inches, and they stood 9 feet 5 inches high. Empty weight was 2,458 pounds; loaded was 3,249 pounds. With the Packard engine, the Boeing fighter could reach 169 mph and had an initial climb rate of 2,100 fpm. Service ceiling was 20,200 feet. The standard fuel load of 100 gallons could be increased with an external tank. Normal range on internal fuel was 323 miles. With

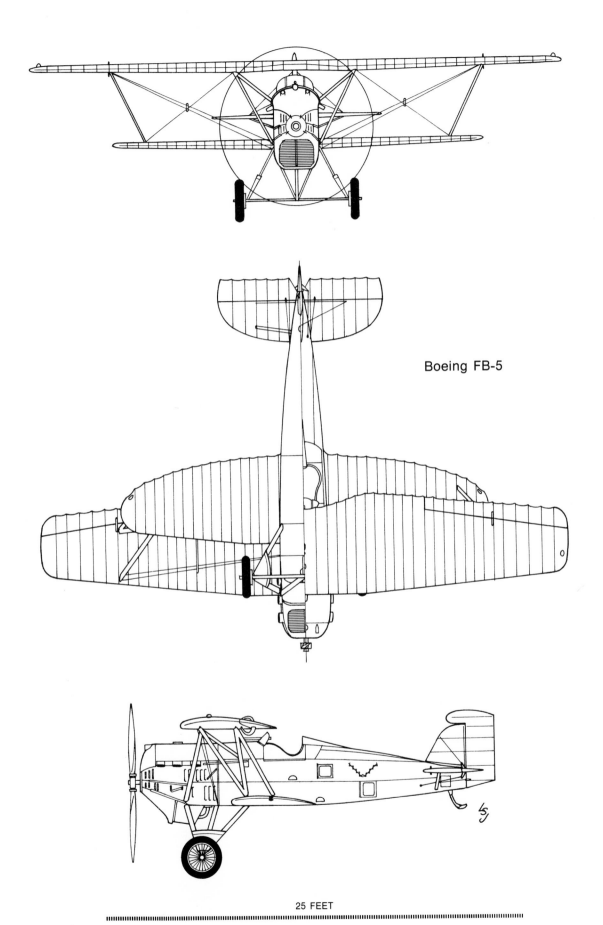

Boeing FB-5

25 FEET

Boeing FB-5's of VF-1 and VF-6. VF-1's High Hat emblem is visible above the wing of the closest plane. These planes were entered in the 1927 National Air Races.   *Gordon S. Williams*

The Boeing FB-4 with a Wright P-1 engine. The extra drag of the cylinders reduced its speed by 7 mph. Boeing

Ten of these FB-1's were used by the Marine Corps in China during 1927 and '28.   *Gordon S. Williams*

This, one of three FB-3's, was used to evaluate a 525 hp Packard engine.   Boeing

A Boeing FB-1 of the First Marine Fighter Squadron. These planes were land-based only. Gordon S. Williams

the external tank, range could be extended to 530 miles. The FB-5 could be mounted on wheels or a pair of floats; but performance with the floats was somewhat reduced. Two .30 cal. Browning machine guns were used for offensive weapons.

For comparative evaluation between air-cooled and liquid-cooled engines, Boeing built one experimental model with a Wright P-1 radial engine of 450 hp. Flight tests were made with twin floats, but although the installation was more than 200 pounds lighter, the added drag of the exposed cylinders reduced the performance by 7 mph. This version was tagged FB-4, but when the Wright engine was replaced by a 450 hp Pratt & Whitney R-1340-B Wasp, it became the FB-6. A proposed Wasp-powered FB-7 was cancelled before any work had begun on the project.

WRIGHT
F3W-1 APACHE

Because of problems with the Wright engine, the F3W-1 received the first Pratt & Whitney Wasp and became famous as a research plane.
Gordon S. Williams

When the Navy Department made it known that it wanted to standardize on an air-cooled radial engine for its air fleet, both Wright and Pratt & Whitney set about engineering a powerplant to meet the requirements. While the Wright designers were working on the new engine, their aircraft division set to work on an airframe which they hoped would also win the Navy's approval. It was named Apache and received the Navy designation F3W-1 and BuNo A-7223.

The Apache was to serve a dual purpose. As a scout, it would be mounted on a single float with a pair of small stabilizing pontoons under the wings. Thus outfitted, it could be catapult-launched from most naval vessels. In its alternate role with wheels, the F3W-1 would be a fighter suitable for carrier duty. The Apache was to be fitted with a 220 hp Wright J-5 Whirlwind, but tests soon made it clear that this engine could not supply sufficient power to make the fighter competitive.

By this time, the new Wright P-1 Simoon radial engine was being tested; and after a conference between Wright's engineers and the Navy, it was agreed that the Simoon

would be mounted to the Apache. The new engine, with its 325 hp, made a substantial improvement in the Apache's performance, but the Simoon was beset with technical problems and there was no assurance that it would even go into production. At this time, one of aviation's strange ironies occurred when the F3W-1 was selected to become the vehicle upon which the competing Pratt & Whitney Wasp engine was to be tested. This mating was destined to secure a permanent place in the record books for an airplane which would otherwise have vanished into obscurity.

The Wasp-powered Apache first soared into the air on May 5, 1926, and its performance was reported with exuberance by those who flew it. For the next three years, the Apache and its Wasp engine literally stacked altitude record upon record. Since its role was now purely experimental, the Apache was classed as the XF3W-1—a reversal of the usual application of designators. For the record flights, the Wasp was fed air from a new supercharger. The supercharger was activated by a spring-mounted control which was held by the pilot. This "dead-man" type system would

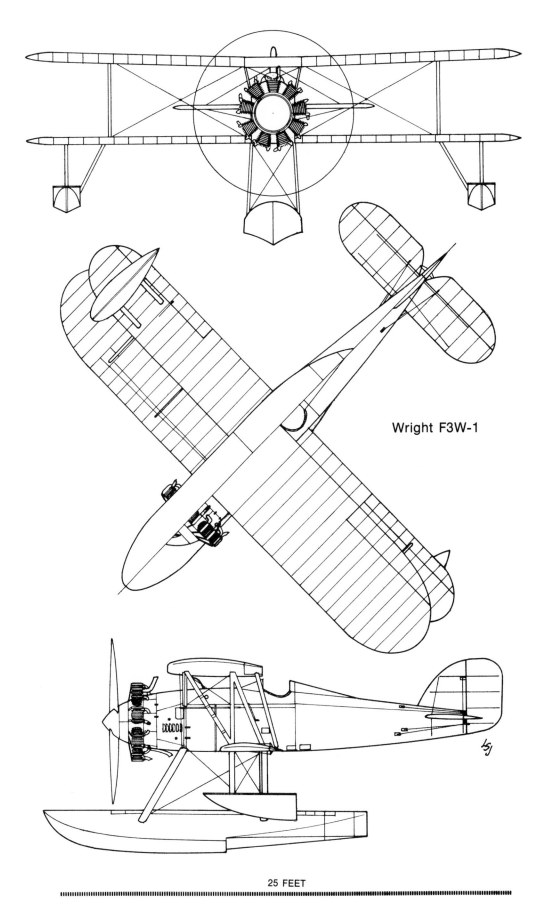

Wright F3W-1

25 FEET

shut down the supercharger and cause the plane to lose altitude if the pilot lost consciousness. The pilot breathed pure oxygen through a hose held in his mouth; and if he should drop the hose at some 40,000 feet, he was not likely to recover it soon enough to avoid passing out. Pin holes were drilled into the goggles to enable the flier to see his instruments when the clear lenses froze in the -65 degree temperature.

Under these conditions, Lt's. C. C. Champion and Apollo Soucek lifted the Apache through a series of altitude records during 1927—30. The flights were made in both seaplane and landplane configurations, thus setting records in two categories. By the time the flights were concluded, Lt. Soucek and the Apache had set the seaplane record of 38,560 feet and a landplane record of 43,-166 feet.

As the Wasp test vehicle, the XF3W-1 had a wingspan of 27 feet 4 inches with a wing area of 215 square feet. Length was 22 feet 1 inch and height was 8 feet 6 inches. Empty weight was 1,414 pounds, gross weight was 2,128 pounds. Fuel load was 47 gallons. Top speed was 162 mph.

The Wright P-1 Simoon engine was abandoned without reaching production, and the aircraft division of the Wright Aeronautical Corp. was dissolved.

It was originally planned to catapult the float version of the Apache from ships. Here the float gear is being tested.
Gordon S. Williams

CURTISS
F6C HAWK

The Curtiss F6C-1 was the Navy's equivalent of the Army P-1 Hawk.   Gordon S. Williams

The second Army fighter to don the Navy's colors was the Curtiss P-1 Hawk, suitably altered and designated F6C. (The F5C classification was reportedly passed over to avoid confusion with the Curtiss F-5 flying boats of an earlier designation system, some of which were still in service.) An order was placed in January 1925, for nine F6C's. Five were to be -1's, essentially P-1's, and four -2's with carrier fixtures. The F6C-1's were delivered in September to VF-2 for evaluation while the four F6C-2's were fitted at the Curtiss plant for carrier operations. This consisted of reinforcing the fuselage to withstand the strain of the arresting hook as it snagged the cables and adding a bar between the landing gear axles. To this spreader bar was attached a group of hook-like guides which tracked between a series of longitudinal wires on the carrier deck. The object of this system was to steer the plane straight down the deck during the landing.

The F6C-3 appeared with the improvements recommended by VF-2 and were supplied with float kits which could be interchanged with wheels. The Navy planned to use the F6C-3 on catapults, but tests showed they were not suitable for this operation. A total of thirty-five F6C-3's were received, these being the equivalent of the Army's P-1A. These planes were assigned to both Navy and Marine units.

Since the F6C Hawks, like the Boeing FB's, were actually adaptations of Army fighters already in production, they were also equipped with the Army's favored water-cooled inline engines. The F6C-1 through -3 used the Curtiss V-1150-1 twelve-cylinder engine with 435 hp. As noted before, the Navy was not inclined to encourage the use of this type of powerplant due to the extra weight of the cooling system and its added maintenance.

In May of 1926, Pratt & Whitney had first sent aloft their new air-cooled Wasp. This engine was expressly devised for the Navy; and with its success came the conviction that such a unit would become the standard Navy power system. In October 1926, the Navy ordered 200 of the new Wasp engines.

The first of the original F6C-1's, BuNo A-6968, became the prototype of a new Hawk for the Navy. Mounting one of the

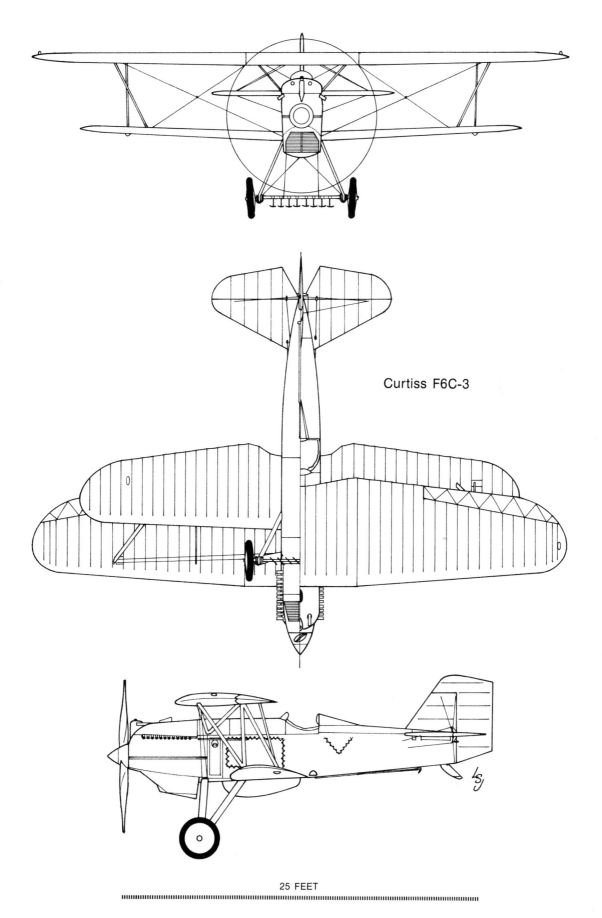

Curtiss F6C-3

25 FEET

This F6C-3 Hawk was assigned to Marine Squadron VF-8M at Quantico, Va., 1928.   Wayne Morris

410 hp Wasps and designated F6C-4, the air-cooled Curtiss fighter proved everything the Navy had hoped; and an order was placed with Curtiss for thirty-one F6C-4's. At last, naval fighter design was heading on a course of its own.

All the F6C Hawks used the same wing arrangement with a span of 31 feet 6 inches and an area of 252 square feet. The F6C-3, with the Curtiss inline engine, was 22 feet 10 inches long and 10 feet 8 inches high. Maximum speed was 154 mph at sea level. Service ceiling was 20,300 feet. With 50 gallons of fuel, the range was 351 miles.

The F6C-3 airframe weighed 2,161 pounds; loaded normally, it tipped the scales at 2,963 pounds.

The Wasp-powered F6C-4 was 22 feet 6 inches long and stood 10 feet 11 inches high. Empty weight was only 1,980 pounds while gross was 2,785 pounds. Normal fuel capacity was 50 gallons giving a range of 361 miles. Speed with the Wasp was 155 mph, 1 mph faster than the heavier F6C-3; but the ceiling, at 22,900 feet, was 2,600 feet higher than the Curtiss-powered fighter. Armament on all F6C fighters was two .30 cal. machine guns.

An F6C-3 of the Red Rippers, at the time designated VB-1B.   Navy

The prototype F6C-4 was again re-engined, this time with a Pratt & Whitney R-1690 of 525 hp, to become the sole XF6C-5. One XF6C-7 came into being when an inverted-V air-cooled Ranger SGV-770 was installed in an F6C-4. The XF6C-6 was a parasol-winged monoplane rebuilt from F6C-3, #A-7147, for the 1930 Thompson Trophy Race at Chicago. A beautiful aircraft, it led the race until its pilot was overcome by carbon-monoxide fumes from the engine and plunged into the ground.

The air-cooled engine was more to the Navy's liking so they ordered thirty-one of these F6C-4 Hawks.
Gordon S. Williams

The XF6C-6 was a Hawk modified into a racer for the 1930 Thompson Trophy Race. Gordon S. Williams

Curtiss F6C-4

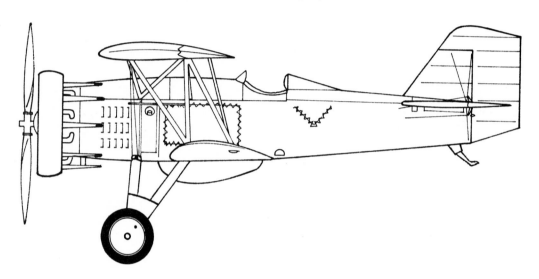

Boeing's Model 69 became the Navy's XF2B-1. The spinner was used on the prototype only. *Boeing*

Perhaps the best known Navy fighter of the 1920's was Boeing's Wasp-powered F2B-1. "The Three Sea Hawks" was a name familiar to nearly every racing and air show fan, and it identified the Navy's first aerobatic demonstration team. This group of three naval aviators thrilled the race-going crowd by putting on a spectacular show of the F2B-1's nimble abilities while flying in close formation.

The subject of the "Sea Hawks" demonstrations began as Boeing Model 69. On the basis of the tests with the Wasp-powered FB-6, Boeing undertook the construction of a radial-engined fighter expressly for carrier service. Flying first on November 3, 1926, the Navy obtained it as the XF2B-1 and put it through its paces before placing a production contract for thirty-two more of the type. The XF2B-1 was initially flown with a large streamlined spinner and an unbalanced rudder. Production F2B-1's had no spinner and an enlarged rudder. Like the earlier Boeing fighters, the F2B-1's were constructed with fabric-covered welded steel tubing fuselages and wooden-frame wings. An internal tank held fifty gallons of fuel and external attachments provided mounting for an additional fifty gallon tank. Either two .30 cal. guns or one .30 and one .50 cal. machine gun were mounted on these fighters. Four 25 pound bombs could be attached under the wings and a fifth bomb could be fitted to the fuselage.

The F2B-1's were assigned to fighter squadron VF-1B and bomber squadron VB-2B on board the USS Saratoga. Deliveries began on January 30, 1928. No further orders were received from the Navy, but Boeing did export two examples of the plane as Model 69B, one each to Japan and Brazil.

The proportions of the F2B-1 were: wingspan 30 feet 1 inch; length 22 feet 11 inches; height 9 feet 2¾ inches. Wing area was 243 square feet. The 425 hp Pratt & Whitney R-1340B Wasp gave a top speed of 158 mph at sea level and an initial rate of climb of 1,890 fpm. Service ceiling was 21,-500 feet. Range on internal fuel was 372 miles. Weight was 2,058 pounds empty, 2,-804 pounds gross.

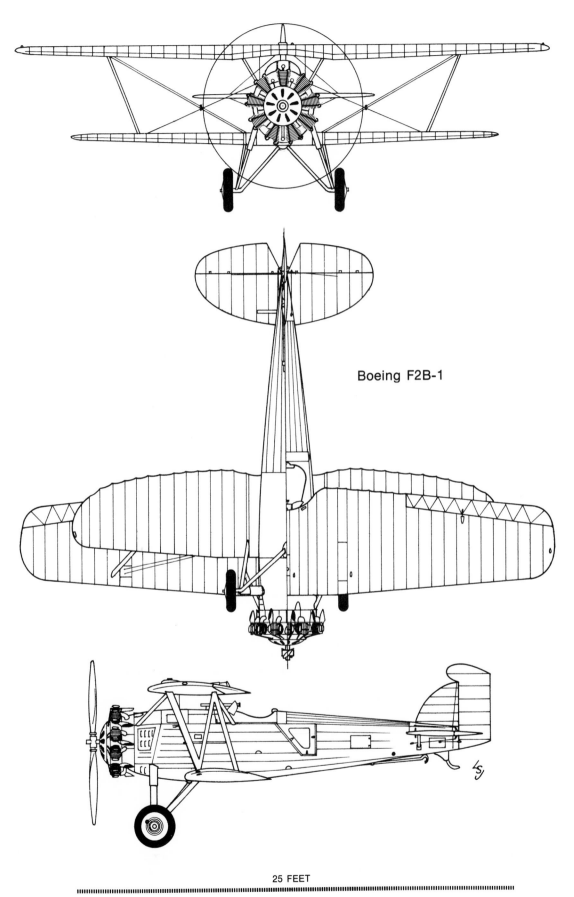

Boeing F2B-1

25 FEET

The sleek lines of the XF2B-1 helped the prototype reach a speed of 154 mph. Note the Boeing emblem. Boeing

Production F2B-1's had an enlarged balanced rudder.   Boeing

A spanking new F2B-1 tries out its powerplant. At this time the finish is natural linen.   Boeing

CURTISS
F7C SEAHAWK

The Commanding Officer's Seahawk from VF-5M. Notice here the U.S. MARINES appears under the wings.
Wayne Morris

At last, the requirements for a shipboard fighter had been defined to the extent that airframe builders were no longer modifying Army types to suit the Navy. The first Curtiss fighter expressly designed for this role was their Model 43, called Seahawk and designated XF7C-1. In appearance, the XF7C-1 was obviously a descendant of the Hawk line, but with a bullet-like spinner and untapered wings it was much cleaner looking. Mounted to the nose was the Navy's new Pratt & Whitney Wasp radial engine.

First flown on February 28, 1927, the XF7C-1 received the usual scrutiny from the Navy. The Seahawk was stressed for use as a dive bomber and could be operated with a single float and wing pontoons. It was over a year before a contract was issued for sixteen more Seahawks, and these showed evidence of some of the problems encountered during the testing. The straight-winged prototype had been excessively tail heavy; but by sweeping the top wing back seven degrees and increasing the span 2 feet this fault was eliminated. The first three production Seahawks were subjected to further testing and a beefier landing gear

was devised for the remaining production F7C-1's. The fourth Seahawk, BuNo A-7656, tried out a set of leading-edge slots. By the middle of the year, the F7C-1's were finally released for service, all joining Marine Squadron VF-5M at Quantico, Virginia, and serving into 1933 before retirement.

The swept-back top wing of the F7C-1 was constructed of spruce covered with fabric. The span was 32 feet 8 inches, and both wings together had an area of 276 square feet. The fuselage was built-up of aluminum and steel tubing, also fabric covered. The Seahawk's overall length was 22 feet 2 inches. Height was 10 feet 4 inches. The F7C-1 weighed 2,105 pounds empty and had a gross of 2,782 pounds. Maximum weight was 3,219 pounds. Fuel load was 100 gallons which provided a range of 330 miles.

The Seahawk's Pratt & Whitney R-1340B provided 450 hp to give the fighter a speed up to 151 mph at sea level. Service ceiling was 23,350 feet, the first 5,000 feet of which could be reached in 2½ minutes. Two .30 cal. machine guns were located in the cowl firing between the engine cylinders.

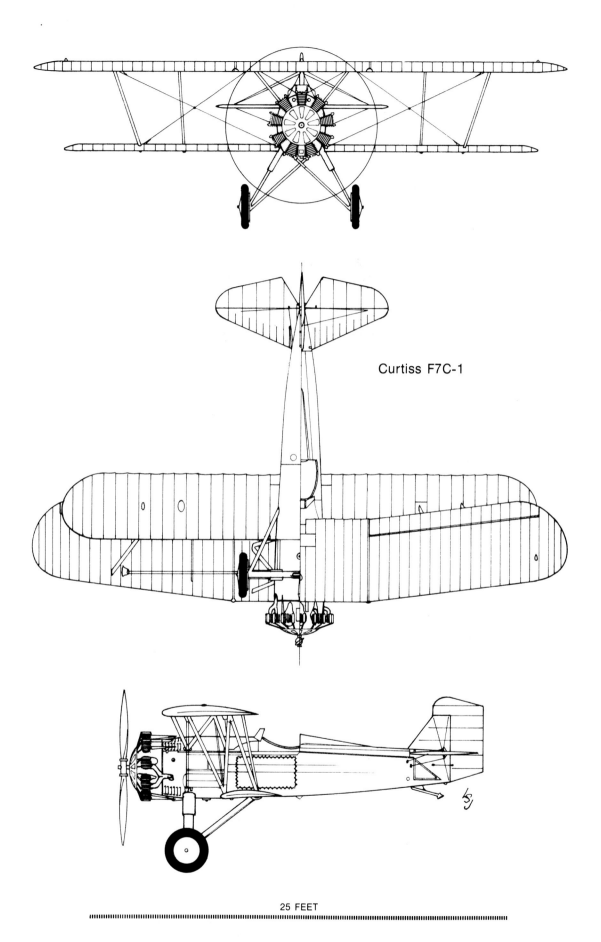

Curtiss F7C-1

25 FEET

All production Curtiss F7C-1 Seahawks were assigned to Marine Squadrons. This one belongs to VF-9M.
Wayne Morris

The F7C-1's were initially delivered to VF-5M at Quantico, Va. Of interest is the U.S. MARINES on top of the wing.
Wayne Morris

VOUGHT
FU

The Vought FU-1 was essentially a two-place airplane with the front cockpit covered over. *Vought*

Due to the success of the VE-7 series by Vought in 1922, this company received $459,709 from the Navy in 1926 to supply twenty examples of a convertible land/sea based fighter. Already in production at the Vought plant was a fast two-seat observation plane, the UO-1. This was essentially a refined VE type with the boxy fuselage padded by stringers into a streamlined shape. The wings and stabilizer were identical with the earlier plane, but it was powered by a Wright J-3 radial engine of 200 hp.

Elimination of the front cockpit in the observation plane brought about the transformation of the fighter. A new designation was assigned declaring the plane was indeed a fighter—the FU-1. Up front, the FU-1 mounted a 220 hp Wright R-1790 (J-5) Whirlwind with a Roots integral supercharger to permit operation at higher altitudes. With the supercharged engine, the FU-1 found its best speed at 13,000 feet, this being 147 mph. At sea level, the maximum speed was 125 mph. The FU-1's were the last of the convertible float/wheel planes ordered by the Navy.

All twenty FU-1's were delivered to VF-2B in San Diego where they were operated with their float gear from the twelve battleships assigned to the Pacific Fleet. One plane was assigned to each of the big

vessels and they were launched from shipboard catapults. After 8 months as seaplanes, the FU-1's were brought ashore; and as the squadron converted to carrier operations, the pilots began to complain about the poor visibility from the aft-placed cockpit. The solution was quite simple since the FU-1 was based on a two-seat design. The forward position was opened up and they became two-place FU-2's with dual controls, although they were no longer considered suitable for the fighting role. Many of the FU-2's were reassigned to trainer duties. Their performance made them ideal as a medium to introduce student pilots to the more modern fighters beginning to reach the fleet. Others were used for various utility duties where their good handling characteristics made them popular with their pilots.

The FU-1 had a 34 foot 4 inch wingspan and a wing area of 290 square feet. Length of the landplane was 24 feet 5 inches and height was 8 feet 10 inches. Empty weight of the landplane was 1,715 pounds, gross was 2,409 pounds. The seaplane version weighed 365 pounds more. Forty-six gallons of gasoline were carried and this provided a range of 430 miles for the landplane. The FU-1 had a service ceiling of 27,300 feet, but it could be pushed up to nearly 30,000 feet. Two cowl-mounted .30 cal. machine guns provided offensive armament.

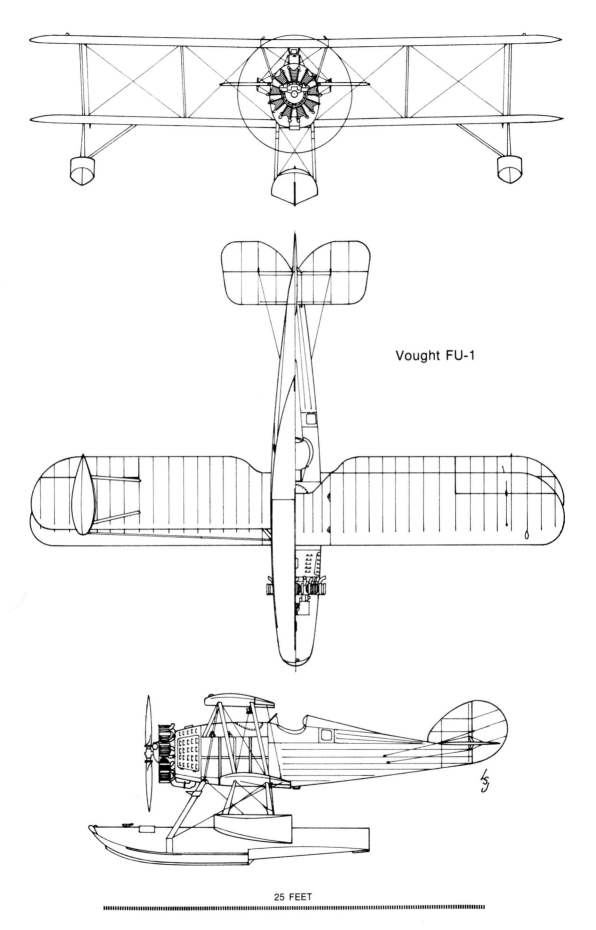

Vought FU-1

25 FEET

EBERHART
FG-1, F2G-1 COMANCHE

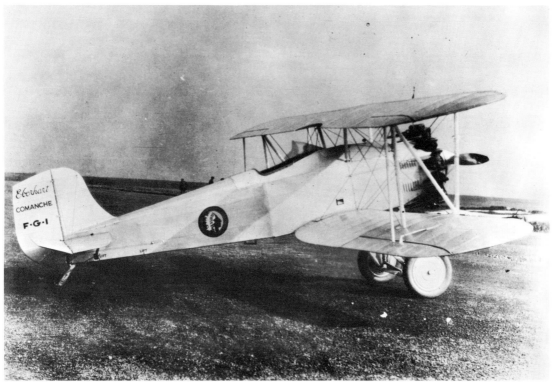

The Eberhart Comanche suffered from poor lateral stability. It first appeared as the XFG-1. Gordon S. Williams

One of the aeronautical novelties of the 'twenties was the Eberhart Comanche. The Eberhart Aeroplane and Motor Company was formed in 1925 as a branch of the Eberhart Steel Products Company. The full extent of their experience in the aircraft industry was in the rebuilding of fifty British Scouts into SE-5E trainers for the U.S. Army. Undaunted by their lack of aerodynamic experience, the Eberhart designers set about building a single-seat Wasp-powered fighter for the Navy.

The plane was dubbed Comanche by its builder and boldly proclaimed by an Indian head insignia on the fuselage sides. The placement of the Comanche's wings was quite unique. The upper wing was swept back seven degrees while the lower wing was swept forward five degrees, giving a rhomboid appearance. It was claimed that this arrangement would give the pilot good visibility during landing. The fuselage and tail surfaces were formed of welded steel tubing and the wings were constructed of aluminum. The entire framework was then covered with fabric. A Pratt & Whitney R-

1340D 450 hp Wasp provided power.

The Navy agreed to conduct tests of the Eberhart fighter, but on a contractor-owned basis. It was given the designation XFG-1 and the BuNo A-7944, but was not immediately purchased by the service. The XFG-1 was first tested by the contractor before submitting it for official trials. During these initial tests, several problems manifested themselves; and, following an accident which caused some minor damage, the builder made several corrections to the design. The most noticeable of these was an increase in the span of the upper wing by three feet.

When the Navy began testing the XFG-1, it was equipped with wheels. In this form it had a speed of 154 mph and had a gross weight of 2,938 pounds. The design of the Comanche allowed for conversion to a float plane and additional testing was done in this form. Apparently the float gear was much more streamlined than the wheel-type landing gear, because the maximum speed was nearly 2 mph greater when thus rigged, despite an increase in loaded weight of 204

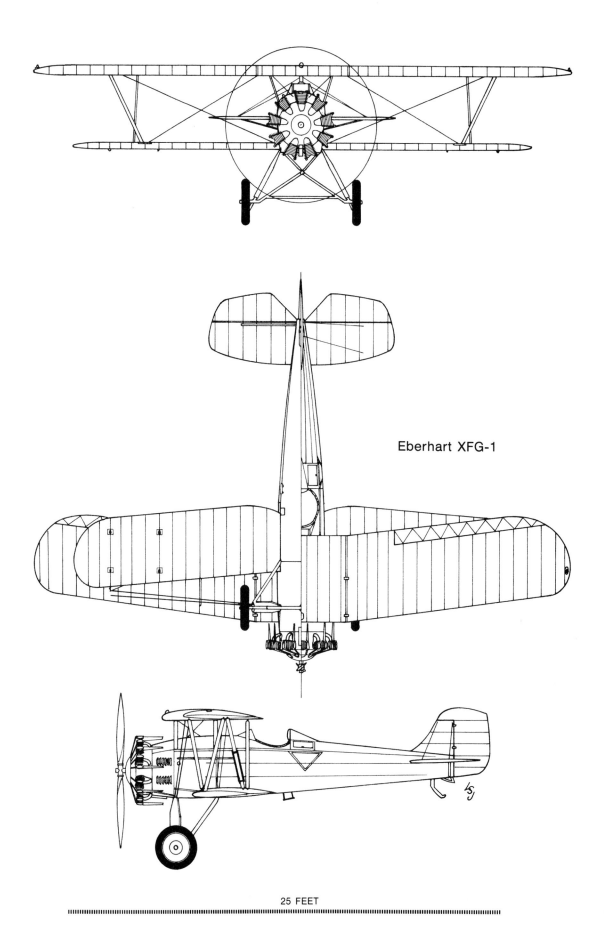

Eberhart XFG-1

25 FEET

pounds.

Following the float tests, the Comanche again visited its makers for additional corrections and a change back to wheeled landing gear. Further flight testing continued to uncover faults, but the basic underlying problem was simply that it was a poor design and suffered from a bad case of lateral instability. Even the construction techniques were considered impractical for production. So many modifications were made to the airframe during the testing program it was redesignated XF2G-1. Even-

tually the Navy purchased the Eberhart fighter but no production was ever considered and the company returned to manufacturing metal parts for the aircraft industry.

Final dimensions of the Comanche show a wingspan of 32 feet with an area of 241 square feet. Length was 22 feet 6 inches and it was 9 feet 10 inches high. With the float attached, the length was 18 feet 6 inches. Service ceiling as a land plane was 20,400 feet. Two .30 cal. machine guns intended for armament were never installed.

This view of the Comanche shows the fore and aft angle of the wings. In this form it was known as the XF2G-1.

Gordon S. Williams

HALL ALUMINUM
XFH-1

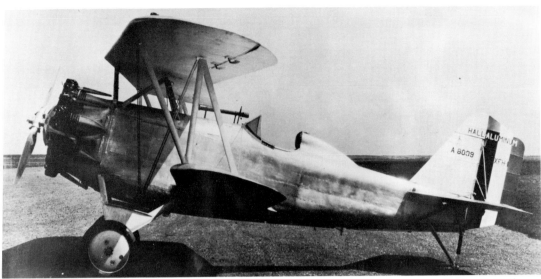

The all-metal Hall Aluminum XFH-1 was built with watertight compartments·   Gordon S. Williams

The metal aircraft specialist Charles W. Hall was given the opportunity of designing the Navy's first all-metal fighter in November 1927. Though not strictly all-metal by today's standards, since the wings and tail surfaces were fabric-covered, the entire structure was built of metal-frame and the fuselage was covered with dural sheeting.

In its proposal to Hall, the Navy was explicit in its design requirements for the metal fighter. The all-aluminum fuselage was to be of metal-covered monocoque construction and completely water-tight to permit the aircraft to float in the event of a water landing. Another specification was to include an emergency release mechanism which would jettison the entire landing gear should a forced landing be necessary.

The Hall XFH-1 was presented to the Navy at their testing ground at Anacostia on June 18, 1929. Even before test flights began, it was apparent that the XFH-1 would not be suitable as a combat machine. But, the Navy was greatly interested in the all-metal construction of the plane and proceeded with its evaluation. It was no surprise that the flight trials were unsuccessful. It was tail heavy and did not respond well to the controls. Buffeting was so violent it damaged the plane, controls froze, and the﹒upper wing nearly collapsed during one severe maneuver. It is interesting to note

that, like the ill-fated Eberhart design, the upper wing was swept to the rear while the lower wing angled forward.

With a new wing installed, the XFH-1 was returned to the Navy for carrier-suitability trials. During one of these tests, the engine failed and the pilot suddenly found himself with the opportunity to evaluate the metal craft's ability to survive an emergency water landing. According to the report, the plane hit the water with the landing gear still attached and the nose pitched upward momentarily, then settled downward. It floated for three-quarters of an hour before it was recovered with about one-fourth of the fuselage filled with water. This did not necessarily indicate that the construction was defective, however, since the plane had been subjected to some pretty severe forces during testing.

The XFH-1 weighed 1,773 pounds empty and had a gross of 2,514 pounds. It had a high speed of 152½ mph. The manufacturer's estimated time to climb to 5,000 feet was 2.8 minutes; but during testing, it required ten minutes to reach 2,530 feet. Service ceiling was only 14,250 feet. The wingspan was 32 feet with 255 square feet of area. Length was 22 feet 6 inches and the XFH-1 was 11 feet high. The fuel tank could hold 80 gallons, giving a range of 275 miles. A 450 hp Pratt & Whitney R-1340B Wasp provided the necessary power.

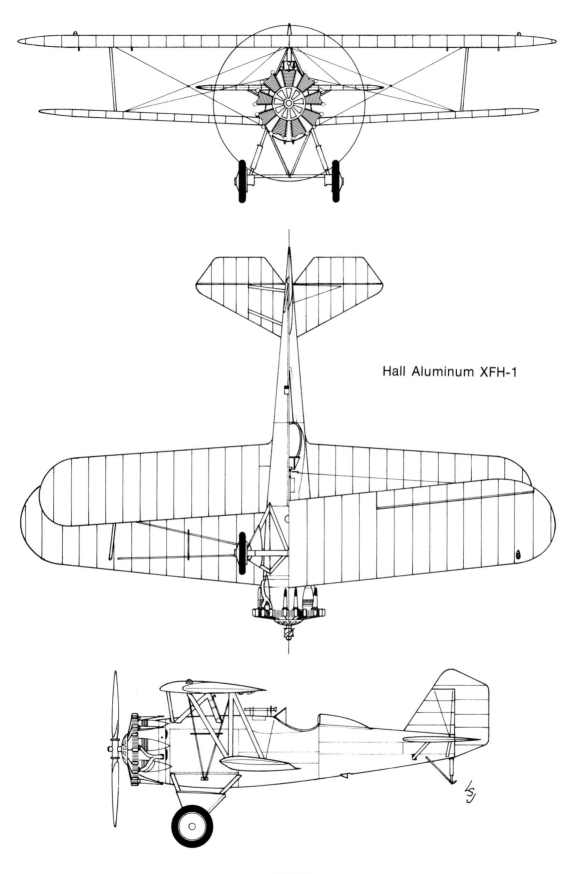

Hall Aluminum XFH-1

25 FEET

BOEING
F3B-1

This Boeing F3B-1 is operating with Fighting Squadron Three. The pilot is LCDR Ginder, Commanding Officer.
Boeing

Continuing refinement of their basic naval fighter design, Boeing offered their Model 74 for the Navy's approval. As the XF3B-1, the Navy subjected the new plane to a test program which indicated a few changes would be necessary before it would be acceptable. In its original form the XF3B-1 had tapered wings of the type used by the F2B's. It was felt that better handling at high altitudes could be attained by increasing the wing area; and to improve lateral stability the top wing was swept back. The entire tail unit was also to be revised before the XF3B-1 would be suitable for service. The XF3B-1 had been built as a single-float seaplane, but with the availability of aircraft carriers, the need for float fighters did not exist.

When the redesigned F3B-1 flew on February 3, 1928, it was a totally different land plane with corrugated aluminum tail and aileron surfaces. The fuselage, with the typical fabric-covered steel tube structure, was common to Boeing's fighters. In its altered form, the F3B-1 turned in a very acceptable performance and the Boeing Company was rewarded with a contract for seventy-three more of the type.

Some refinement was made by the Navy to a few of the F3B-1's during their operational careers. A Townend ring was mounted around the engine to smooth the airflow, and some planes were fitted with streamlined wheel covers. The Navy flew the F3B-1's in the role of fighter-bomber for some five years before replacing them with more modern equipment. Those that remained in service after that were relegated to transport or other menial duties.

The F3B-1 had a wingspan of 33 feet with an area of 275 square feet. Length was 24 feet 10 inches, and the fighter was 9 feet 2 inches high. Unloaded, the plane weighed 2,180 pounds; fully laden with crew, fuel, ammunition and five 25 pound bombs, the F3B-1 weighed 3,340 pounds. Normal gross was 2,950 pounds. Armament was the typical pair of synchronized .30 cal. machine guns. The internal fuel tank held 60 gallons for a range of 340 miles. Maximum speed at sea level was 157 mph, and the F3B-1 cruised at 131 mph. Initial climb rate was 2,020 fpm with a service ceiling of 21,000 feet.

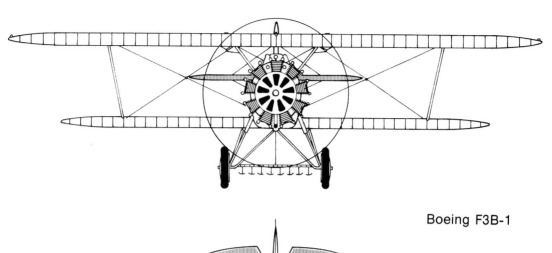

Boeing F3B-1

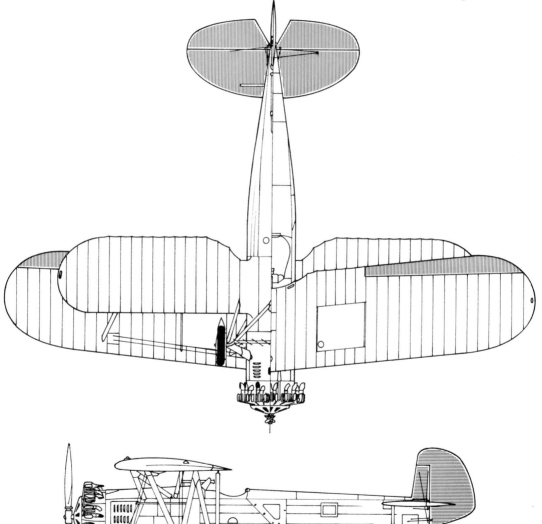

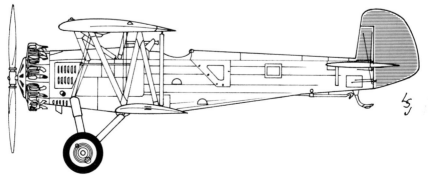

25 FEET

One of Boeing's F3B-1's before delivery to the Navy.   *Boeing*

The XF3B-1 poses beside Puget Sound in Seattle. The rudder striping is unusual on a Navy plane. Boeing

This F3B-1 is from VF-2 of the USS Langley. Pilot is CDR E.E. Wilson.   *Navy*

CURTISS
F8C FALCON/HELLDIVER

The XF8C-7 at Anacostia. This version provided the two-man crew with an enclosed cockpit. Note the parachute on the wing.   Gordon S. Williams

The F8C designation was applied to two distinctly different Curtiss two-seat aircraft. The original F8C-1 was based on the Curtiss Falcon observation plane designed for the Army in 1924. The Army's Falcon was powered by a liquid-cooled engine, but the Navy's preference for the air-cooled radial led to the installation of the Pratt & Whitney Wasp on the Naval craft. Six F8C-1 Falcons were supplied to the Marine Corps during the spring of 1928, to become the first of a series of two-place fighters. Regrettably, even with the Wasp, the performance of the F8C-1 was more like its observation counterpart than a fighter. In fact, they were soon reclassed in this role and the designation changed to OC-1. In this guise, they continued serving as fighters to a limited degree, along with their other duties.

Since the Falcon had proved only marginally suited as a two-seat fighter, Curtiss scaled the basic design down, still retaining the two seats, and created a new machine which was offered as the XF8C-2. Not only was it conceived as a fighter, but it was seen as a dive bomber. During testing, the dive bombing capabilities of the XF8C-

2 so impressed the pilots that it became known as the Helldiver, a name that was officially applied and eventually came to identify all Curtiss dive bombers. Even though the prototype of this new series was lost in a terminal-velocity dive, its potential was well recognized and steps were taken to strengthen the fighter-bomber.

Meanwhile, the F8C-3 came along. Again an attempt was made to convert the large Falcon to the fighting category and one XF8C-3 and twenty F8C-3's were delivered to the Marines. There was little difference between the later Falcons and the first F8C-1's; and, once again, they were relegated to observation duties with the designation OC-2.

In order to continue development of the more suitable F8C-2 Helldiver, a refined example of this plane was ordered as the XF8C-4 which flew in August 1929. This one was followed by twenty-five production F8C-4's equipped with carrier gear. A follow-up order was placed for 63 more as F8C-5's, but it was not long before complaints from the fleet led to changes in the production line. In operation, the Helldivers had proven slower than the

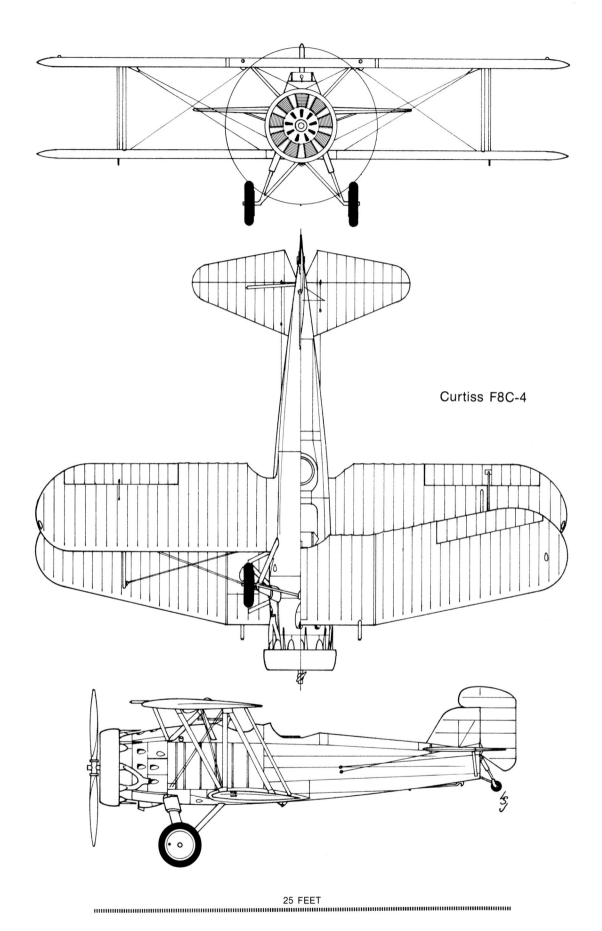

Curtiss F8C-4

25 FEET

The first F8C's were based on the Army's Falcon observation planes. Classed by the Navy as F8C-1's, they were not suitable for the fighting role and were reclassed as OC-1's.   *Gordon S. Williams*

This OC-2 was formerly an F8C-3 two-seat fighter. Too heavy and clumsy for a fighter, it has been relegated to a utility role.   *Gordon S. Williams*

Sixty-three of the F8C-5's were used by the Navy. This plane eventually became an O2C-2. Gordon S. Williams

The prototype XF8C-2, showing the rear machine gun arament. Here a pair of Lewis guns are mounted.
Gordon S. Williams

A-8425 is an F8C-4 Helldiver from VF-1B, the "High Hat" squadron. The arresting hook and extra fuel tank are seen in this view.
Gordon S. Williams

single-seat fighters. This was a serious problem since the more nimble single-seaters were to fly in a protective formation with the two-seat types. Obviously, the speed of the formation was dictated by the performance of the slowest planes. Therefore, the first twenty F8C-5's on the production line were altered to delete the deck landing fixtures and the remaining Helldivers were completed as land-based observation planes, later to become O2C-2's.

The F8C-4 was powered by a cowled Pratt & Whitney R-1340-88 of 400 hp. This gave a top speed of 137 mph. The empty weight was 2,513 pounds; maximum weight, with 136 gallons of fuel, was 4,238 pounds. The forward part of the fuselage was formed by the external skins of the fuel tanks. The balance of the fuselage structure was fabric-covered steel and aluminum tubing. Two .30 cal. machine guns were install-ed in the leading edge of the upper wing and fired outside the propeller. A single .30 or .50 cal. gun was mounted behind the rear cockpit and controlled by the gunner-observer. One 500 pound bomb or two 116 pound bombs could be fitted to wing and fuselage racks.

Length of the F8C-4 was 25 feet 11 inches, height was 10 feet 6 inches. The wingspan was 32 feet with an area of 308 square feet. The XF8C-6 designation was given to two Helldivers when experimental wing flaps, slots and Frise ailerons were installed. BuNo A-8845 was the sole XF8C-7, ordered to test a Wright R-1820E Cyclone with 575 hp. This Helldiver sported enclosed cockpits, wheel pants, and other trim which permitted an increase of over 35 mph above the standard F8C-4. There were three more Cyclone-powered Helldivers that were iden-tified as XF8C-8's, but they also failed to reach production.

The Vought XF2U-1 was already outclassed when it was ready for testing in 1929.   *Vought*

While Curtiss was revising its Falcon reconnaissance planes to Navy fighter standards as the F8C, Vought was undertaking a similar task with their O2U Corsair. The O2U, which was delivered to the Navy in 1927, featured a welded steel tube fuselage structure with the forward part of this unit being formed by the fuel tank. The reliable R-1340 Wasp engine was the prime mover of this series; and with its 450 hp, the Corsair established four speed and altitude records in 1927. As a result of these achievements, every new O2U was guaranteed in writing that "each standard stock production Corsair is guaranteed to equal or exceed the world record performances officially credited to this model."

It was this design that became the basis of Vought's two-seat fighter, the XF2U-1. Two years in development, the XF2U-1 was already outclassed by the time it was completed in June 1929. It was attractive in appearance and a large cutout over the front cockpit provided good upward visibility. However, the long cowling over the engine did cause some concern about the forward view during carrier operations. The plane was taken to Norfolk, Virginia, where it was evaluated on a simulated carrier deck. The pilots found no difficulty seeing over the long nose, and the XF2U-1 was then turned over to the Naval Aircraft Factory. It was operated until March 6, 1931, when it was written-off in a crash landing.

The XF2U-1, BuNo A-7692, had a wingspan of 36 feet, a wing area of 318 square feet, a length of 27 feet, and was 10 feet high. A 450 hp Wasp R-1340D gave the erstwhile fighter a maximum speed of 146 mph. Weight was 2,539 pounds light; 4,208 pounds gross including a fuel load of 110 gallons. With this it could fly 495 miles. Service ceiling was 18,700 feet. Two .30 cal. Browning machine guns were located in the top wing firing forward. The rear cockpit was fitted with a single Lewis gun on a swivel mount.

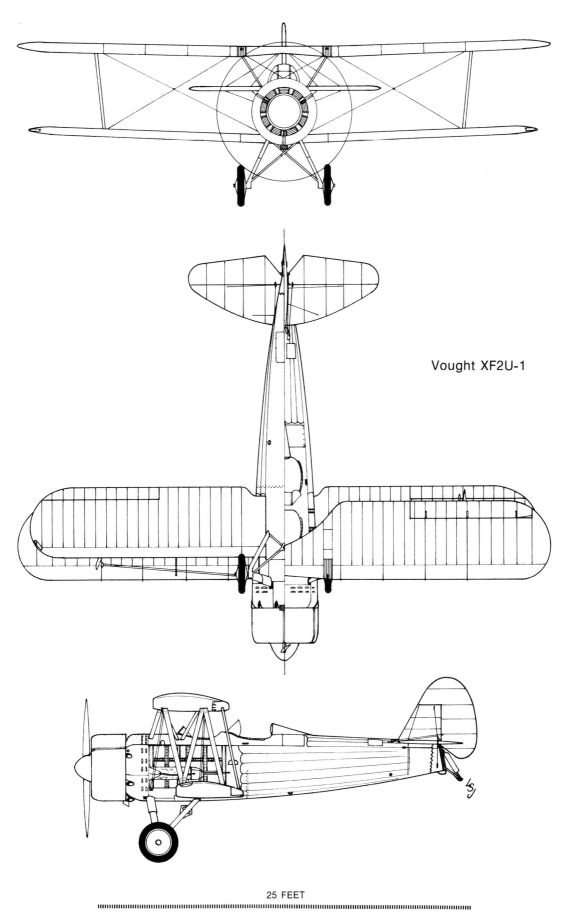

Vought XF2U-1

25 FEET

The single XF2U-1 was attractive and offered good upward visibility due to the large cutout in the upper wing.
Vought

5-B-7 on the fuselage shows that this F4B-4 was used as a bomber with VB-5. The bomb racks are visible under the wings.
Boeing

By the late twenties, the aircraft manufacturers had begun to learn the lessons of aerodynamics dictated by the performance drawbacks of their earlier designs. In 1928, the Boeing Company produced two new fighter prototypes at their own expense. Drawing from the experiences of their past stable of military types, the engineers chose an uncomplicated approach which resulted in a configuration with a great growth potential. The efforts of the company were directed toward development of a fighter suitable for the Navy, but the new planes quickly caught the attention of the Army and one of the most renowned series of biplane fighters was created.

The two test aircraft of the new Boeing fighters were almost identical. The main difference was the landing gear structure. The Model 83 had an axle connecting the two wheels, and an arresting hook; while the Model 89 used a double-tripod system as seen on the F3B's. This latter arrangement allowed the installation of a bomb rack with a 500 pound capacity under the fuselage. The planes were compact, relatively light, and much attention was given to aerodynamics. With Pratt & Whitney's 450

hp Wasp, they completely outperformed all the Navy's latest equipment.

The initial flights were made on June 25 and August 7, 1928. The Model 83 was the first of the two into the air. Both planes were sent to the Navy for their study and received the designation XF4B-1. Production was ordered for twenty-seven F4B-1's which combined the best features of both prototypes. The split-axle tripod gear with the bomb rack and the arresting hook were included when the first production model of the Boeing fighter flew on May 6, 1929. Minor design changes appeared during the life of the F4B-1 to refine its outstanding performance even further.

The Army found its fighters were outclassed by the Navy's new Boeing fighter and ordered it themselves as the P-12, which alongside the F4B, was also developed to high degrees of success. Some of the Army's ideas crossed over to the Navy fighters and an improved F4B-2, with a cowling and Frise ailerons appeared. This model also reintroduced the Model 83's landing gear with the straight-across axle. Forty-six F4B-2's were produced.

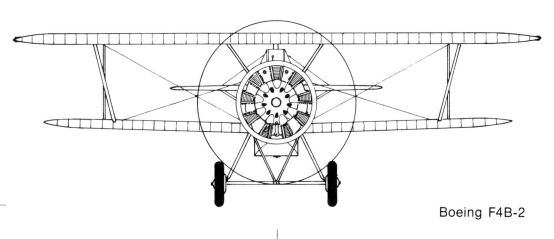

Boeing F4B-2

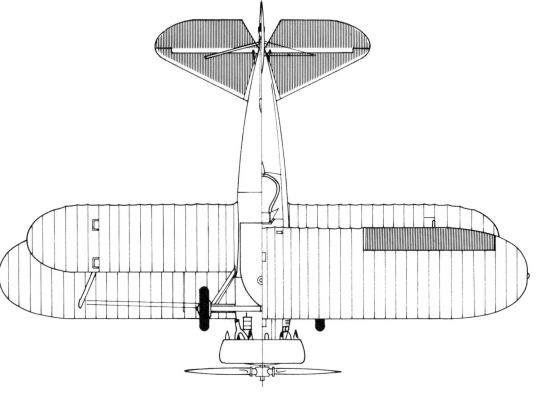

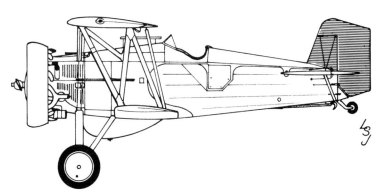

25 FEET

These F4B-3's are with Marine bombing squadron VB-4M, also known as the "Red Devils." The bomb racks can be seen behind the landing gear.   *Boeing*

The F4B-1 originally had streamlining shrouds over the exhaust stacks.   *Boeing*

The seventh plane of the "Red Rippers" takes off from the carrier deck. The fuselage stripe is true blue edged in black. The squadron was designated VB-1B at this time.   Navy

The F4B-1 and -2 were equipped with fabric-covered metal tube fuselages. To extend the production life of their fighter, Boeing showed the Navy a new fuselage of all-metal semi-monocoque construction. Thus outfitted, the maximum speed increased even more, impressing the Navy into placing an order for twenty-one F4B-3's, followed by ninety-two F4B-4's with enlarged tail surfaces. With the last half of the F4B-4 order, a taller headrest was faired into the rear of the fuselage. The F4B-1's and -2's benefitted from the new tail surfaces mounted to the F4B-4 when most of the earlier types still in service were retrofitted with the -4 vertical tail unit.

Both the Navy and Marine Corps flew the little Boeing fighter which had a service life extending from 1929 to 1941. During the last years, several were converted to radio-controlled drones. In 1940, twenty-three P-12's were received from the Army and became F4B-4A's.

The F4B-2 used a Pratt & Whitney R-1340-8 delivering 500 hp. With this, it had a top speed of 186 mph at 6,000 feet. Wingspan was 30 feet with an area of 227½

square feet. Length was 20 feet 1 inch and height was 9 feet 1 inch. It weighed 2,067 pounds empty and grossed at 2,799 pounds. Up to 110 gallons of fuel could be carried in both internal and external tanks for a maximum range of 812 miles. Operational ceiling was 26,900 feet.

The final model of the series, the F4B-4 had a 550 hp Pratt & Whitney R-1340-16 with which it could attain a speed of 188 mph at 6,000 feet. Wings were the same on all F4B's, but the overall length was four inches greater and the plane stood 9 feet 9 inches high. This model weighed 2,354 pounds empty and 3,611 pounds gross. Fuel capacity equalled that of the F4B-2 but range was 734 miles maximum. Service ceiling of the -4 was also 26,900 feet.

All F4B's were armed with the standard pair of .30 cal. machine guns in the nose, with 1,200 rounds of ammunition; or alternately, one .30 cal. and one .50 cal. gun. The F4B-1 could carry ten 24 pound bombs under its wings and a single 500 pound bomb beneath the fuselage. From the F4B-3 on, two 116 pound bombs could be hauled.

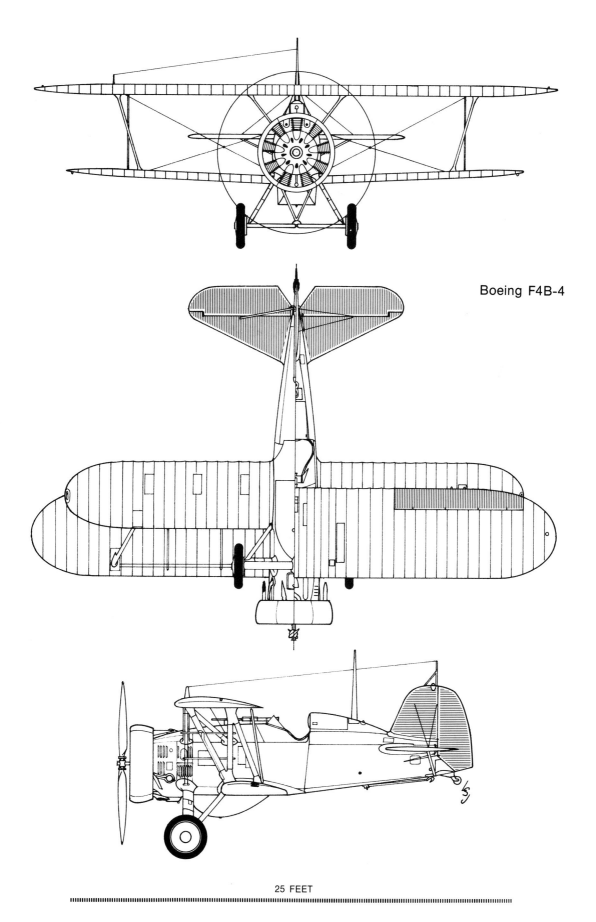

Boeing F4B-4

25 FEET

BOEING
XF5B-1

The Boeing XF5B-1, the Navy's first monoplane fighter type.   **Boeing**

In 1929, Boeing again invested their own funds in the development of the first monoplane to bear the Navy's fighter designation. By 1930, the Army was testing a series of monoplane bombers—the Douglas XB-7 and Fokker XB-8. And Boeing had begun on their twin-engine monoplane bomber, the XB-9. In May 1930, the all-metal Monomail low-wing transport took to the air; and, although it was twice as large as contemporary fighters, its single 575 hp Pratt & Whitney Hornet gave it a speed of 158 mph. Clearly, the age of the monoplane was dawning.

Boeing had already made one monoplane fighter for the Army, but it proved totally unsuitable. Their second attempt utilized the successful F4B structure, but a single all-metal wing was mounted on struts above the fuselage, parasol style. As with the F4B, a pair of the planes was assembled, one with equipment suited to the Army's requirements, the other fitted for carrier use. The Navy's version was given the designation XF5B-1 and assigned BuNo A-8640, although it was initially tested with civil registration.

The XF5B-1 was first flown in February 1930, and delivered to the Navy at Anacostia. At first, the Wasp engine was uncovered, then a close fitting cowling was installed and the maximum speed rose 16 mph. Comparison flights were made with F4B-1's and, in spite of the monoplane configuration and a marginally lighter weight, the XF5B-1 was only 7 mph faster. In order to make the directional stability acceptable, it became necessary to replace the vertical tail with one of the type used on the F4B-3, which had gone into production by this time. Maneuverability was good and the XF5B-1 did exhibit many of the qualifications of a good fighter, but with performance so near that of current biplanes, the Navy decided it was not practical to invest in the new design.

On the other hand, the all-metal construction of the Boeing XF5B-1 was of great interest to the Navy and the airframe was subjected to extensive tests. The fuselage was steel and dural, an aluminum alloy, and the parasol-mounted wing was made of dural ribs. The entire airframe was then covered by sheets of aluminum, forming a smooth, strong unit. There were also some side benefits to this method of construction including a watertight wing which eliminated the need for added flotation gear.

The XF5B-1 was finally destroyed in 1932, after severe structural testing. In the final analysis, it was found that the airframe

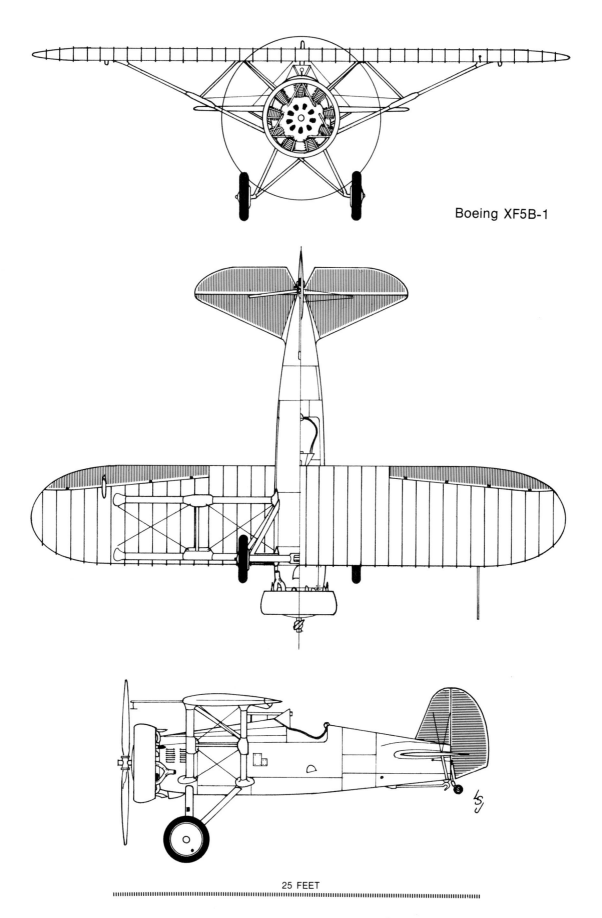

Boeing XF5B-1

25 FEET

The parasol-winged XF5B-1 was company-owned but officially designated as a fighter prototype by the Navy. **Boeing**

This flight view shows the similarities between the monoplane and the F4B series. **Boeing**

had withstood one-third more stress than the engineering design requirements.

The single wing of the XF5B-1 had an area of 157 square feet and measured 30 feet 6 inches tip to tip. Overall length of the plane was 21 feet, and its height was 9 feet 4 inches. Empty weight was 2,091 pounds and maximum weight was 2,848 pounds with 132 gallons of fuel. Service ceiling was 27,100 feet under the best conditions. While undergoing flight testing, the XF5B-1 was alternately fitted with a Pratt & Whitney R-1340B and R-1340C Wasp for comparison. With supercharging, the highest rating produced by these engines was 485 hp. Highest speed obtained during the tests was 183 mph.

The XF5B-1 did not provide the production contracts Boeing desired, but the progressive construction techniques displayed by the fighter advanced the state of the art a measurable degree.

Here the XF5B-1 has received a larger tail and a cowling over the engine. Notice the Boeing insignia and civil registration.
Boeing

The Berliner Joyce XFJ-1 in its original configuration. The cushion between the hook and fuselage was to prevent damage to the fuselage by the banging of the hook.   *Rockwell*

The name Berliner enters the aviation scene in 1922 when a dual-rotor helicopter, designed by Emil Berliner, was successfully flown and hovered for Army officials on July 16. The Berliner Aircraft Co. was formed in 1926. By 1929, Berliner-Joyce Aircraft was incorporated for the production of aircraft under military contracts; and a few months later, the new corporation became a division of North American Aviation. That same year, the Berliner-Joyce Aircraft Corp. submitted its first fighter design to the Navy. Conforming their design to the Navy's requirements, their offering was an all-metal biplane with the top wing attached directly to the fuselage and the lower wing on struts, slung between the body, thus inverting the normal biplane configuration. This concept was similar to the Wright NW-1 racer previously described. The fuselage was of all metal monocoque construction with the stressed skin taking some of the flight loads, a method soon to become standard in airframe manufacturing.

As the XFJ-1, the Berliner-Joyce fighter was first flown in May 1930, and sent to Anacostia for Naval evaluation. From the very beginning of flight testing, difficulty was encountered during landings. The XFJ-1 had an overwhelming tendency to ground-loop. Examination of the design indicates that perhaps the very low position of the bottom wing, scarcely two feet from the ground, made it a victim of air compression caused by ground-effect. It was not a complete surprise, then, that the XFJ-1 was severely damaged during a landing accident. It was returned to the manufacturer for repair and modification before testing was resumed.

When first delivered, the Berliner-Joyce fighter had an uncowled 450 hp Pratt & Whitney R-1340C. The upper wing sprouted directly from the top of the fuselage at a noticeable dihedral angle. Following the return visit to the factory of its origin, the plane reappeared with a Townend ring cowling over a new 500 hp R-1340-92 Wasp. This cowling, named after its English inventor, directed the air between the cylinders, thus helping to cool the engine. It also had an airfoil-shaped section which added enough forward force to cause a noticeable increase in airspeed. These factors, plus a large spinner and streamlined wheel fairings, combined to increase the top speed of the fighter by 16½ mph. During the reconstruction, the

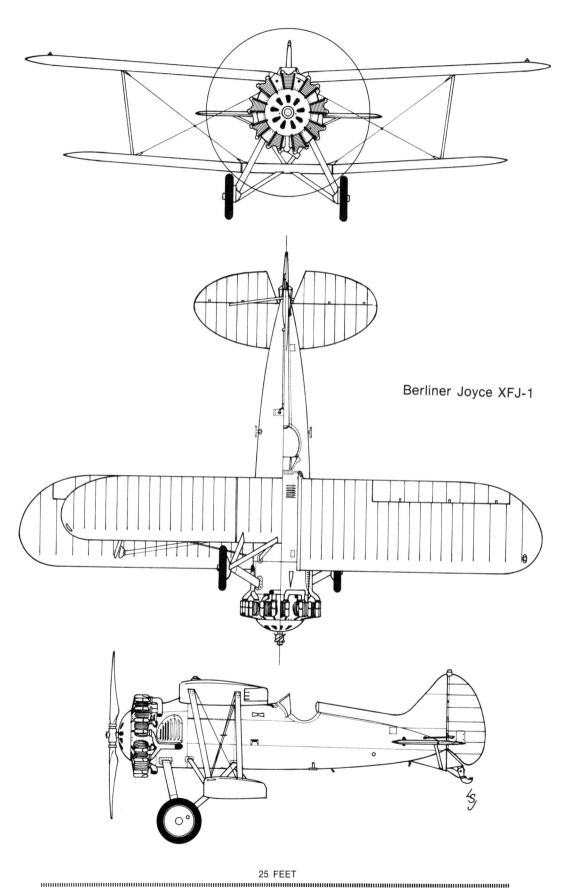

Berliner Joyce XFJ-1

25 FEET

The XFJ-1 with the modified gull wing. **Rockwell**

The rectangular panel under the top wing covers the flotation bags for emergency water landing. Rockwell

The final shape of the Berliner Joyce fighter. The Townend ring cowling had been installed, low pressure tires added and the designation changed to XFJ-2.   *Rockwell*

dihedral in the upper wings was eliminated, and in its new form, the wing root was gulled downward onto the fuselage. So extensive were these modifications, the Navy assigned a new designation to the plane and it became the XFJ-2. The performance of the XFJ-2 had increased notably but at the expense of stability. This, along with its continued tendency to ground-loop finally led to its abandonment as a potential fighter, though it continued as a medium for other tests for several years.

As the XFJ-2, it was capable of attaining a maximum speed of 193 mph and had a service ceiling of 24,500 feet. Wingspan was 28 feet 6 inches with an area of 178.6 square feet. Length was 20 feet 7 inches and height was 9 feet 10 inches. Empty weight was 2,-102 pounds, normal gross was 2,847 pounds, but it could be loaded up to 3,116 pounds. Internal fuel tanks holding 91 gallons gave the XFJ-2 a range of 400 miles. No armament was installed.

CURTISS
F9C SPARROWHAWK

A-9056 is the first F9C-2. It was assigned to the USS Macon.   Lowell Dixon

A unique specification for a compact fighter was drawn up and presented by the Navy on May 10, 1930. The requirements were precisely outlined, giving gross weight, dimensions, airfoil to be used, even the propeller diameter and tire size were prescribed. Not mentioned in the Bureau of Aeronautics Design No. 96 was the fact that the accepted fighter was to be the strong-arm of an airborne aircraft carrier.

The U.S. Navy had become the owner of a large German-built Zeppelin as part of the repatriations of World War I. It had been christened USS Los Angeles, and though it was not designed to carry airplanes, it was the catalyst of the flying aircraft carrier concept. The Los Angeles was received by the Navy on October 14, 1924, and became a vehicle to refine the aerial recovery system required for the carrier concept.

In 1926, the Akron and Macon airships were ordered by the Navy—each to have a 60 by 75 foot hangar for the stowing of four small fighters. The specific dimensions called out in Design No. 96 would permit the little fighter to be raised through the hangar opening.

Strictly speaking, the "airship fighters" were not actually fighters, but were scouts to be operated at a distance from the parent airship in much the way that modern carrier-based reconnaissance planes are used.

Curtiss and General Aviation answered the request for the new proposal and both received contracts for prototypes of a compact carrier-based fighter. The Curtiss XF9C-1 was completed and flew on February 12, 1931. A month later, it was delivered for qualification tests at Anacostia Naval Air Station, Washington, D.C. Initial tests of the XF9C-1, called Sparrowhawk, were not entirely satisfactory; perhaps due to the strict design parameter presented to the airframe builders. In the original form, it was unstable, had a vicious spin, and pilot visibility was poor. In fact, it was hard to find anything encouraging about the plane. However, a comparison of the performance of the prototype Sparrowhawk with the Design No. 96 requirements shows the plane actually met or exceeded them.

The XF9C-1, along with a list of recommended corrections, was returned to the Curtiss plant. The changes were so extensive that virtually a new airplane was called for. Since the No. 96 requirements were so strict, and the resulting aircraft was clearly not suited for conventional carrier use, Curtiss engineers suspected another use

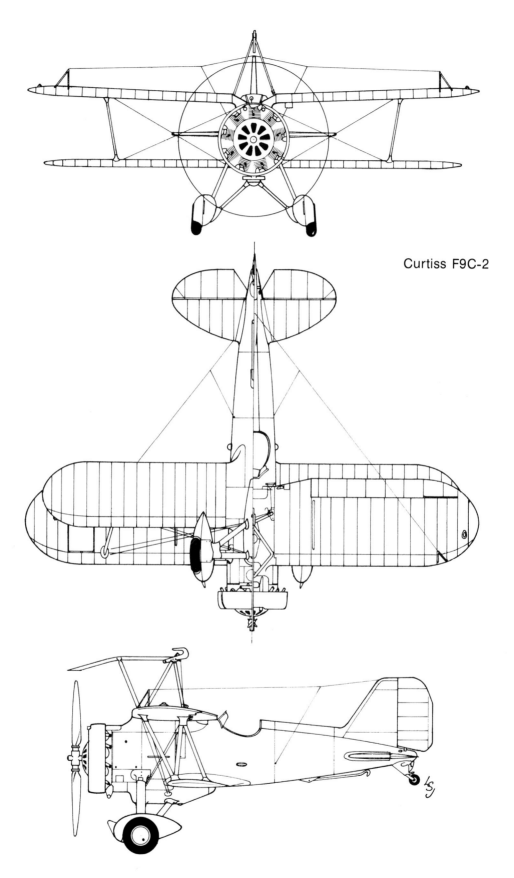

Curtiss F9C-2

25 FEET

A classic shot of the second Sparrowhawk engaging the trapeze on the USS Macon.   *Navy*

Here a Sparrowhawk is seen from the opening in the dirigible. The V stripe on the top wing was for alignment in formation. The shadow of the Macon trails on the water below.   *Wayne Morris*

for the plane may have been intended. At the company's expense, they set about designing an improved model with characteristics aimed at airship operation.

This model became the XF9C-2, although Curtiss operated it with a civil license during its development. The improved performance of the revised design was sufficient to

The fins on the front of the wheel pants were to deflect the arresting cables beneath the wheels during a carrier landing. The Sparrowhawks had both airship and carrier hooks, both of which can be seen in this photo.

Wayne Morris

The Sparrowhawk cockpit was simple and compact. *Wayne Morris*

warrant an order for six F9C-2's, and the civil prototype was eventually purchased as well.

The first hook-up trials with the F9C-2 were performed with the Akron on June 29, 1932, and some directional instability was encountered. This was corrected by the addition of 3 inches to the rudder. The Sparrowhawks became operational in September 1932. After the pilots had become thoroughly familiar with their little scout/fighters, they found they could **operate the planes without the heavy landing gear. Since launch and recovery was** made in the air, wheels were not always needed. When the landing gear was removed, a 30 gallon fuel tank was usually installed in its place. In this condition, the top speed of the Sparrowhawk was increased by 14 mph.

Operational experience unveiled many shortcomings in both the Sparrowhawks and the concept for which they were created. In mock combat, they were unable to defend the giant airship; and navigation involving a moving aerial base with the instruments available at that time caused much difficulty. It all became academic when the Akron was destroyed on April 4, 1933; and the Macon went down on February 12, 1935. The latter took four Sparrowhawks with it. This left only two F9C-2's and the

XF9C-2 prototype. The XF9C-1 had been previously scrapped due to its poor performance. These were sent to North Island NAS, San Diego, and within a year the two production Sparrowhawks were scrapped. The original XF9C-2 was spared this fate and continued to serve the Navy in a utility role until 1939, when it was turned over to the Smithsonian Institution. It has been fully restored to its former splendor for display in the National Air and Space Museum in Washington, D.C.

The diminutive F9C-2 Sparrowhawk had a wingspan of 25 feet 6 inches with an area of 175 square feet. It measured 20 feet 1 inch in length and stood 9 feet 10½ inches from the ground to the top of its airship hook. Empty weight was 2,114 pounds, gross was 2,776 pounds with a maximum weight of 2,888 pounds. A Wright R-975-22 was mounted to the Sparrowhawk and its 420 hp gave it a speed of 176.5 mph with the landing gear in place. With the gear off, the top speed was 190 mph. Internal fuel tankage was 60 gallons and the bullet-like external tank had a capacity of 30 gallons more. As usual, two .30 cal. machine guns were installed in the forward fuselage. These were Browning M-2's with 600 rounds of ammunition per gun. Service ceiling was 19,200 feet.

The XFA-1 was an unsuccessful competitor for the airship fighter role.   *Rockwell*

The second company to submit a proposal for the Navy's Design No. 96, which was to evolve into the airship-fighter program, was General Aircraft Corporation. This company was a descendant of the American branch of the famous Fokker Company, which had already been reorganized as Atlantic Aircraft. Realignment of management following the formation of the new company led to a delay in completing their offering, but it was finally delivered to Anacostia on March 5, 1932, where the contractor proceeded to demonstrate its abilities.

Obviously, due to the very strict specifications set forth in the Navy's requirements, the XFA-1, as it was called, was a virtual twin of the Curtiss Sparrowhawk. And, like the Curtiss plane, it suffered from similar handling flaws, mainly longitudinal instability. The manufacturers received the plane for a series of recommended changes which included increasing the area of all the tail surfaces and the addition of trimming tabs to the elevators.

The XFA-1 was returned to the Navy for continuation of the flight testing, but the new reports were even more unfavorable than before. The modifications seemed to have had an opposite effect to those desired and some even less desirable traits had developed. As the throttle was advanced, the plane began to nose up abruptly, but upon reducing the power, it became overly nose heavy. Within a month it was back at the factory for more alterations.

By the time the XFA-1 was again in the hands of the Navy's testing facilities, it was being considered with some skepticism and following weight and balance tests by the Navy, the General Aircraft people were asked to report on the XFA-1's spinning characteristics. After three attempts ended in near disasters, the plane was classed unsafe and further testing was abandoned.

The sheet metal application on the fuselage of the all-metal XFA-1 is worth noting. Usually, metal-skinned aircraft of the period were lap-jointed; that is, the edges of the metal panels were overlapped about an inch and rivets were driven through this overlap into the internal bulkheads. In the case of the XFA-1, the edges of the sheets were bent inward and the

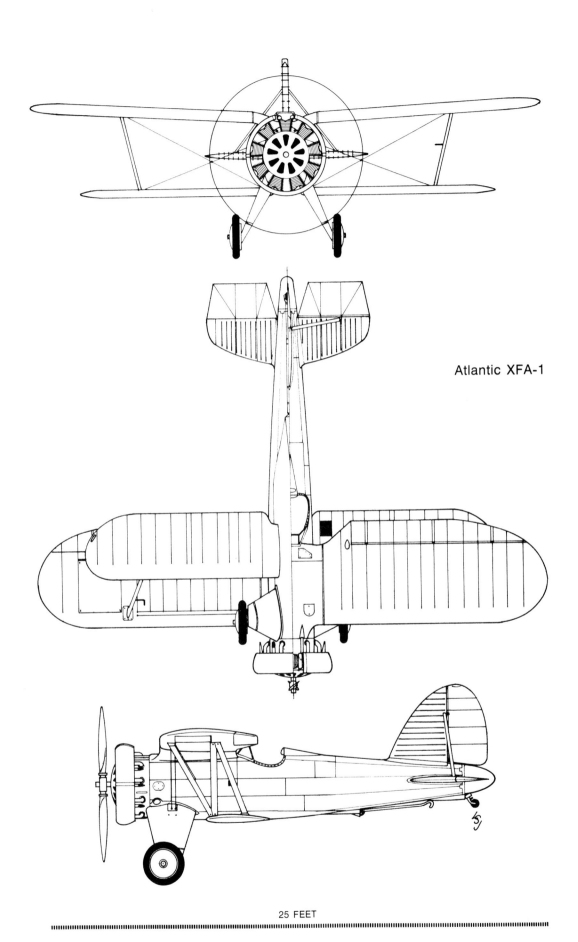

Atlantic XFA-1

25 FEET

rivets were applied to this flange. When the assembly was complete, the rivets were inside the fuselage, out of the airstream, and a much smoother finish was obtained.

Dimensions of the General XFA-1 show a wingspan of 25 feet 6 inches, a length of 22 feet 2 inches and a height of 9 feet 3 inches. Wing area was 175 square feet. The empty airframe weighed 1,837 pounds, and loaded for flight it tipped 2,508 pounds. The fuel tank held 60 gallons and gave a range of 375 miles. The XFA-1 had a top speed of 170 mph and could operate at a ceiling of 20,200 feet. The armament, consisting of two .30 cal. guns with 200 rpg, were mounted and ground tested. Even this prov-ed unsatisfactory, however, because of a high rate of jamming due to improper belt feeding.

Thus ended the airship fighter experiment. Some articles indicate that the Berliner-Joyce XFJ-1 was also conceived to meet the Design No. 96 requirements, but this appears unlikely since it was proposed in May 1929, while the Navy's specifications were not released until May 10, 1930—after the XFJ-1 had been completed. Perhaps the proportions of the XFJ-1 had some influence on the Navy's concept, but it's very doubtful that there was ever any serious consideration given to its use in this specialized role.

Grumman's FF-1 was popularly known as "Fifi" by its pilots. *Grumman*

With the signing of an agreement on April 2, 1931, the Navy began a relationship that was to produce a series of the most successful naval aircraft in history. This agreement was to lead to the delivery of an entirely new two-seat fighter prototype whose novel, yet practical features, and un-excelled performance was to obsolete the Navy's existing fighter force.

Grumman Aircraft Co. was a spin-off of the Loening Aircraft Corp. which had just been sold. Grover Loening, president of the earlier company, was the inventor of a landing gear retraction system which had been used successfully on his famous amphibians. The rights to this invention were assigned to the new Grumman Company, of which Loening was a major stockholder. Relying on its past experience of building metal aircraft floats and truck bodies, Grumman designers set about developing their XFF-1 to include retracting wheels and a sliding cover for the double cockpit.

The bulging fuselage of the XFF-1 contrasted sharply with the trim shapes which had finally evolved among its contemporaries. The pot-belly was necessary to provide ground clearance for the squat landing gear. The Grumman fighter was first flown on December 29, 1931, and it was flown that same day to Anacostia to begin its trials. The powerplant was a Wright R-

1820E with a maximum of 620 hp and was intended for civil operation instead of military. However, this did not prove a hindrance since the XFF-1 proceeded to breeze through her tests with little difficulty and achieved a speed as high as 197 mph.

Recommendations for changes were few and Grumman was presented with a contract for 27 FF-1's in December 1932. Production FF-1's were outfitted with a military R-1820-78 which delivered 700 hp and increased the maximum speed to above 200 mph. With this performance, the big two-place fighter easily outdistanced the Navy's single-seat fleet. At first, the enclosed cockpit and folding gear were greeted with skepticism by the Navy pilots. The spidery-looking landing gear caused some misgivings among the carrier pilots used to slamming their planes onto a carrier deck. And, the enclosed canopy . . . "What if you had to get out in a hurry?" Operational experience dispelled these fears and the FF-1 earned the affectionate name "Fifi" among its crews.

The two-seat arrangement of the FF-1 made it a candidate for scouting operations, and to this end the SF-1 was developed. This now gave the Navy a scouting plane that could outperform every fighter in its inventory, except, of course, Fifi. Thirty-three SF-1's were delivered.

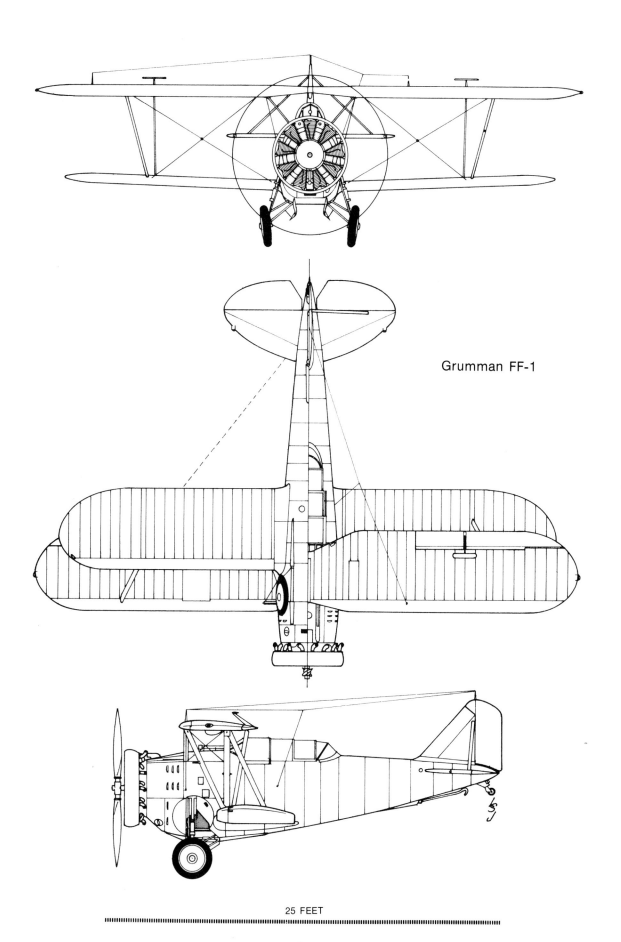

Grumman FF-1

25 FEET

The FF-1 introduced retractable landing gear to Navy fighters.   Grumman

Navy pilots were somewhat apprehensive about the enclosed cockpit on the FF-1.   Grumman

This FF-1 belongs to the Red Rippers, VF-5, based on the USS Lexington.   Gordon S. Williams

The FF-2, shown here, was a dual-control trainer converted from an FF-1.   Gordon S. Williams

By 1935, the FF-1's were being replaced by single-seaters which were equalling their performance and the Grumman fighters were modified into dual-control trainers as FF-2's. The last Fifi was retired from its duties in 1942, after a decade of service, quite an accomplishment for a plane that represented the first offering of a new company.

The FF-1 wingspan was 34 feet 6 inches, area was 310 square feet. Length was 24 feet 6 inches and it was 11 feet 1 inch high. With an empty weight of 3,250 pounds, it had a gross of 4,828 pounds. Fuel load was 140 gallons for a range of 921 miles. The 700 hp Wright R-1820-78 gave the FF-1 a high speed of 207 mph at 4,000 feet. Service ceil-ing was 21,100 feet. The barrels of two .30 cal. machine guns could be seen in the nose and the rear crewman had a single .30 that he could mount in a socket for rear defense, if needed.

The FF-1's role in the U.S. Navy was passive, but license-built versions of the Grumman fighter were assembled in Canada and several of these were actually involved in combat during the 1938 Spanish Civil War. This would make them the earliest American-designed Navy fighter to participate in any significant warfare. Incidentally, the foreign version of the FF-1 used an 800 hp R-1820-F52 Wright Cyclone which gave it a maximum speed of 216 mph!

The Berliner-Joyce XF2J-1 had open cockpits when delivered to the Navy.   Rockwell

The Navy was still serious about two-place fighters when they discussed the possibility of producing such a machine with Berliner-Joyce in 1931. This company had produced the P-16 two-seat fighter for the Army as the result of a 1929 competition. Based on this experience, Berliner-Joyce received a development contract for the XF2J-1 fighter.

Original plans called for the installation of a Pratt & Whitney R-1690C Hornet, with 525 hp. As development of the plane proceeded, the 625 hp Wright R-1510-92 double-row radial became available and it was decided to mount the larger engine to the frame. Engineering on the XF2J-1 moved slowly and it was two years after the contract was signed before the fighter saw the light of day.

In keeping with the trend of the time, the XF2J-1's upper wing was gulled at the roots to blend into the fuselage top. This represented better streamlining than the more conventional strut-mounted wing, but it had the disadvantage of obstructing the pilot's view of the carrier deck during landing. When the plane was finally delivered to the testing facilities, it had two open cockpits for its crew. With the appearance of the Grumman FF-1 and its enclosed crew

quarters, the XF2J-1 was treated to the same fixture, but it did little more than keep the crew out of the slipstream.

Aside from the aforementioned factors, the XF2J-1 was a fairly good performer considering it had been conceived some two years prior to its testing program. However, during its gestation period, the newly-formed Grumman Company had revolutionized the two-seat fighter concept and the XF2J-1 was simply outclassed. Since the FF-1 was proving eminently successful, it was pointless to expend additional funds and effort in attempting to improve the B/J fighter.

The XF2J-1 recorded a maximum speed of 196 mph at 6,000 feet and had a service ceiling of 21,500 feet. The wingspan was 36 feet with an area of 303½ square feet. It was 28 feet 10 inches long and had a height of 11 feet 2 inches. Empty weight was 3,211 pounds, gross was 4,539 pounds. Maximum overload brought the total up to 4,851 pounds. Normal fuel capacity was 80 gallons which gave a range of 522 miles, but with an additional 80 gallons the range could be extended to 1,015 miles.

The final blow to the XF2J-1 came when production of the double-row Wright engine used to power the fighter was cancelled.

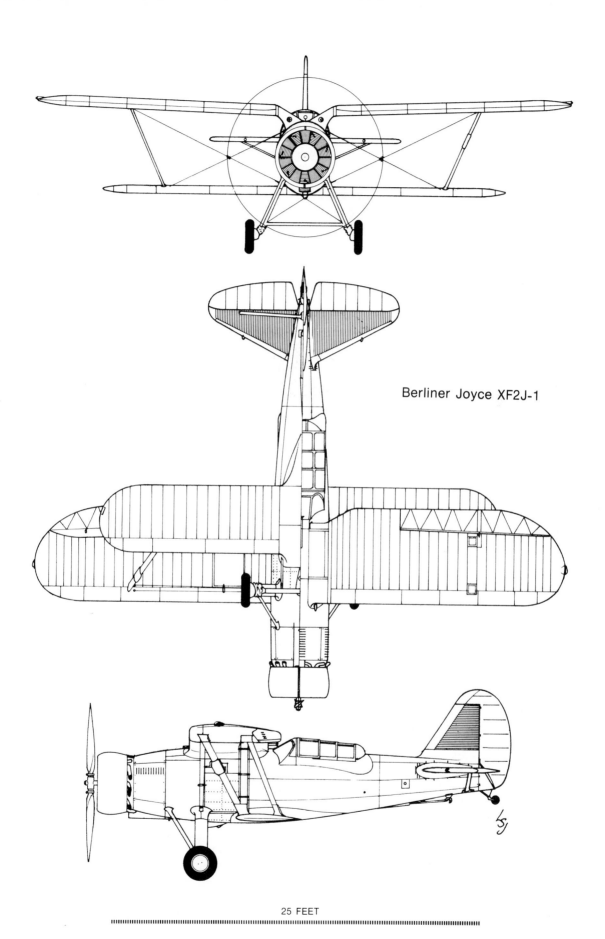

Berliner Joyce XF2J-1

25 FEET

A fully-enclosed cockpit was added to the XF2J-1 after testing had begun.   *Rockwell*

With fixed landing gear and open cockpits, the XF2J-1 was outclassed by the FF-1.   *Rockwell*

This view shows the wide sliding canopy and gulled upper wing of the B/J fighter.   *Rockwell*

VOUGHT
XF3U

The XF3U-1 was Vought's entry in the two-place fighter competition of 1932.   *William T. Larkins*

Bureau of Aeronautics Design No. 113 outlined a two-seat biplane fighter of conventional layout with fixed landing gear and a set of landing flaps attached to the upper wings. Either the double-row Pratt & Whitney Twin Wasp or Wright Whirlwind 14 could be used. Each engine delivered 700 hp, was geared, and supercharged.

Both Douglas and Vought responded to the Navy's request and Vought was the first to receive an order, this for one XF3U-1, BuNo 9222, on June 30, 1932. On May 9, 1933, the new fighter made its maiden flight from Vought's field at East Hartford, Conn. The most noticeable difference between Vought's fighter and the Navy's current crop of two-seaters were the XF3U-1's tapered wings. The cockpit was protected by a large greenhouse-like canopy.

But again, the Navy began to have misgivings about the suitability of two-place carrier fighters; and despite the respectable performance of the XF3U-1, no orders for the fighter were forthcoming. However, the Navy was very interested in a scout bomber with a performance that matched its fighters and directed the company to alter its XF3U-

1 to fit such a role. If it was successful, there would be a contract for twenty-seven of the scout bombers.

The XF3U-1 reappeared as the XSBU-1 in the summer of 1934—highly modified but bearing the same BuNo. The wings were enlarged and strengthened to withstand the high "g" forces at the end of the dive. It had a new cockpit, but it still was an interim design pending its qualifications as a dive bomber. At the conclusion of the tests, the promised contract was increased to eighty-four SBU-1 dive bombers which became a major element in the Navy's attack fleet.

According to Navy records, the single XSBU-1 was assigned the BuNo 9746, but Vought records indicate there was a second XF3U-1 with that serial. It appears that the original airframe may have been renumbered after the SBU-1 acceptance flights, since only single examples of these experimental fighters were ordered in all other instances. In any case, #9746 was sent to Pratt & Whitney for the testing of new engines.

As the XF3U-1, the Vought fighter displayed these characteristics: wingspan was

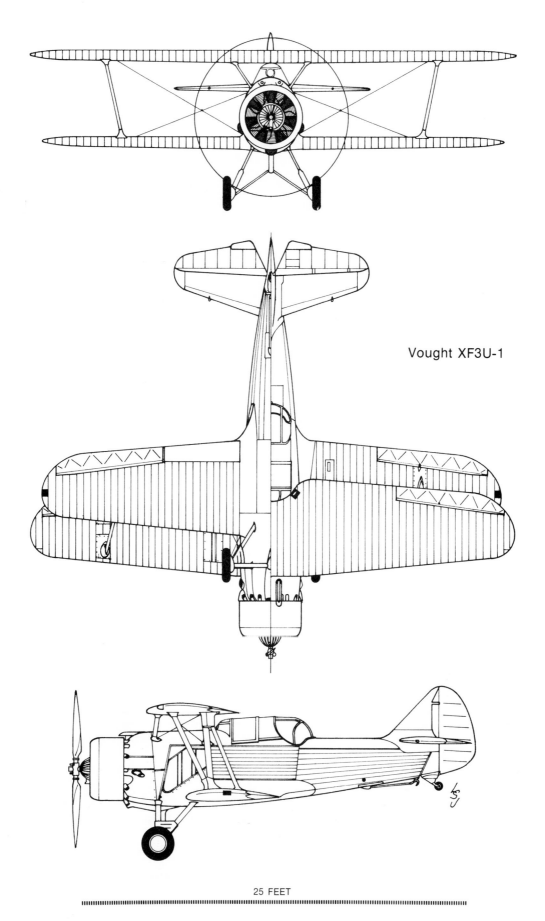

Vought XF3U-1

25 FEET

The XF3U-1 was not suited for the fighter role.   *William T. Larkins*

As the prototype XSBU-1 dive bomber, the former XF3U-1 still carries its original Bureau Number, 9222.
                                                                              Vought

Here 9222 has virtually completed the transformation into the SBU-1 bomber with a revised rudder. Vought

31 feet 6 inches, wing area was 295 square feet, length was 26 feet 6 inches, and it was 10 feet 11 inches high. With its 700 hp Pratt & Whitney R-1535-64 engine, it had a top speed of 214 mph and a service ceiling of 24,600 feet. With its landing flaps lowered, the XF3U-1 could touch-down at 64 mph. Empty weight was 3,078 pounds, gross was 4,616 pounds. One hundred ten gallons of gasoline could be carried to provide a range of 570 miles.

Another victim of the Navy's second thoughts about two-place fighters was the Douglas XFD-1. Douglas

The second company to submit an acceptable proposal for the Navy's Design No. 113 was Douglas. This company also received a development contract on June 30, 1932, for a single prototype of their concept of the requirement.

Douglas was no novice at designing military aircraft; their first was a large torpedo bomber, the DT-1, in 1921. Within ten years, the company's engineers had produced a very advanced twin-engined amphibian featuring retractable landing gear. Twenty of these were operated by the Navy and Coast Guard as "Dolphins." Their first fighter, however, was slated for a less than spectacular existence.

As Vought had with the XF3U-1, Douglas also chose to develop their fighter around the 700 hp Pratt & Whitney R-1535-64 Twin Wasp engine. This power unit was slightly smaller in diameter than the similar Wright engine mentioned in the Navy's design requirement, and therefore, offered less aerodynamic drag. Douglas designers wrapped a long-chord cowling tightly around the engine to reduce drag even more. The newly-accepted cockpit enclosure covered the crew positions, but the landing gear was rigidly affixed to the fuselage un-

derside. The wings had a straight taper on both leading and trailing edges, similar to those of the Vought XF3U-1 and also had landing flaps on the top wing. In fact, there was very little difference to distinguish one machine from the other.

Douglas presented the XFD-1 to the Navy for trials on June 18, 1932, preceding the Vought by four days. The tests showed the XFD-1 could reach a top speed of 204 mph at an altitude of 8,900 feet. It could climb to 5,000 feet in 3.1 minutes and had a service ceiling of 23,700 feet. With a full load of 110 gallons of fuel, the XFD-1 could fly for 576 miles. Structural weight of the fighter was 3,227 pounds empty, with a gross of 4,745 pounds. Highest permissible weight was 5,000 pounds. Wingspan was 31 feet 6 inches, length was 25 feet 4 inches, height was 11 feet 1 inch. The XFD-1 had two fixed forward-firing .30 cal. machine guns and a swivel-mounted .30 for rear defense. One 500 pound bomb or two 116 pounders could also be carried.

The results of the tests gave the edge to the Vought XF3U-1, which went on to become the SBU dive bomber, but the Navy was no longer desirous of a two-seat fighter and the XFD-1 faded into oblivion.

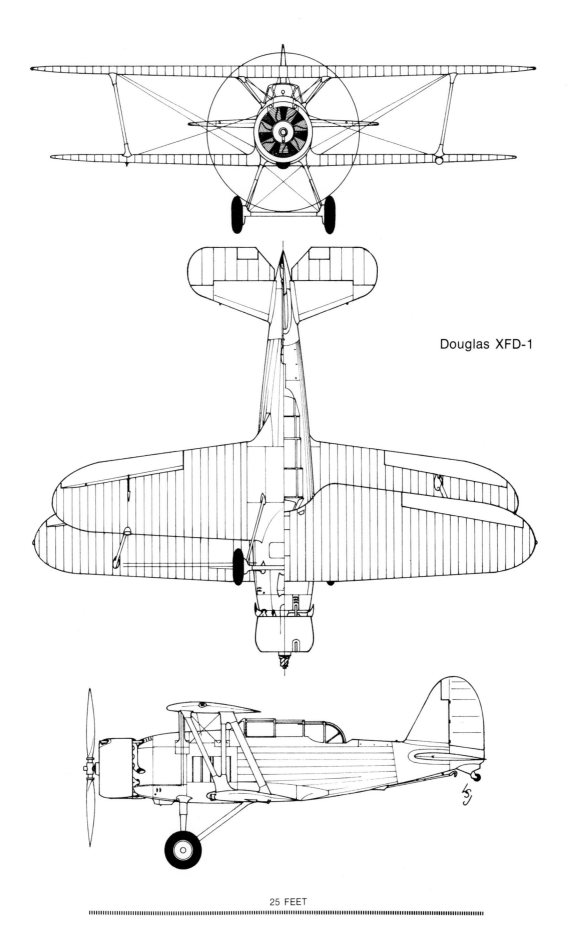

Douglas XFD-1

25 FEET

The Douglas fighter was remarkably similar to the Vought design.   Gordon S. Williams

The two-man crew monitors an engine run-up prior to a test flight of the XFD-1.   Gordon S. Williams

This plane was temporarily designated XF10C-1 during its construction.   Gordon S. Williams

The designation XF10C-1 does not appear on any list of Naval fighters, yet such a title was briefly assigned to one Curtiss airplane. In fact, this particular ship bore no less than four separate designations!

The airframe bearing BuNo A-8847 began as the first of a group of three Curtiss XF8C-8 twin-seat fighters. Originally constructed with a Wright R-1510 14 cylinder Whirlwind, #8847 was slated to receive a Wright R-1820 Cyclone. At this time the entire empennage was redesigned; and with the new tail surfaces and engine, the plane became the O2C-2. Further modifications included replacement of the tripod landing gear assembly with single struts braced by wire. At this point, A-8847 became the XF10C-1 and was to serve as the prototype of a new Helldiver series. However, the Navy's sudden lack of interest in two-seat fighters brought about a designation change to XS3C-1.

Despite the wide range of designations applied to #8847, the Navy lists it in its original role of O2C-2. The following specifications are for the O2C. Span was 32 feet with a 308 square foot wing area. Length was 27 feet 8 inches, height was 10 feet 3 inches. Empty and gross weights were 2,520 pounds and 4,627 pounds respectively. This version of the Helldiver had a maximum speed of 174 mph.

The O2C-2's were relegated to utility duties and underwent many individual changes. These included the addition of wheelpants, and even an enclosed cockpit to create an executive-type transport.

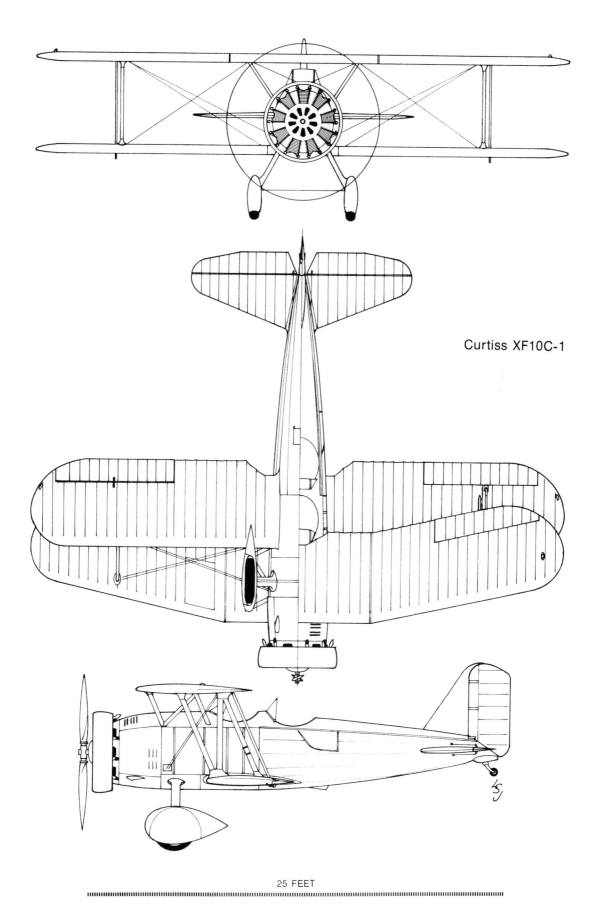

Curtiss XF10C-1

25 FEET

The "XF10C-1" differed from the XF8C-8 mainly in the shape of the tail assembly and modifications to the landing gear. *Gordon S. Williams*

The lines of the F8C are seen in this view of the Curtiss scout. *Gordon S. Williams*

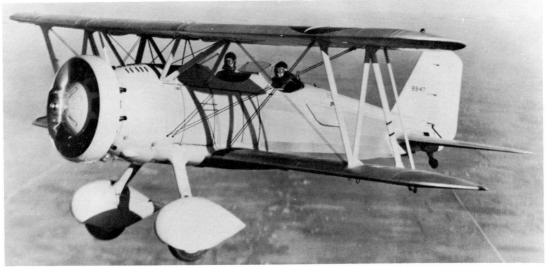

A-8847 was finally designated XS3C-1 when the Navy abandoned the two-seat fighter category. *Gordon S. Williams*

CURTISS
F11C (BFC & BF2C) GOSHAWK

A BF2C-1 of Bombing Squadron Five. The V shaped marks on the fuselage are access areas covered by zippered panels.

Gordon S. Williams

While the Navy had lost interest in the two-place fighter concept, they did find the ability of these planes to deliver bombs very intriguing. At this time, the Army's P-6E Hawk was also attracting the Navy's attention, especially an experimental version constructed of metal, the XP-23.

The Curtiss Company had financed the construction of a radial-powered Hawk for their own evaluation in the hope of either selling it to the Navy or exporting it to gain a new lease on the Hawk's life span. This plane had been undergoing flight testing since March 25, 1932. The next month, on April 16, the Navy ordered one prototype as the XF11C-1 and purchased the Curtiss demonstrator, designating it the XF11C-2.

The XF11C-2 arrived on May 2, at Anacostia for the Navy's Bureau of Aeronautics evaluation. It mounted a 700 hp Wright SR-1820-78 Cyclone. Flight testing was not without its mishaps and the plane was severely damaged on several occasions, but in general its performance was outstanding.

When the XF11C-1 was delivered, it differed from the -2 in several respects. Its deeper cowl enclosed a double-row Wright

R-1510-98 with 600 hp. This arrangement made the XF11C-1 two feet longer than later production models. The wings were those of the rejected Army XP-23, which had been dismantled after its Army tests were completed. The Navy, pleased with the new ships, ordered twenty-eight F11C-2's with 700 hp Wright R-1820-78 Cyclones. All of these were assigned to VF-1B on the Saratoga.

Since these new fighters, called Goshawk in keeping with the Hawk lineage, were also capable of dive-bombing as well, the Navy chose a new designation class to distinguish them from the pure fighters. The XF11C-1 had been changed to XBFC-1—the "B" indicating its bombardment role. In keeping with this, the F11C-2's became BFC-2's.

The F11C-2/BFC-2 wings were formed of spruce covered with fabric. Span was 31 feet 6 inches and the area was 262 square feet. Overall length was 23 feet, height was 10 feet 7 inches. The production F11C-2 was a composite of the two Goshawk prototypes, plus some features of its own. The landing gear was similar to the -1 but the engine cowl was slightly wider than that of the -2. Ten BFC-2's on a second order featured a

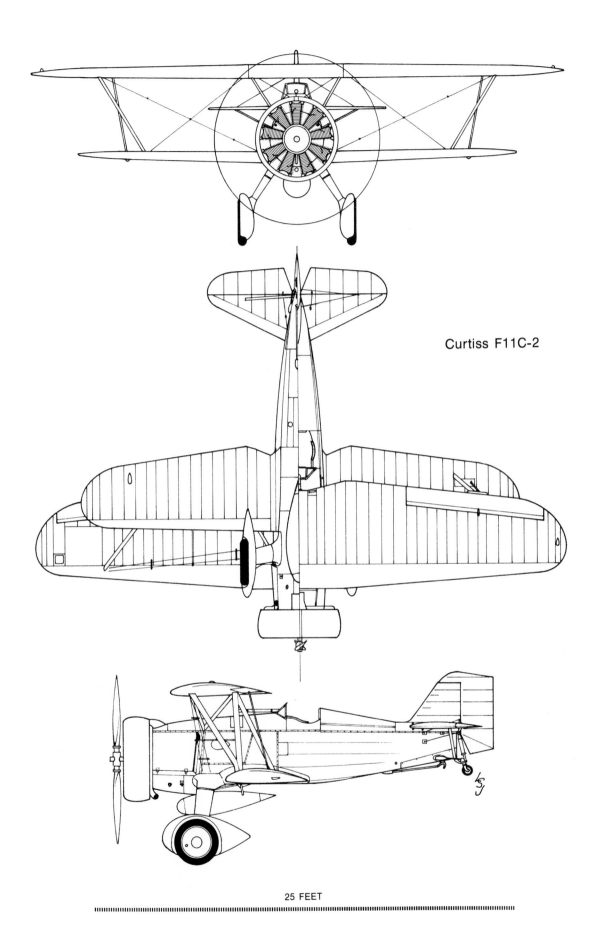

Curtiss F11C-2

25 FEET

Although performance was good, the BF2C-1's suffered from structural weakness and were withdrawn from service.
Gordon S. Williams

The Navy was so impressed with Grumman's retracting landing gear that Curtiss installed it on the Goshawk.
Gordon S. Williams

The F11C-2 was classed as a bomber-fighter and redesignated BFC-2.   *Gordon S. Williams*

raised turtle deck which held the pilot's life raft.

The BFC-2 weighed 3,037 pounds empty and grossed 4,120 pounds. Performance varied as the roles were changed. As a fighter it had a top speed of 205 mph while the heavy, drag-producing bombs slowed it to 195 mph. As a dive bomber, one 500 pound or four 112 pound bombs were carried. Service ceiling was 24,300 feet. Up to 150 gallons of fuel could be carried internally and another 50 gallon tank could be attached to the fuselage bomb rack. Thus equipped, the BFC-2 had a range of 628 miles. Two .30 cal. guns were installed on the cowling, firing between the cylinders.

The retractable landing gear of Grumman's FF-1 had so favorably impressed the Navy that, at Curtiss' suggestion, the fifth F11C-2 became the recipient of a similar system. As the XF11C-3, it arrived at Anacostia on May 23, 1933. The retracted gear cleaned up the airplane sufficiently to increase the maximum speed to 216 mph. The engine used on the XF11C-3 was an R-1820-80 of 700 hp. Twenty-seven of the new Goshawks were ordered in February 1934, and labeled BF2C-1. These planes had a

partial sliding canopy on a modified turtle deck and controllable pitch propeller. To further strengthen the new dive bomber/fighters, the all-metal wing structure of the XP-23 was adopted. First deliveries of the BF2C-1 took place on October 7, 1934, and the entire group was turned over to VB-5B on the USS Ranger.

Soon after operations had begun, the BF2C-1's began to react strangely. The plane suffered from severe vibrations, especially when a bomb or drop tank was attached to the fuselage rack. The air flowing through the recessed channel between the retracted wheels became turbulent when the stores were in place. This problem was corrected by the installation of a tubular airfoil just in front of the attachment point, but there was still a noticeable airframe vibration in the cruise regime of the fighter. Further tests disclosed that the vibrations of the R-1820 engine, combined with the controllable-pitch propeller, complimented the vibrations of the metal in the wings and set up a dangerous harmonic reaction. Within months of their acceptance into the service, all the BF2C-1's were withdrawn, classed as unsafe, and destroyed.

The wingspan and area of the BF2C-1

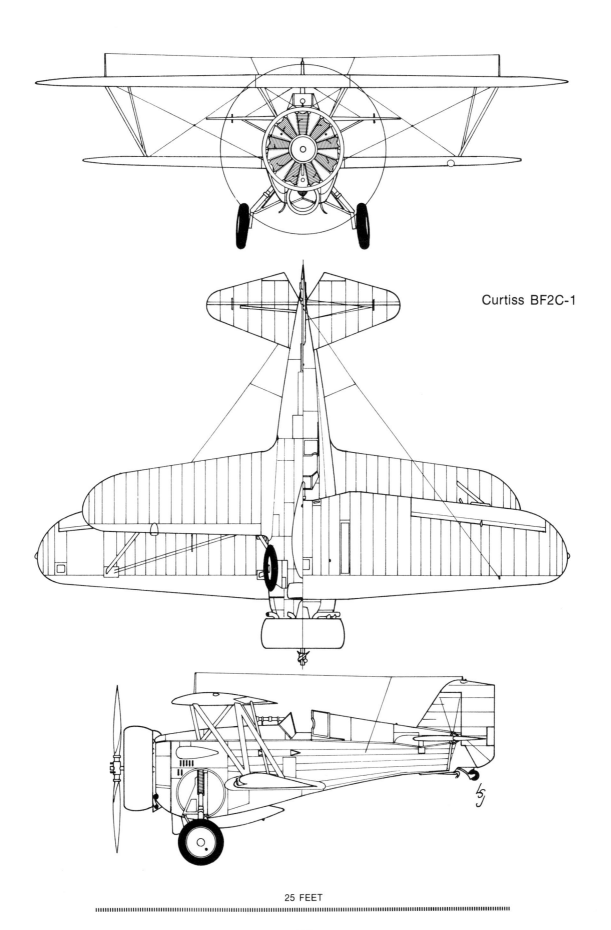

Curtiss BF2C-1

25 FEET

The XF11C-1. This plane had a double-row engine that necessitated a deeper cowl.   Gordon S. Williams

A production F11C-2 under test before delivery to a squadron.   Gordon S. Williams

was the same as the BFC-2. Length was 23 feet, height was 10 feet 10 inches. Its empty weight was 3,329 pounds, gross was 4,555 pounds. Maximum weight came to 5,086 pounds. Highest speed, as a fighter, was 225 mph. With a 474 pound bomb load, this was reduced to 210 mph. Alternatively, two 116 pound bombs could be carried under the wings. Two .30 cal. Browning machine guns were carried in the nose. Service ceiling was 27,000 feet; and with a fuel load of 160 gallons, both internal and in the auxiliary tank, a distance of 1,054 miles could be flown.

BOEING
XF6B-1/XBFB-1

The XF6B-1 after it was reclassed and designated XBFB-1 for its bomber-fighter role.   *Boeing*

Boeing's last biplane offering showed more improvement in the area of appearance than performance. The most significant change from the final F4B series was the use of a 625 hp Pratt & Whitney R-1535-44 Twin Wasp. The basic construction of the XF6B-1 was of metal with only the wing skins of fabric. It was ordered by the Navy on June 30, 1931. By February 1, 1933, the XF6B-1 was airborne on her first test-hop, but was delivered to the Navy for their phase of the testing program nearly two years later.

During the early part of the 'thirties, the Navy was studying several approaches to the operations of their aircraft. One of these was the two-seat fighter concept. Another was the dual use of a single type as both a fighter and a bomber. In the case of the two-place types, the resultant aircraft was invariably too large and heavy to perform effectively as a fighter. These planes had been relegated to the scout/observation roles. On the other hand, the alterations of a single-seat fighter to carry bombs was relatively minor. In some cases it merely meant attaching bomb racks to the fighter. The fighter was already capable of sustaining the high "G" loads needed for bomb delivery. Therefore, the Bomber-Fighter had been defined; and it was in this class that the Boeing fighter found itself.

In March, 1934, the XF6B-1 became the XBFB-1 and flight testing revolved around its dual capabilities. Because of its all-metal structure, the XBFB-1 was extremely rugged and could safely withstand as much as nine times the force of gravity during maneuvering. But the very factor that assured its safety under great stress went against it when it was evaluated as a fighter. Its gross weight in the latter role was 3,704 pounds—nearly 600 pounds heavier than the F4B-4. The XBFB-1 was seven miles per hour faster than the F4B, but the higher gross weight compromised maneuverability.

The XBFB-1 underwent many alterations in attempts to improve its fighter

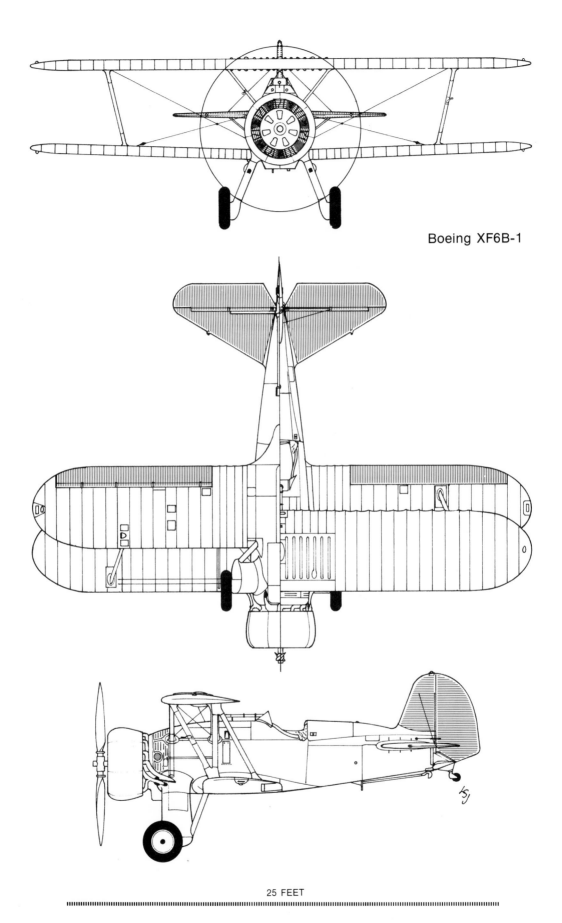

Boeing XF6B-1

25 FEET

The XF6B-1 was the final evolution of the F4B design.   *Boeing*

Several different cowlings and landing gear designs were tried on the XF6B-1.   *Boeing*

qualities. These were mainly in the area of streamlining the engine cowling and landing gear struts. At one point, the plane appeared with a three-bladed propeller, but it was plainly evident that it was not suitable for the dual-role concept. The sole XBFB-1 terminated its service in 1936 by ramming crash barriers at Norfolk Naval Air Station, Virginia.

The XF6B-1/XBFB-1 had equal-span wings measuring 28 feet 6 inches with a total area of 252 square feet. Overall length was 22 feet 2 inches, and it was 10 feet 6 in-

ches high. Maximum speed was reached at 6,000 feet and was 195 mph in level flight. Climb rate was 5,000 feet in 4.2 minutes. Service ceiling was 20,700 feet. Empty weight was 2,823 pounds. As a bomber, the XBFB-1 had a gross weight of 4,282 pounds. Two .30 cal. Browning machine guns were installed in the cowling. Bomb racks could hold one 500 pound bomb or two 115 pound bombs. On-board fuel capacity was 64 gallons which gave a range of 437 miles and external tanks could extend that to 737 miles.

With the leading-edge slats and landing flaps extended as shown here, the XF12C-1 had a landing speed of 64 mph.
William T. Larkins

By the early 1930's aircraft powerplants were delivering well over 700 hp with continued development pointing toward even greater outputs. On the other hand, aside from a few adventuresome forays into monoplane design, the airframe was still hindered by the external struts and rigging needed to support a second wing. Part of the reluctance to dispense with the biplane configuration was due to the strict size limitations imposed on a carrier-borne craft. The average Navy fighter wingspan was around thirty-five feet and even this caused a great deal of crowding on a carrier deck. The biplane had one advantage in providing the necessary wing area within the restricted dimensions. However, the convenience of parking is of little value when the pilot is tangling with an aerial foe. Clearly, the only way to take advantage of the increased engine power was to pursue the development of the monoplane.

Concurrently with the orders of the Douglas XFD-1 and Vought XF3U-1 biplanes on June 30, 1932, the Navy authorized Curtiss to proceed with construction of a monoplane with generally similar characteristics to those specified in B of A

design 113. In order to obtain the necessary lifting area, the high strut-mounted wing extended to a span of forty-one-and-a-half feet. The 272 square feet of area was comparable to contemporary biplane fighters, but it became necessary to provide a wing-folding system for carrier stowage. Thus, the XF12C-1 became the first U.S. Navy fighter to utilize this feature.

Although the wing folding concept was basically simple—it hinged on the rear main spar and swung aft—it was complicated by the parasol-mounting of the wing with its supporting struts which were also hinged. In addition to the folding wings, Curtiss also included a retracting landing gear on their new fighter. In keeping with the B of A specifications, the XF12C-1 seated two crewmen and derived its power from a Wright R-1510-92 Twin Whirlwind with 625 hp.

The XF12C-1, BuNo 9225, was completed by January 1933, and began the contractor's flight testing phase. General characteristics of the plane were found to be satisfactory, but it did not display the performance felt necessary for the new generation of fighters being sought by the Navy.

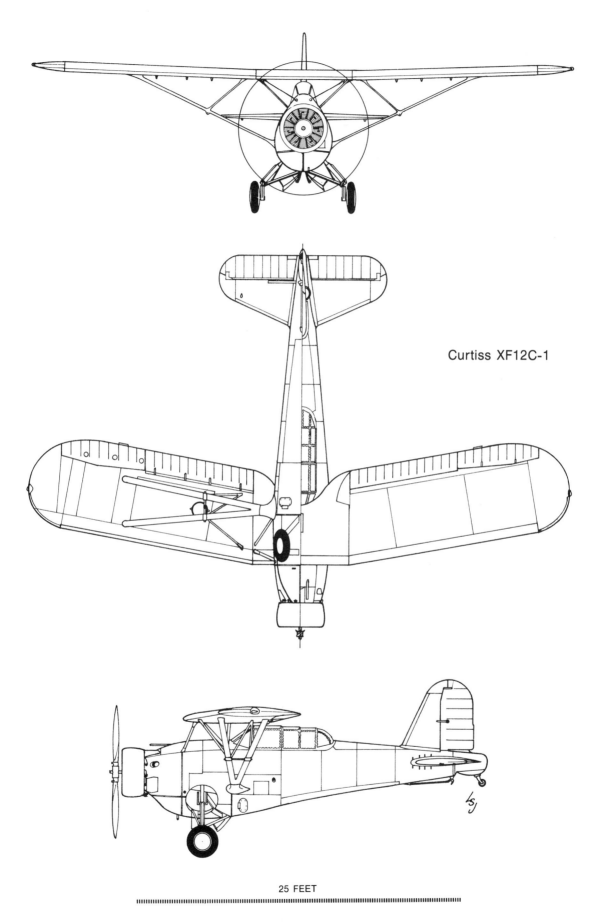

Curtiss XF12C-1

25 FEET

So, before delivering the plane to the Navy, Curtiss installed a 745 hp SR-1820-80 nine cylinder Wright Cyclone.

The XF12C-1 arrived at Anacostia in October 1933, for the Navy's evaluation. Conversion to the Cyclone engine did not improve the plane's fighter characteristics, but the Navy had been studying a new class of light attack bombers. In this new category, the XF12C-1 showed some promise, so flight testing proceeded with an eye toward adapting the plane to the role of a scout bomber. For this duty, the plane was designated XS4C-1 in December 1933; but a month later it became the XSBC-1. In June 1934, the prototype scout bomber was damaged in a crash. The damage was not too severe and the XSBC-1 was rebuilt and returned to the Navy for testing. Among the requirements for the new scout bomber class was the ability to deliver bombs at the end of a near-vertical dive, then climb sharply away. During one of these tests, the strut-mounted parasol wing failed and the craft plummeted into the ground. The Navy felt the plane did have some potential as a dive bomber in spite of the accident, but had some misgivings about the monoplane wing. Construction of a biplane version was authorized, to be designated XSBC-2, assigned the same BuNo, and powered by a Wright R-1510-12 of 700 hp. This new plane was designed expressly as a scout bomber and flew on December 9, 1935. This new machine responded to the test program so well that a production order for 83 SBC-3's was placed and another Helldiver was born. Ironically, what had been originally intended as the Navy's first production monoplane fighter actually became the prototype of the Navy's last operational biplane.

In its initial form the Curtiss XF12C-1 had a wingspan of 41 feet 6 inches with 272 square feet of area. It was 29 feet 1 inch long and 12 feet 11 inches high. With the original R-1510-92 engine, it had a maximum speed of 217 mph at 6,000 feet. With the use of trailing-edge flaps and leading edge slots, the XF12C-1 could be landed as slow as 64 mph. The empty airframe weighed 3,884 pounds, and normal gross was 5,461 pounds. Service ceiling was 22,500 feet; and with a fuel load of 110 gallons, the XF12C-1 had a range of 738 miles. Nose armament consisted of two .30 cal. machine guns in the cowl.

The first Curtiss monoplane design for a Navy fighter, the XF12C-1 proved to be better suited as a dive-bomber and was modified into the biplane SBC Helldiver.
William T. Larkins

At this stage of testing the XF12C-1 is powered by a Wright SR-1820-80 Cyclone engine. William T. Larkins

BERLINER-JOYCE
XF3J-1

The XF3J-1 was the last fixed-gear biplane fighter to be considered by the Navy. *Rockwell*

A Bureau of Aeronautics design proposal in 1932 brought forth the final fixed-gear biplane fighter to be considered by the Navy. Design No. 120 specified the use of a 625 hp Wright R-1510-26 engine on a single-seat carrier fighter. Two companies were awarded development contracts on June 30, and both submitted drawings for the approval of the Navy. The Grover Loening Aircraft Company reviewed their proposal with the Navy and both concluded it would not be sufficiently advanced to merit further development. Thus, the Loening XFL-1, as it was to have been known, was stillborn.

On the other hand, the Berliner-Joyce Company was allowed to continue with their proposal and eventually began construction of their XF3J-1. Completion of the fighter was delayed while the company underwent administrative changes which ultimately led to their becoming part of North American Aviation.

The XF3J-1 finally saw the light of day in January, 1934, and was sent to the Navy the following April. For a plane designed in 1932, the B/J fighter was a good performer, but its prolonged gestation period had made it obsolete in the face of more ambitious types already flying. As far as its lines were concerned, it was one of the most attractive planes on the flight line. It displayed some of the aspects of a racing plane, and its elliptical wings caused many to compare the XF3J-1 to a butterfly.

Construction of the Berliner-Joyce fighter was typical of the period. It was formed of metal with a semi-monocoque aluminum-covered fuselage. The elliptical wings were of metal framework covered with fabric. A long-chord cowling faired the big double-row Wright engine into the lines of the fuselage, and the cockpit was provided with a sliding cover. In keeping with the Navy's dual fighter-bomber concept, the XF3J-1 had attachment points for two 116 pound bombs under each wing.

The XF3J-1 could attain a speed of 209.3 mph at 6,000 feet, but the airframe was beset by an excessive amount of vibration and the tests were terminated in September, 1935. The XF3J-1 wings spanned 29 feet with an area of 240 square feet; and the plane measured 22 feet 11 inches long with a height of 10 feet 9 inches. The B/J fighter could climb to 5,000 feet in 2.7 minutes and

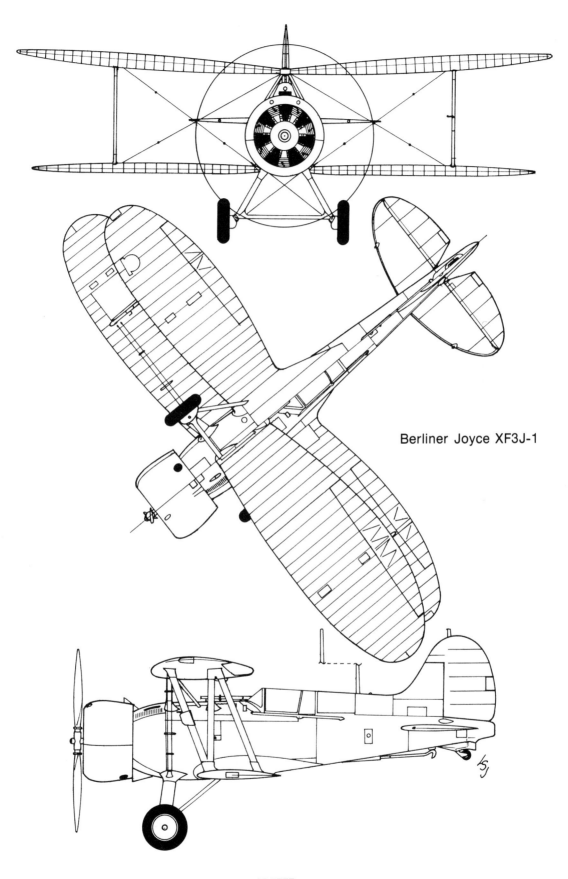

Berliner Joyce XF3J-1

25 FEET

This view shows the trim lines of the XF3J-1. It was rejected because of excessive vibration.   Rockwell

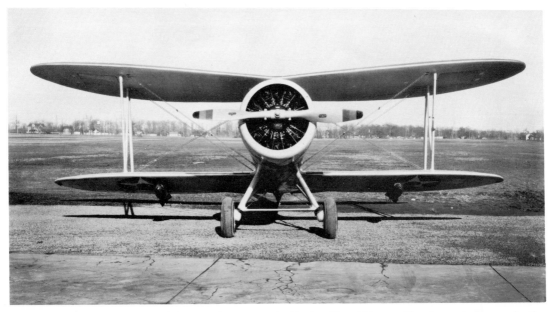

The unique "butterfly" shape of the wings is apparent in this shot. Two 116 pound bombs can be seen under the wings.
Rockwell

had a service ceiling of 24,500 feet. The plane had an empty weight of 2,717 pounds with its normal gross weight being 4,016 pounds. With a fuel load of 120 gallons, the B/J XF3J-1 could deliver two 116 pound bombs to a target 719 miles from its point of take-off. The standard defensive armament, in the form of two .30 cal. machine guns, was built into the nose and synchronized to fire through the propeller arc.

124

9624, the second production F2F-1 shows its plump lines in this view.   *Grumman*

In December, 1933, Grumman had completed deliveries to the Navy of its highly successful FF-1. But by this time, Grumman designers had been busy paring the lines of their plump two-seat fighter to provide an even more outstanding carrier-based single-seater. With a contract which had been awarded on November 2, 1932, Grumman was well into the construction of the single-place XF2F-1 when the final FF-1 rolled out the door onto the company runway on Long Island.

Mounted to the firewall of the XF2F-1 was a fourteen cylinder Pratt & Whitney XR-1535-44 Twin Wasp Jr. capable of delivering 625 hp to Grumman's new standard bearer. Behind this was a pudgy metal fuselage supported between the two wings, for despite the obvious trend to monoplanes, the Navy was still reluctant to sever relations with the proven bi-wing format. Besides, no suitable monoplane had yet been tested; and to put all their efforts into an, as yet, unproven area could lead to disaster.

On October 18, 1933, the XF2F-1 followed its two-place sisters into the sky. It was soon apparent that Grumman's new fighter was in every way as great as the FF-1 With an initial climb rate in excess of 3,000 feet per minute, the XF2F-1 was soon at its service ceiling of 29,800 feet. At 8,400 feet, the XF2F-1 could move along at 229 mph.

In its initial state, the cowling of the

XF2F-1 curved smoothly over the big Twin Wasp engine. To improve cooling and overall streamlining, the cowl was wrapped so tightly around the engine that it was necessary to bulge the metal over the rocker box covers. Few additional changes were dictated by the Navy's tests, although one disconcerting characteristic did become apparent. Because of the very short fuselage, the F2F suffered some directional instability and had a tendency to spin if the pilot's attention wandered. This was not considered too serious, however, as a recovery could be made without a great deal of pilot experience due to the inherent stability of the biplane design. Nevertheless, production F2F's were four inches longer than the prototype to give some improvement to the longitudinal stability.

Retractable landing gear was still somewhat of a novelty when the F2F-1 made its debut. The mechanism was operated from the cockpit by a handcrank which was turned some thirty revolutions. The gear was activated by a chain, and when it was fully extended a lock would fall in place to secure the wheels in a down position. In the event of a landing approach being made with the gear still snug against the wells, a buzzer would sound when the throttle was closed as an audible reminder of impending embarrassment.

The Navy ordered 54 F2F-1's on May 17, 1934, with supercharged R-1535-72 Twin

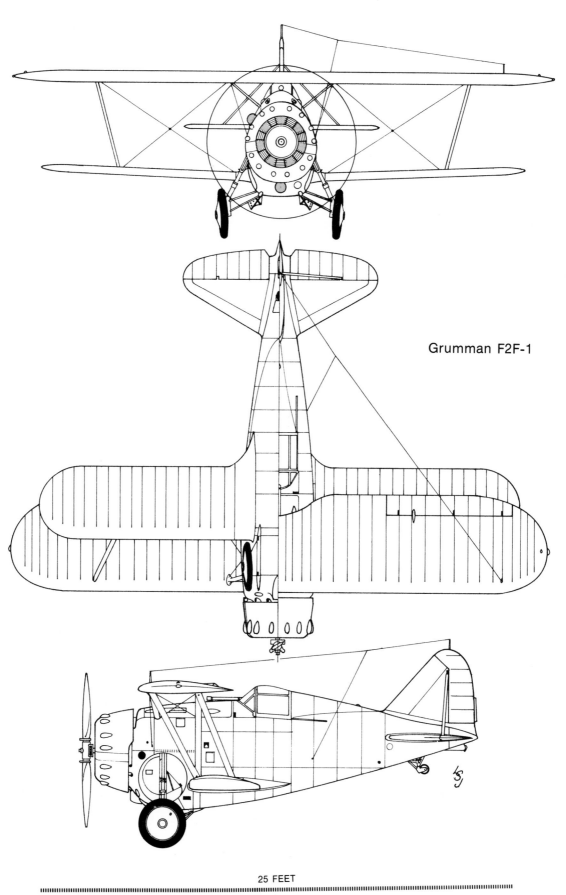

Grumman F2F-1

25 FEET

Here is the first production F2F-1 at Anacostia during evaluation.

Gordon S. Williams

2-F-12, an F2F-1, is the third plane in the 4th Section of VF-2. Cowl and chevron color are black.

Gordon S. Williams

Wasp Jrs. These engines provided 650 hp at 7,500 feet. Two .30 cal. Browning machine guns were situated above the cowling, and two bomb racks provided attachment points for 116 pound bombs. Delivery of the first F2F-1's took place on January 28, 1935, and VF-2B became the first squadron to receive the bulbous Grumman fighter on February 19, 1935. An additional F2F-1 was ordered on June 29, 1935, to replace one lost during its delivery flight from Grumman.

The F2F-1's were in squadron use for five years until September 30, 1940, when the machines of VF-2B were relegated to the status of advanced trainer. As late as 1941, a handful of these ex-fighters could still be seen as squadron "hacks" on some Navy bases.

The fuselage of the F2F-1 was of all-metal stressed-skin monocoque construction. The wings, which spanned 28 feet 6 inches with an area of 230 square feet, were framed with metal and then fabric covered. The control surfaces were also fabric covered metal frames. The F2F-1 was 21 feet 5 inches long and stood 9 feet 1 inch high. The production model of the Grumman fighter was slightly faster than the prototype, with a top speed of 231 mph at 7,500 feet. Landing speed was 66 mph. The F2F-1 weighed 2,691 pounds empty and grossed at 3,847 pounds including 110 gallons of fuel. Range with full internal tanks was 985 miles. Service ceiling was 27,-100 feet, and the F2F-1 had an initial rate of climb of 2,050 feet per minute.

The Curtiss XF13C-1 in its original monoplane form.   *Gordon S. Williams.*

One of the more interesting approaches to monoplane development was the Curtiss XF13C (Model 70), which was built with two sets of detachable wings to enable comparative flight tests as a biplane or monoplane. A great deal of interest was shown in the Curtiss-funded design, and the potential value of a plane with such versatility was also apparent to the Navy.

Although the XF12C-1 (Curtiss Model 73) carried a lower Navy designation, it was actually preceded by the XF13C-1. Financing for the engineering and construction was provided by Curtiss; and the Model 70 was nearly completed when the Navy signed a formal contract for the plane on November 23, 1932. (The XF12C-1 had been ordered on June 30, 1932, hence the lower designation). Only one airframe was assembled; and during its five year life, was operated under three designations, the subtype number depending on its configuration. However, the number painted on the tail remained "XF13C-1" until the final modifications had been completed.

A month after the contract had been signed, the XF13C was first flown. For this occasion, the biplane wings were fitted. Subsequent flights were made in both configurations. The constantly changing appearance of the XF13C-1 had the effect of thoroughly confusing the press corps of the day, and the plane soon became known as the "Curtiss Mystery Fighter" to the newspapers.

The original concept of the XF13C was to provide a carrier-type fighter which could be altered for the best performance depending on its base of operations. For carrier service, the biplane wings could provide shorter takeoff runs and slower landing speed than the monoplane surface. On the other hand, a monoplane operating from the longer runways of a land base would have a greater maximum speed. To reduce the drag factor to a minimum, the upper wing was mounted directly to the canopy, the frames of this structure effectively serving as intercabane struts. The bracing struts that supported the monoplane wing were attached to the same fuselage points that held the lower biplane wing in place. Although the span of the upper wing was the same in both versions, they were in fact two different units.

The upper wings of the XF13C-2 biplane contained full-span ailerons and a compartment for flotation gear outboard of the inter-plane struts. The two wings had a total area of 282 square feet; and thus con-

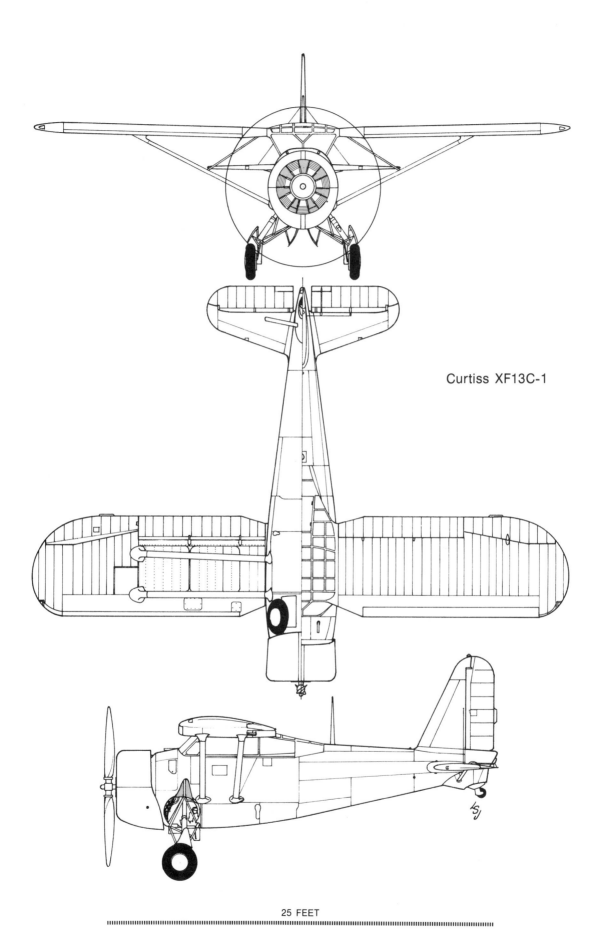

Curtiss XF13C-1

25 FEET

Although the tail still carries the designation with a -1, the biplane configuration was designated XF13C-2 on paper.
Gordon S. Williams

figured, the Curtiss fighter could lift off after a run of 504 feet and land at 58 mph. Service ceiling of this version was 23,900 feet and it could reach 5,000 feet in 3.6 minutes. Range on its 110 gallon fuel capactiy was 863 miles. Empty weight of the biplane was 3,183 pounds, while it weighed 4,343 pounds loaded. Maximum speed in this form was 205 mph at 7,000 feet.

For comparison, the monoplane XF13C-1 wing featured trailing-edge flaps between the ailerons and leading-edge slats to reduce the landing speed. With these devices, the monoplane was only 3.5 mph faster on touchdown. On takeoff, the -1 covered 113 feet more on the ground before it was airborne. These negative factors were not unexpected, of course; and in the area of top speed, the -1 was 19 mph faster due to the decreased drag. With a wing area of only 205 square feet, the XF13C-1 also lagged behind the biplane in service ceiling to the extent of 100 feet. The rate of climb was virtually the same regardless of configuration. Due to the beefy struts and fittings required to secure the single-wing assembly, the XF13C-1 weighed 87 pounds more than the biplane. The fuel capacity remained the same and the maximum range was barely improved by the reduced drag.

Irrespective of the use of one or two wings, the powerplant remained the same—a Wright XR-1510-94 of 600 hp. The overall span of each of the versions was 35 feet, while the biplane had a 24-foot span lower wing. Aircraft length was 25 feet 8 inches and the rudder was 12 feet 9 inches tall.

Curtiss evaluated their polymorphic fighter for a year before delivering it to Anacostia as a monoplane on February 10, 1934. The biplane wings arrived a few days later and the XF13C was again put through its paces by Navy personnel. Carrier trials took place aboard the USS Saratoga and the plane was generally satisfactory throughout the tests. That is not to indicate there were no problems, but none seemed insurmountable.

Among the recommendations to improve the characteristics of the bi-mono fighter was the replacement of one of its twin .30 cal. machine guns with a .50 cal. weapon. The complaints centered around poor visibility for the pilot, whose head was between the upper wing halves, and the excessive vertical height which caused handling problems on the hangar deck of the carrier.

The many changes to the XF13C durings its testing confused the press and they labeled it the "Curtiss Mystery Fighter."
Gordon S. Williams

The monoplane XF13C-1 weighed 87 pounds more than the biplane version, due to the heavier fittings required to support the single wing.
Gordon S. Williams

The final shape of the plane. Here it is designated XF13C-3 and displays an altered vertical stabilizer.

Gordon S. Williams

In November, 1934, the Army was given an opportunity to examine the XF13C and it was flown to Wright Field. Once again its handling characteristics were considered acceptable, but the Army rejected the fighter on the grounds that it was unsuited for any military role. Yet, during World War II, the Army received over 200 Curtiss 0-52 Owl observation planes which were virtual carbon copies of the rejected XF13C!

In February 1935, the XF13C was returned to the Navy, who then sent the fighter back to Curtiss for the recommended changes. In May 1935, the final configuration change to the XF13C was completed. About the only visible difference was a reduction in the height of the vertical stabilizer which was 9 inches shorter and a bit broader. The tail designator proclaimed this was now the XF13C-3, although the Bureau Number remained the same. An ex-

perimental 700 hp Wright XR-1510-12 engine occupied the cowling; and the gross weight had increased over 300 pounds, but this was also accompanied by an increase in maximum speed of 9 mph.

The new engine became a source of constant servicing problems, and by now even the latest biplanes were outperforming the XF13C. Further testing was considered futile and the aircraft was delivered to the National Advisory Committee for Aeronautics (NACA), based at Langley Field. Here it was utilized as a test vehicle for engines, propellers and high-lift devices.

At the end of 1937, the XF13C-3 found itself back in the service, this time with the Marine Corps. For a year, the venerable Curtiss fighter was used as a utility ship by VMJ-1 at Quantico. On its return to NACA at the end of 1938, it was finally retired and disassembled.

The Boeing XF7B-1 was very similar to the XP-29 built for the Army. The fairings behind the wheels were removed during testing.
Boeing

The transition from an established mode to one which is largely conceptual is a difficult one, filled with new ideas, and sometimes extending beyond the existing technology. As we have seen, one such transitional period in aviation history is evidenced by the arrival of the monoplane configurations. By 1933, it was clear that the future of fighter design lay with this arrangement. After a couple of false starts, the Army Air Corps had finally begun this transition with the Boeing P-26.

Following the successful introduction of the P-26 into the Army, Boeing expanded the design to incorporate fully cantilevered wings and semi-retracting landing gear. Development proceeded in two directions as the engineers considered both Army and Navy requirements. Two separate planes were proposed. Model 264 became the Air Corps YP-29, while the Navy ordered the similar Model 273 as the XF7B-1 on March 20, 1933. The XF7B-1 was slightly larger than the Army fighter but both mounted a 550 hp Pratt & Whitney R-1340 Wasp engine with a controllable pitch propeller.

The XF7B-1 was constructed of, and entirely covered with, metal. Several features of the P-26 were apparent in the Navy

fighter, such as the engine cowling and nose plate; and many of the fittings were the same as those on the Army plane. Such interchangability would help keep production costs down if a contract was awarded.

The first flight of the XF7B-1 took place on September 14, 1933, and for the next two months, Boeing pilots examined the capabilities of their new machine. Some refinements were made even before the Navy had the opportunity to fly it. A long-chord NACA cowling replaced the short P-26 fixture and the nose plate was eliminated to provide more efficient engine cooling. A pair of fairings had originally been installed behind the landing gear wells to smooth the air flow around the semi-exposed wheels. The preliminary flights indicated the fairings were responsible for more drag than the wheels themselves so these were also removed.

The XF7B-1 was shipped to the Navy at Anacostia in October 1933, but was routed by way of the Pratt & Whitney factory at Hartford, Connecticut for a final engine tune-up. The Navy received the Boeing monoplane on November 11, 1933, and testing began a few days later.

The performance part of the test program

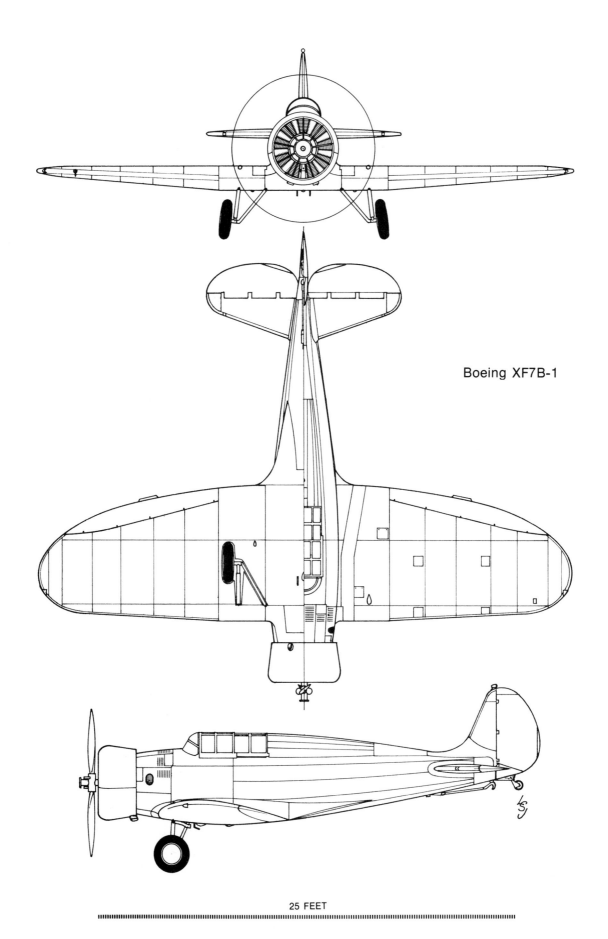

Boeing XF7B-1

25 FEET

was encouraging as the top speed of 239 mph at 10,000 feet and a service ceiling of 26,900 feet exceeded the ratings of the current front line biplane fighters. This, of course, was to be expected of a monoplane. But then, so was the negative response to the tests: the landing speed was too high for safe carrier approaches, the enclosed cockpit impaired the pilot's view of the Landing Signal Officer, and the plane was not as responsive as a biplane.

By April 1934, the XF7B-1 was back in Boeing's Seattle plant for the inevitable series of modifications that befall an experimental aircraft. The Army had also complained about the relatively high landing speed of their P-26's and Boeing engineers succeeded in reducing the speed with landing flaps. The XF7B-1 received a set of these and the approach speed came down from 78 mph to a more reasonable 66 mph. The enclosed cockpit was redesigned, and the sliding canopy was removed at the Navy's insistence.

Flight testing was resumed after the required revisions were completed and the plane was prepared for the final phase of the program. One of the most crucial tests of a fighting plane of that era was the terminal velocity dive in which the aircraft was aimed

straight down from nearly 20,000 feet and dived at full throttle. At about 8,000 feet, the stick was pulled back and the test aircraft was subjected to up to nine times the force of gravity during the pullout. This became known as the "9G" dive; and it was guaranteed to detect any potential structural weaknesses in the airframe, and no doubt, a few in the pilot.

It was in March 1935, that the XF7B-1 was subjected to the grueling high-speed dive. There was no question in the minds of the designers that the fighter could withstand the "9G" pull; but during the dive the pilot's windshield shattered and, as pieces of plexiglass cut his face, he was momentarily delayed in beginning his recovery. By the time the stick was pulled back, the XF7B-1 had reached the incredible speed of 415 mph. The fighter was abruptly pulled out of its dive and the "G" factor reached 12.1 before the plane fully recovered. Despite the crushing force of the high "G" loads, the fighter remained fully controllable and returned to the field. An examination of the plane revealed that damage from the overstressing could be repaired, but in light of the development still required to produce a suitable fighting machine, it was decided to abandon further

In this picture some of the changes to the original design can be seen. The wheel fairings are gone and a long-chord NACA cowling covers the engine.
Boeing

The cockpit of the XF7B-1. The round object at the top center is the eyepiece for the gunsight.   Boeing

work on the project. The XF7B-1 was written off, and Boeing did not attempt another fighter design until the world was in the midst of the Second Great War.

The span of the XF7B-1's all-metal wing was 32 feet and it had 213 square feet of area. Its length was 27 feet 7 inches and height was 10 feet. Weights were 2,698 pounds empty and 3,868 pounds loaded. A capacity of 112 gallons of fuel gave a range of 824 miles. The highest speed attained in level flight was 231 mph at 10,000 feet.

Two .30 cal. Browning M-2 machine guns were located in the fuselage sides with their barrels protruding between the engine cylinders.

The Northrop XFT-1 was a direct descendent of their Gamma transport and featured some of its characteristics.
Northrop

The Navy was serious about incorporating the monoplane into the fleet; and in May 1933, they turned to an airframe manufacturer with a great deal of experience in the field of single-wing types.

In 1927, aeronautical engineer John K. Northrop came to the attention of the aviation world with his record setting Vega cantilever monoplane. Northrop was a design engineer for the budding Lockheed Aircraft Company at that time, and the excellence of his progeny put the young company firmly on the road to success. In 1928, Northrop helped establish the Avion Corporation, which became the Northrop Aircraft Corporation a year later.

By 1933, Northrop was responsible for the design and production of three all-metal monoplane types, two of which were in airline service and had performance similar to contemporary military craft. On May 8, 1933, Northrop held a contract for his first Navy fighter.

Northrop's Navy fighter was designated XFT-1 and bore an obvious relationship to that company's Gamma transport. In spite of the trend to retract the landing gear, the XFT-1 sported a fixed gear shrouded in a prominent metal fairing. Nevertheless, the exposed gear arrangement seemed to have little effect on its performance when the Northrop fighter made its appearance at Anacostia. It was one of the fastest Navy fighters yet tested. The XFT-1 was powered by a Wright R-1510-26 which delivered 625 hp at 6,000 feet. The engine was covered by a unique cowl comprised of seven streamlined panels which were held in place by two cables.

Flight testing of Northrop's fighter revealed the same shortcomings which had plagued the previous monoplanes. The XFT-1 was fast but lacked adequate maneuverability, and it had a wicked tendency to spin. To accomplish a reasonable approach speed for the XFT-1, Northrop had devised an interlock between the flaps and ailerons which depressed the latter when the flaps were lowered. This brought the landing speed down to 63 mph.

The oversized wheel fairings were another source of complaints among Navy personnel associated with the XFT-1. It was a major operation to service the brakes, shock absorbers and hydraulic systems inside the metal fixtures. Although many field

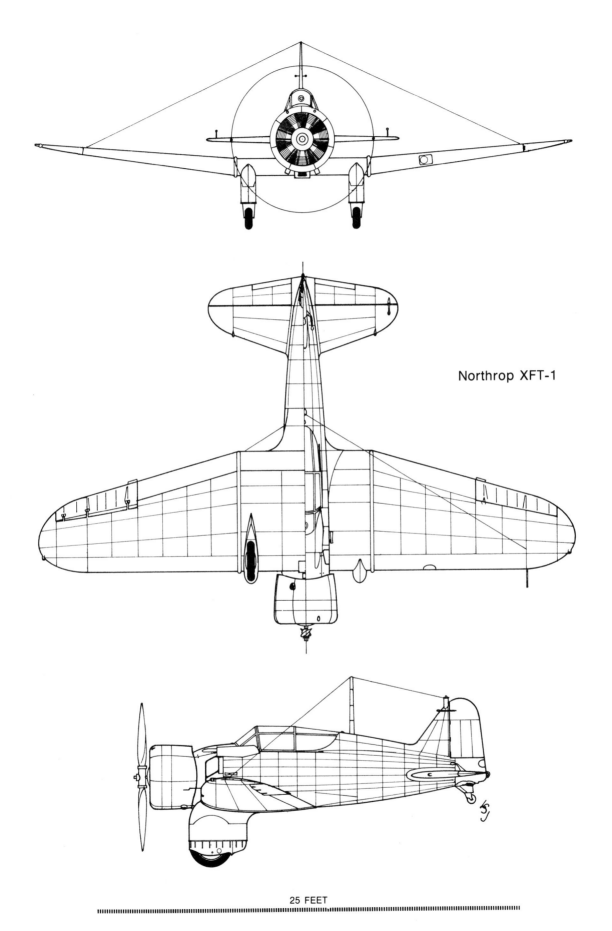

Northrop XFT-1

25 FEET

Although the Northrop fighter underwent several changes, it still retained a dangerous tendency to spin. Here it is revised as the XFT-2.   *Northrop*

modifications were made to the plane at the testing center, it was finally returned to the Northrop factory in the summer of 1935 with its list of recommended fixes.

At this time the XFT-1, when weighed empty, was 2,469 pounds and had a gross weight of 3,756 pounds. The fuel tanks could hold 120 gallons to give a range of 976 miles. Two 116 pound bombs could be carried, and the cowling held a pair of .30 cal. machine guns. The wing was 32 feet in span and 177 square feet in area. The length of the XFT-1 was 21 feet 1 inch; height was 9 feet 5 inches. Maximum speed was 235 mph at 6,000 feet, service ceiling was 26,500 feet. The XFT-1 could reach 6,000 feet in 2.6 minutes.

Northrop was told to replace the Wright engine with a 650 hp Pratt & Whitney R-1535-72 in a more conventional cowling with cooling gills. The wheel pants were replaced with a pair providing access panels on the outboard side for ease of servicing. The designation was now changed to XFT-2. The empty weight had been increased to 2,730 pounds, but the gross had only risen 14 pounds due to a reduction in fuel capacity to only 80 gallons. This also had the undesirable effect of limiting the combat usefulness of the Northrop ship.

The XFT-2 was returned to Anacostia in April, 1936, where the Navy learned that the recommended changes had done nothing to improve the fighter's performance. It still had an unhealthy desire to spin, and retained this nasty habit even through several attempts to rectify it. Pilots became wary of the little ship and finally the Navy ordered it grounded. The manufacturer was informed of the XFT-2's spinning problem and asked to arrange for its return to the Northrop plant for corrections.

Northrop's test pilot arrived at Anacostia to retrieve the XFT-2 and was told of the grounding order. This applied also to any ferry flights—the plane was simply too unstable to be safely flown — and arrangements were to be made for other means of transport back to the factory. However, the pilot had been sent to fly the plane back and it was his intent to do so. Somehow he succeeded in gaining access to the fighter one July morning in 1936, and took off into the predawn darkness. The XFT project was terminated a couple of hours later when a combination of turbulence over the Alleghenies and the little fighter's propensity to spin planted the airplane in a Pennsylvania farmyard. The daring test pilot recovered from his injuries and Northrop squared with the Navy by reimbursing them for the entire expense of the XFT program.

Three XF3F-1's carried the Bureau Number 9727 due to crashes. This one would be the third as indicated by the fact it survived long enough to have the Anacostia name painted on the fuselage.   Grumman

The performance of Grumman's F2F-1 was clouded only by the poor directional stability and spinning characteristics caused by its short fuselage. While the Navy felt the F2F-1 was an excellent fighter in the other aspects which determine the value of such a machine, they also believed the design could be refined to correct its deficiencies. Even before the first production F2F-1 was scheduled for completion, the Navy awarded Grumman a development contract for its successor, the XF3F-1.

Increasing the length and span were considered the most important steps toward correcting the stability problems. The fuselage of the XF3F-1 was stretched 22 inches beyond that of the F2F-1, and the wings were expanded three-and-a-half feet, adding 31 square feet to the overall area. Although the extensions tended to give a slimmer appearance, there was no doubt about its heritage. The powerplant was a 700 hp Pratt & Whitney R-1535-72, the same type being installed in the F2F-1's on the production line.

The prototype XF3F-1 was completed and ready for its first flight on March 20, 1935, and three flights were completed that morning. Again, Grumman was certain they had a winner. Two days later, the XF3F-1 was subjected to the mandatory terminal-velocity dives. Ten dives had been scheduled and the first nine were completed without mishap. On the tenth plunge, however, it appeared that the pilot pulled the nose up too abruptly causing the overstressed fighter to disintegrate and tumble to the ground. The Navy immediately ordered a replacement and the second XF3F-1, bearing the same BuNo as the original, #9727, was completed in two months and flew on May 9.

Misfortune struck again two days later when the second prototype failed to recover from a spin during a demonstration for the Navy. This time, however, the pilot successfully abandoned the stricken plane and parachuted to safety. The pilot's report indicated that high speeds induced directional instability. This caused the XF3F-1 to enter a flat spin from which recovery was impossible.

Now that the problem was known, the Navy ordered yet a third XF3F-1—again with the same bureau number—and this one continued the test program on June 20,

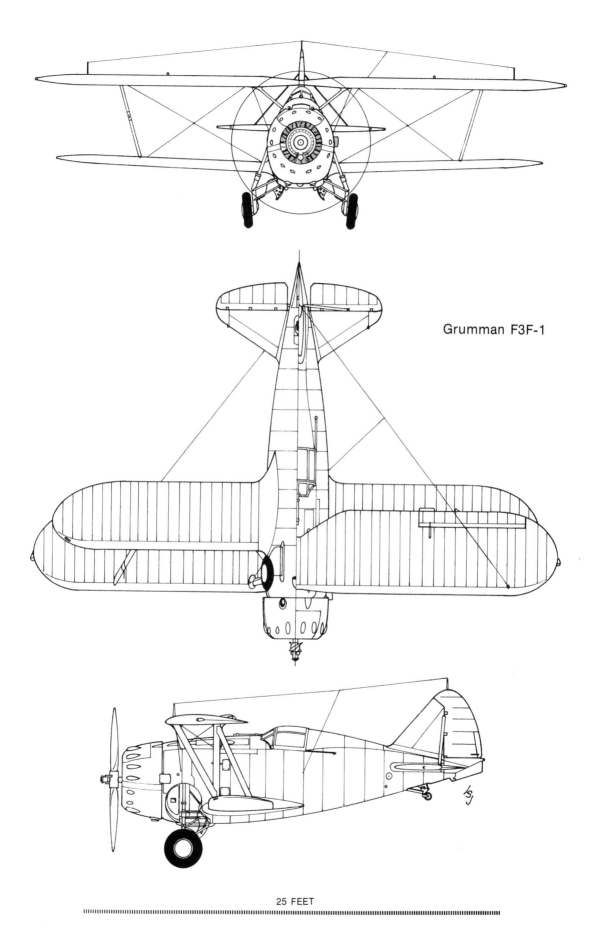

Grumman F3F-1

25 FEET

An F3F-1 in its most dazzling glory. The tail is glossy black, indicating its assignment to the carrier Wasp. A bright insignia red cowl and fuselage stripe was standard for the leader of the 1st Section. This plane is from VF-7, the Blue Burgler Wasps. Of interest is the location of the U.S. national insignia on the cowl, signifying neutrality just before WW 2.   Gordon S. Williams

1935. Some parts of the second prototype had been salvaged and were incorporated into the third ship, hence the short construction time. The Navy accepted the XF3F-1 on August 1, and three days later ordered 54 F3F-1's.

The production F3F-1's had a small fin-like extension on the empennage for increased area. These planes used Pratt & Whitney R-1535-84 engines with a normal rating of 650 hp, but delivering 700 hp for take-off. Their gross weight was nearly 100 pounds more than that of the prototype, but with a speed of 231 mph at 7,500 feet, they were 5 mph faster than the XF3F-1. This was the same as the maximum speed of the F2F-1.

The controls of the F3F-1 were extremely sensitive and manueverability was far better than the F2F. The F3F still had a dangerous spin, but would respond well if the pilot treated it properly. For safety though, intentional spins were prohibited. During the first four months of operations a structural weakness caused four of the fighters to crash. A reinforcing of the upper wing spars and aileron controls solved the problem and the planes were returned to service with their Navy and Marine squadrons.

Though the Navy could no longer dispute the fact the biplane was a lost cause, they still clung to the hope that, at least while the monoplane was being perfected, they could have a two-winged fighter of comparable performance. Since Grumman had been able to improve upon the F2F, they were asked to perform a similar task on the new ship. On March 6, 1936, Grumman received a contract for their fourth biplane fighter design, the XF4F-1. This one was to utilize an experimental Wright XR-1670 engine. Grumman suggested that the performance sought from the new design might be achieved by installing a supercharged 750 hp Wright R-1820-22 on the F3F. The engineering effort could then be directed toward developing the F4F as a monoplane. Grumman had already begun such a conversion and the Navy took this alternative under consideration. The Navy agreed to the proposal and a contract was approved for the XF3F-2 on July 28, 1936—one day after the modified plane was delivered to Anacostia.

The single-row Wright engine was larger in diameter than the Pratt & Whitney and necessitated a revision to the cowling. To absorb the increased power, a three-bladed controllable pitch propeller was mounted to the shaft while the rudder was enlarged to counter the added torque. Due to problems with the carburetor system for the supercharged engine, flight testing was delayed until January 1937.

Grumman's estimates of improved performance were borne out when the results of the flight tests were evaluated. With the super-charged Wright turning out 850 hp at

The engine cowling was enlarged on the F3F-2 to accommodate a larger powerplant. This one carries Fighting Six's shooting star emblem. VF-6 operated from the USS Enterprise.
Grumman

Grumman F3F-3

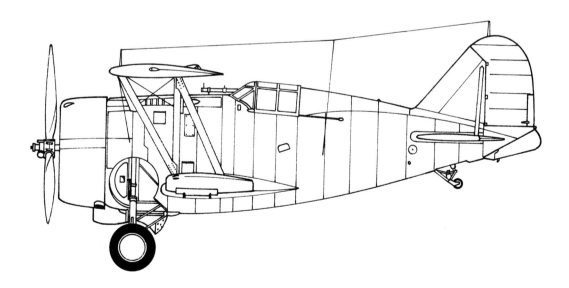

A VMF-2 F3F-2. Note the white-painted cowling half. The position of the plane in a section determined the number, the cowling color and the area painted. This plane was third aircraft in the second section.

Wayne Morris

5,800 feet, the XF3F-2 reached a speed of 255 mph and the service ceiling was raised by 4,000 feet. This merited the award of a contract for 81 examples, the largest order yet received by Grumman. A few minor problems delayed the squadron deliveries, but the first planes began filling the ranks by December 1, 1937.

Development time for the new monoplanes was delaying their anticipated delivery; and by mid-1938 the Navy had planned to add another fighting squadron to the fleet. It was clear that new planes had to be obtained for this expansion, and the Navy was becoming quite concerned about the source of these machines when Grumman once again suggested upgrading the F3F. This time, one of the fighters was sent to the Langley wind tunnel to determine what additional refinements could be made. The resulting F3F-3 had a smaller diameter propeller, modified cowling, a cockpit canopy of the type proposed for the F4F, and a contract for 27 examples. The final

F3F version had a maximum speed of 264 mph and a normal gross weight of 4,543 pounds. Landing speed was 68 mph. It is rather interesting to note that at this point, the landing speed of the later biplanes, in the range of 60-70 mph, was not appreciably slower than the "unacceptable" approach speeds of the new monoplanes.

Dimensions of the F3F series differed only slightly. Wingspan was the same on all versions—32 feet with an area of 206 square feet. The F3F-1 was 23 feet 3 inches long, the -2 and -3 were 23 feet even. The F3F-1 was 9 feet 1 inch high while the -2 and -3 were 9 feet 4 inches.

The entire series carried armament of one .50 and one .30 cal. Browning machine guns in the cowl with 200 rounds for the .50 and 500 rounds for the .30.

The last F3F, a -2 model, was retired from flying in November, 1943, ending almost a decade of service for the Grumman single-seat biplane fighters.

144

The F3F-3 was the last biplane fighter ordered for any U.S. service. The Navy ordered 27 as a stopgap until the first monoplanes were available.

Wayne Morris

SEVERSKY
XNF-1

When first built, the XNF-1 did not have any dihedral in the wings.   *William T. Larkins*

The Air Corps began introducing monoplane fighters into its squadrons in 1934. By 1937, six monoplane types were either in service, entering production, or in some stage of testing prior to production. Curtiss attempted to interest the Navy in a navalized version of their Model 75 Hawk, the prototype for the highly successful P-36 series. The plane was flown to Anacostia where it was demonstrated by Curtiss and the Navy pilots themselves, who were able to compare it to the current carrier types. The Navy was impressed with its speed; but, as with the previous monoplanes subjected to the Navy's scrutiny, the Curtiss ship was also rejected for the same reasons.

Competing with Curtiss for an Air Corps contract was the Seversky Company, producer of a line of high-performance monoplanes, and ultimate winner of the Air Corps contract. Their winning entry became the P-35 and was eventually refined into the famed P-47 Thunderbolt. It was obvious that the Navy would soon be compelled to order a monoplane type; and Seversky, hoping to pull out another plum from the military pie, funded their own version of the plane as a carrier fighter.

The carrier version of the Seversky fighter was classed XNF-1 by the company, for "Experimental Navy Fighter-One." It was based on the lines of the P-35 and featured a retractable landing gear which swung rearward, but remained exposed below the wings. Streamlined fairings were used to smooth the airflow around the retracted gear, and an arresting hook was attached under the fuselage. The wing had no dihedral when the XNF-1 made its appearance in the summer of 1937; the top surfaces of the wing were absolutely flat. Apparently this was responsible for some stability problems, since the outer panels of the wing were eventually tilted upward, A Wright R-1820-22, which could provide 950 hp for takeoff, drove a three-bladed propeller. Company tests indicated the XNF-1 could reach a speed of 267 mph at 15,200 feet while it could land at a reasonable 69 mph.

The Seversky fighter was flown to Anacostia on September 24, 1937, for its Navy evaluation. It was recorded under the company designation XNF-1 for bookkeeping purposes only, and never received an official Navy classification or Bureau Number. The civil number NX-1254 was carried on the wings and tail, but no national insignia was applied to the aircraft.

In comparing the XNF-1 with the Navy's operational biplanes, the only improvement

146

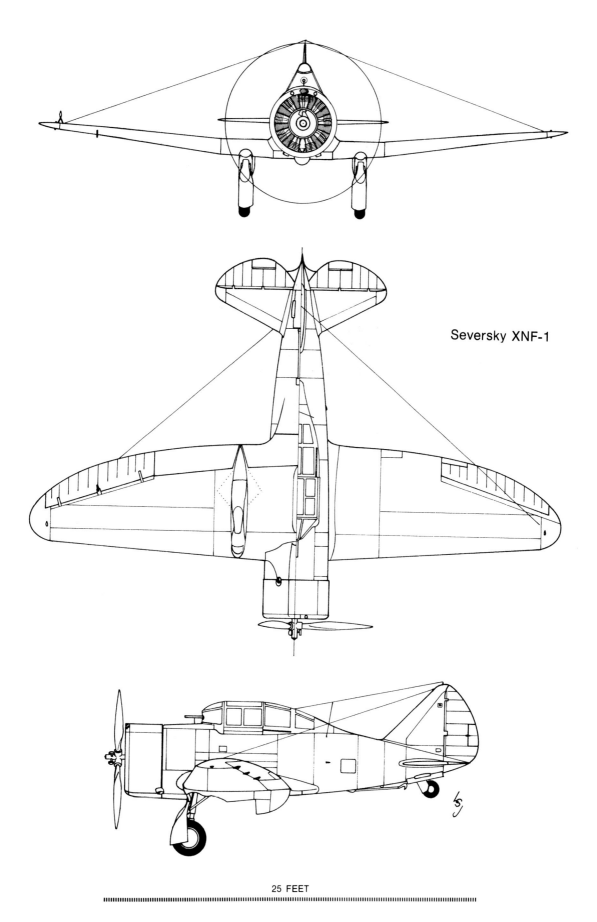

Seversky XNF-1

25 FEET

Wing dihedral was added to the XNF-1 to improve stability. The XNF-1 was not accepted by the Navy and the designation was unofficial. *Ray Wagner*

The Seversky XNF-1 was a modification of the Army's P-35. *Gordon S. Williams*

noted was the greater level-flight speed of 7 mph—hardly enough to warrant further consideration in view of the monoplanes which were being devised expressly for the Navy's requirements by Grumman and Brewster. However, the XNF-1 did provide a point of reference from which to evaluate the Navy's new monoplanes and the Seversky was retained for comparative evaluations. On completion of this phase of its service, the XNF-1 was returned to its builders and ultimately scrapped.

The proportions of the XNF-1 were comparable to the P-35 on which it was patterned. The wings spanned 36 feet and had an area of 220 square feet. The length was 25 feet 2 inches, and height was 9 feet 1 inch. The typical .30 and .50 cal. machine guns were installed in the cowl, and bomb racks could be mounted. Seversky's Navy fighter weighed 4,020 pounds empty and grossed at 5,231 pounds. Fuel content of the tanks was 90 gallons, but an external tank could increase this to 200 gallons. Its service ceiling was 30,700 feet and the XNF-1 had an initial climb rate of 2,600 feet per minute.

BREWSTER
F2A BUFFALO

The popular cartoon cat Felix rides on the side of VF-3's F2A-1. This view shows the white tail, signifying its assignment to the USS Saratoga.
Gordon S. Williams

The demise of the biplane fighter for carrier duty was heralded by the arrival of Brewster's F2A Buffalo. Brewster had been assigned the manufacturer's code letter "A" after the General (Atlantic) Company had been dissolved. Since there had already been an FA-1 on the Navy's roster, Brewster's first offering became the F2A.

The Brewster Company was new to the airframe business. Its only previous experience was in the construction of seaplane floats for the Navy. In 1932, the Brewster Aeronautical Corporation was formed with the ultimate intention being the design and construction of military aircraft. Their first product was an experimental monoplane scout bomber, the XSBA-1, flown in 1936. Brewster was underbid for the production contract of their scout bomber, but on the basis of the design, they received a development contract for the monoplane fighter. It may seem strange that a relatively new company was selected to develop such an important subject as the Navy's first monoplane fighter; but Brewster's engineering methods reflected contemporary ideas, and the XF2A-1 was as modern as current technology permitted. The prototype XF2A-1 was ordered on June 23, 1936, after the

drawings had been reviewed. It was to use a Wright R-1820-22 engine; have hydraulically retractable landing gear; and be of all-metal stressed skin, flush-riveted construction. One of the constant complaints regarding the monoplane configuration was poor pilot visibility. To overcome this, Brewster engineers provided a clear panel in the underside of the fuselage of the XF2A-1; but this was deleted on the -2 and later subtypes.

The first flight of the Buffalo, as it became known, was undertaken in December 1937; however, its original performance did little to encourage the Navy which was counting so heavily on it as a biplane replacement. At 15,200 feet, the XF2A-1 could only reach a speed of 277.5 mph, or 13 mph faster than the F3F-3—hardly an improvement to get excited about. The Langley wind tunnel was utilized and the prototype XF2A-1 was subjected to a series of airflow tests. This was the first time in the United States that a full-size airplane was wind-tunnel tested. Guided by the test results, several minor refinements were made to the Buffalo, and when flying was resumed, a phenomenal speed of 304 mph was reached at 17,000 feet.

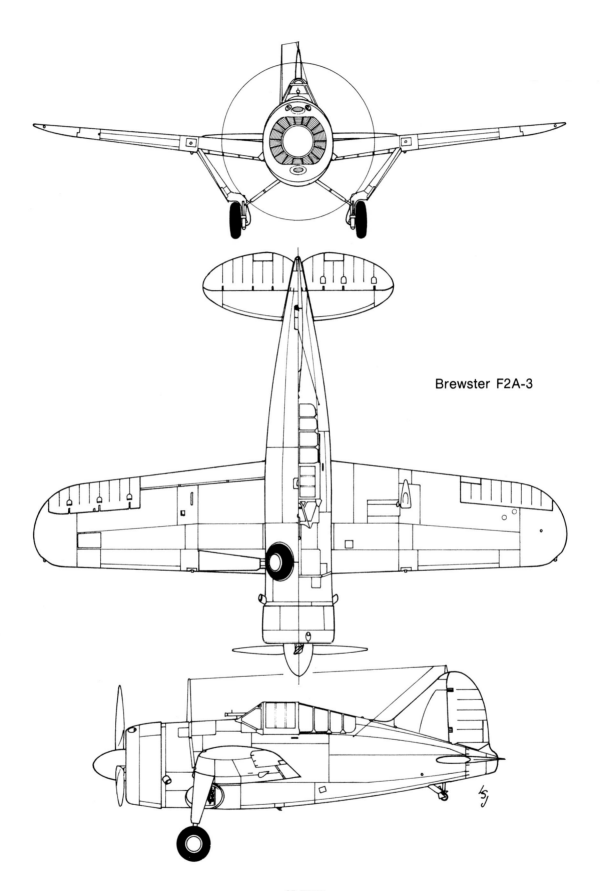

Brewster F2A-3

25 FEET

The XF2A-1 Buffalo prototype. Note the difference between this and the production types. Gordon S. Williams

The F2A-2 was the first major production variant of the Brewster Buffalo. This is the XF2A-2 prototype.
Wayne Morris

The future of the Brewster fighter looked good now, and simulated carrier landings were undertaken. The Buffalo had hydraulically-operated split flaps to help slow it to a speed of 67 mph for carrier approach, but during one hard landing the prototype was severely damaged. By this time, the advanced performance was evident and Brewster received a production order for 54 F2A-1's. So the Buffalo was assured its place in history as the Navy's first operational monoplane fighter. (The Buffalo was actually the second production carrier-based monoplane—it was preceded by the Douglas TBD-1 Devastator torpedo bomber.)

Setting up the production line for their fighter created many problems for the Brewster Company, severely hindering its delivery schedule. The first F2A-1 was finished in July 1939, but they were unable to complete enough planes to outfit a squadron until the following December. On the 8th day of that month, VF-3 received the first ten of the new Buffalos. Before any further F2A-1's were delivered, however, the Navy ordered Brewster to upgrade the remaining Buffalos to the F2A-2 standard based on trials of the rebuilt XF2A-1.

Following its accident during carrier trials, the XF2A-1 had been returned to Brewster where the damage was repaired and a 1,200 hp R-1820-40 Wright engine installed. In addition, the canopy had been raised and a larger vertical stabilizer added. While the F2A-2 production was getting underway, the remaining 43 F2A-1's were completed as Brewster Model B-239's and sold to Finland. This group of Buffalos was to prove the most successful of the type, as the stubby fighter was ideally suited to the conditions under which they were operated in Europe.

Meanwhile, reports from VF-3 on board

Just before World War II began, Navy fighters were painted overall light gray, as seen on this F2A-2 Buffalo.
Gordon S. Williams

the USS Saratoga were revealing serious problems with the F2A-1's. Foremost of these was landing gear failure. The Vee structure of the gear struts was inherently weak and the stresses of an arrested landing were more than they could withstand. This defect remained with the Buffalo throughout its life. By now, it was too late to have second thoughts about the F2A as the Navy needed fighters. The new Grumman F4F's could not be produced fast enough to fill this need, so Brewster received another contract for the Buffalo—this time for 108 improved F2A-3 types.

The F2A-3 was similar to the -2, but the engine was moved forward for greater CG limits. The space behind the engine was used for additional fuel and the capacity was increased by 76 gallons. Brewster was ready to deliver the F2A-3's in July 1941; and by December, three squadrons were using the new Buffalo. Even on the F2A-3, the landing gear collapsed; and now a new problem arose—arresting hook failures which were ultimately traced to deliberate sabotage during assembly.

When the Japanese attacked Pearl Harbor on December 7, 1941, both the Navy and Marines were flying the Brewster fighter. During that month, pilots flying the export model of the Buffalo had learned of the fighter's combat shortcomings; but it wasn't until the Battle of Midway, on June

4, 1942, that American pilots would become aware of them.

It would be unfair to criticize the Navy for the failures manifested by its first monoplane fighter by saying they waited too long before accepting the demise of the biplane. The Buffalo's main opponent was the vastly superior Zero-Sen, and even the more advanced Air Corps types were overwhelmed by this nimble warrior. In addition, the Japanese pilots had been trained with the intent of engaging in warfare. The very existence of the Zero-Sen had come as a startling surprise to the Allies, and here was a plane destined to rank among the world's greatest.

Under different circumstances, where the Buffalo was not overwhelmed by sheer numbers, it proved to be an effective machine. In Finland it was a popular weapon against the Russian invaders, where it was operated for three years before being replaced with Messerschmitt Bf 109's.

When production of the Buffalo had been concluded, 162 had been delivered to the Navy. An additional 346 export models had also been constructed. Just one of these planes survives today, an historic exhibit in a Finnish museum.

Throughout the modifications made to the Buffalo, the wing remained the same with a 35 foot span and an area of 209 square feet. The F2A-1 was 26 feet long, 11

This F2A-3 is assigned to a training squadron. The Buffalo was not satisfactory as a fighter.   Navy

This photo shows the prototype Buffalo after conversion to the F2A-2 form.   Gordon S. Williams

Navy planes were painted light gray just before the U.S. entry into World War II. Seen in this paint scheme is BuNo 01517, the second F2A-3.
Wayne Morris

feet 8 inches high, and weighed 3,785 pounds empty, 5,055 pounds gross. Fuel capacity was 160 gallons. Top speed was 301 mph at 17,000 feet.

The F2A-2 was 25 feet 7 inches long, stood 12 feet high, had an empty weight of 4,576 pounds, grossed at 5,942 pounds, and carried 242 gallons of fuel. Maximum speed for this model was 323 mph at 16,500 feet, making it the fastest of the type.

The length of the F2A-3 was 26 feet 4 inches. It also was 12 feet high. Weight was 4,732 pounds empty, 6,321 pounds loaded, and could reach 321 mph at 16,500 feet.

Initially, the F2A carried the prescribed pair of .30 cal. and .50 cal. machine guns in the nose, but allowance had been made to install a pair of .50's in the wing outside the propeller arc. For combat, all four positions were occupied by .50 cal. weapons. In addition, one 116 pound bomb could be mounted under each wing.

One further attempt was made to improve the Buffalo's capabilities. The first F2A-3 was fitted with a pressurized cabin as the XF2A-4, but evaluation of this system led to rejection and no further development of the series was undertaken.

GRUMMAN
F4F WILDCAT

The F4F-4, shown above, was the first of the Wildcats to have folding wings for carrier stowage. Navy

As previously reported, the original format for the Grumman F4F featured a biplane configuration, and was intended to use a Pratt & Whitney R-1535-92 engine or an experimental Wright XR-1670. The anticipated speed of the XF4F-1 was 264 mph. Since Brewster had already been contracted to supply the Navy with the F2A monoplane, Grumman felt they would be in a more advantageous position if they, too, could develop a monoplane. The improvement of the F3F, with the supercharged Wright, provided an adequate stopgap, and Grumman concentrated on the design of their new prototype.

In light of the less than auspicious performance of the Brewster F2A, the Navy's decision to proceed with the Grumman design was of monumental importance. For it was the F4F that took the brunt of the fighting in the early part of World War II while superior fighting machines were taking shape on American drawing boards for the final blow.

The XF4F-2 retained the distinctive blunt appearance that characterized Grumman fighters. The single wing was mounted squarely on the fuselage centerline, and the now-familiar retractable landing gear was there, still operated by a handcrank. To forestall complaints about poor downward visibility, four windows were located in the lower sides of the fuselage.

Despite its delayed approval, the XF4F-2 was ready for trials four months ahead of the Buffalo and took to the air on September 2, 1937. The Navy received the Grumman fighter at Anacostia on December 23, for its evaluation. During the course of these tests, the XF4F-2 was subjected to several modifications which led to extensive variations in its silhouette. The windshield framing was changed, the rounded flying surfaces were squared-off, and the cowling underwent several alterations. By the early part of 1938, the definitive shape of the future Wildcat was evident. From the outset, the engine was a constant source of trouble. It was a Pratt & Whitney R-1830-66 Twin Wasp with a single-stage supercharger capable of 1,050 hp at takeoff.

In the competition flyoff between the XF4F-2, XF2A-1 and the Seversky XNF-1, the Grumman fighter proved the fastest with a speed of 290 mph at 10,000 feet. The service ceiling fell short of the estimates, but in most respects, the XF4F-2 proved satisfactory. While the plane was making simulated deck landings, the troublesome engine failed and the XF4F-2 flipped over

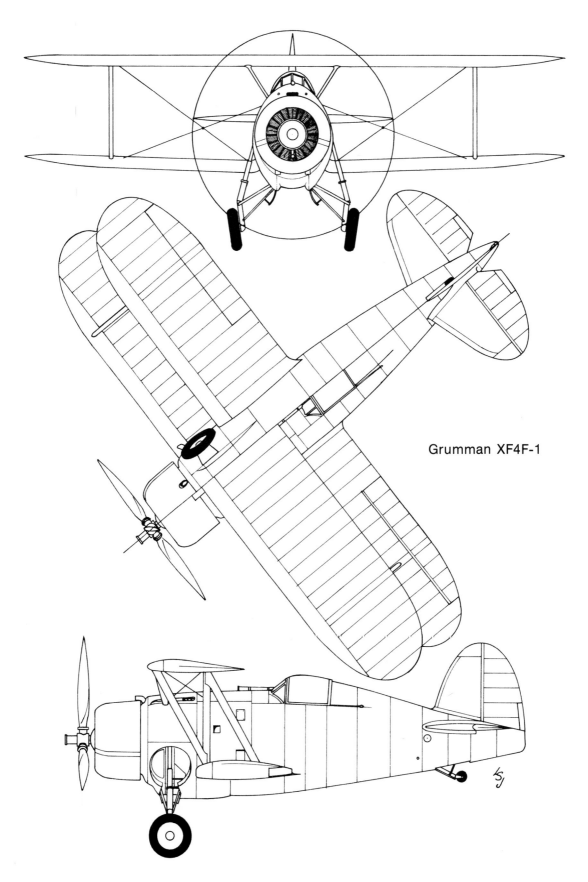

Grumman XF4F-1

25 FEET

The Wilcat prototype with larger, square-tipped wings and tail surfaces.   The spinner was removed later due to excessive engine heating. At this point it is the XF4F-3.   *Grumman*

The XF4F-2 as it first appeared for Navy tests in 1938.   *Grumman*

VF-3 Wildcats on patrol over the Pacific. These are F4F-4's from "Butch" O'Hare's squadron.   *Navy*

The Wilcat production line at Grumman.   *Grumman*

during the ensuing forced landing. While the damaged plane was being repaired at the Grumman plant, the Navy announced the results of its evaluation. Although the performance was notably lower, it was felt that the Brewster had a greater potential for its intended role and the Buffalo was ordered into production.

Certainly disappointed, but not defeated, Grumman proposed a modified F4F with a two-speed supercharged Twin Wasp. Since Grumman's previous attempts at upgrading its designs had resulted in superior aircraft, the Navy was willing to gamble on the F4F. A new contract approved the construction of the XF4F-3. Using the damaged prototype as a basis, the new F4F model was built up and prepared for trials on February 12, 1939.

The XF4F-3 was both larger and heavier than the -2; and to keep its wing loading down, the wingspan was four feet greater to increase the area by 28 square feet. That Grumman's faith in their offspring was justified was proven when the revamped fighter turned in a maximum speed of 335 mph at 20,500 feet, yet touched down at 68 mph. Even by this time, the Navy was recognizing the shortcomings of the Brewster fighter, and a decision was made to order the Grumman on the basis of both its potential capabilities and as a safety factor in the event of the Buffalo's failure. The wisdom of this decision was even more apparent when the first of 54 F4F-3's began flying in February 1940. By this time, the superiority of the F4F over the F2A was clearly established.

Evaluation of the XF4F-3 suggested some refinements and these were incorporated

The General Motors FM-2 was the production version of the F4F-8.　　　　　*Grumman*

These Wildcats are FM-1's, built by General Motors. Of interest is the red surround to the star insignia. FM-1's used only four .50 cal. machine guns instead of the six used by the F4F-4.　　　　　*Navy*

into the production models. Engine overheating was still a problem and attempts were made to alleviate this through various cowling and spinner combinations. The difficulty was finally solved by adding small airfoils at the base of the propeller blades. The roots of the blades were round where they joined the hub and had little aerodynamic pressure. By placing airfoil-shaped cuffs over these areas, a fan effect was created which forced the cooling air between the cylinders.

The war in Europe brought export customers to Grumman; and, as the G-36A, 81 were sold to France. The fall of France to Germany forced the transfer of the contract to England where, as the Martlet, Grumman's fighter had its first taste of combat.

By the time the United States became involved in World War II, the second production batch of F4F's was underway. Now known as the Wildcat, it was the first of a continuing line of Grumman fighters to bear feline titles. The 38 foot wingspan was causing a great deal of crowding on carrier decks, so the F4F-4 was treated to a pair of folding wings which twisted on the rear spar to swing aft and fit vertically alongside the fuselage. This reduced the width of the Wildcat to 14 feet 4 inches and permitted more than twice as many planes to occupy the deck space with adequate clearance. The F4F-4 also was given more armament.

The original F4F was provided with the two .30 and .50 cal. machine guns which the military seemed to feel was suitable during the 'thirties. Certainly, considering the amount of combat they were actually involved in during that period, it was more than adequate. But to pose any kind of threat to a serious foe, more substantial firepower was compulsory. On the F4F-3, the armament consisted of four wing-mounted .50 cal. machine guns. The F4F-4 added two more .50's to the wings, providing them with 1,440 rounds of ammunition. For protection against enemy gunfire, the new Wildcat carried armor plate for the pilot and self-sealing fuel tanks.

The Wildcat was the only Navy fighter on hand at the outbreak of the war that was capable of offering any resistance to the Japanese attackers. Its principal foe was the lighter, faster, and more maneuverable Zero-Sen. Wildcat pilots rapidly learned to develop tactics that took advantage of the rugged construction of their Grumman fighters. The shock of the initial encounters with the Zero-Sen was soon moderated by the Americans' ability to do battle on more even terms.

In May, 1943, Grumman delivered their last F4F and turned their attention to its successor. However, the need for Wildcats still remained and production of the fighter continued at the Eastern Aircraft Division of General Motors, where the F4F-4 was designated FM-1. The first of this type was flown on September 1, 1942. GM introduced a modified version, the FM-2, in September 1943. This model was the equivalent of the XF4F-8, two of which had been tested by Grumman before turning

production over to GM. It used a Wright R-1820-56 Cyclone engine of 1,350 hp for takeoff and had a taller fin and rudder. The FM-2 was a specialized model. It was lighter in weight to improve takeoff and landing performance for use on small escort carriers. With the FM-1 and FM-2, there also came a change in armament; a return to the four wing guns, and six 5 inch rockets could also be carried on underwing mounts by the FM-2.

At the end of production in August, 1945, a total of 7,815 Wildcats had been built. This included over 900 supplied to the British Royal Navy.

The Wildcat was assigned several designations during its service; some sub-types reached -8. The third and fourth F4F-3's were test fitted with two-speed single-stage superchargers to become XF4F-5's. The XF4F-6 became the first of 96 F4F3A's to use an R-1830-90 engine with a single-stage supercharger. The F4F-7 was an unarmed photo-reconnaissance Wildcat which had an enlarged fuel capacity and a 24 hour endurance. Fortunately, this type was equipped with an autopilot. Twenty-one examples were completed.

Three XF2M-1's, with turbo-superchargers, were ordered but cancelled before an example was completed.

The F4F-4 is typical of the Wildcat series with a wingspan of 38 feet, a wing area of 260 sq. feet, a length of 28 feet 9 inches, and a height of 11 feet 10 inches. A single Pratt & Whitney R-1830-86 Twin Wasp engine provided 1,700 hp for a maximum speed of 320 mph at 18,800 feet. Empty weight of the airframe was 5,895 pounds, gross weight was 7,975 pounds. Service ceiling was 34,000 feet.

With the Wildcat, the Navy's late introduction of the monoplane to fleet service now seemed justified, for here indeed was a fighter that could do what was needed when it was needed. It is recorded that the Wildcat was inferior to its foes, yet official records show that they were responsible for the destruction of 6.9 planes for each Wildcat lost. That's not too bad, considering the Navy's original opinion of the design.

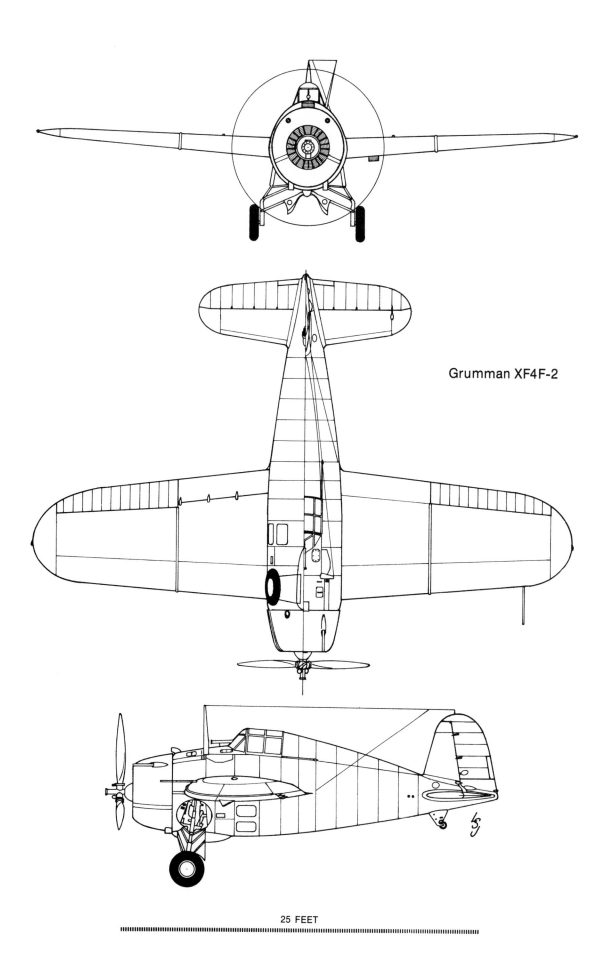

Grumman XF4F-2

25 FEET

This XF4F-8 was the prototype for the FM-2, but has a shorter fin and rudder. *Grumman*

Several Wildcats survive and can be seen at air shows on occasion. The tall tail identifies this as an FM-2, still in flying condition. *Air Museum*

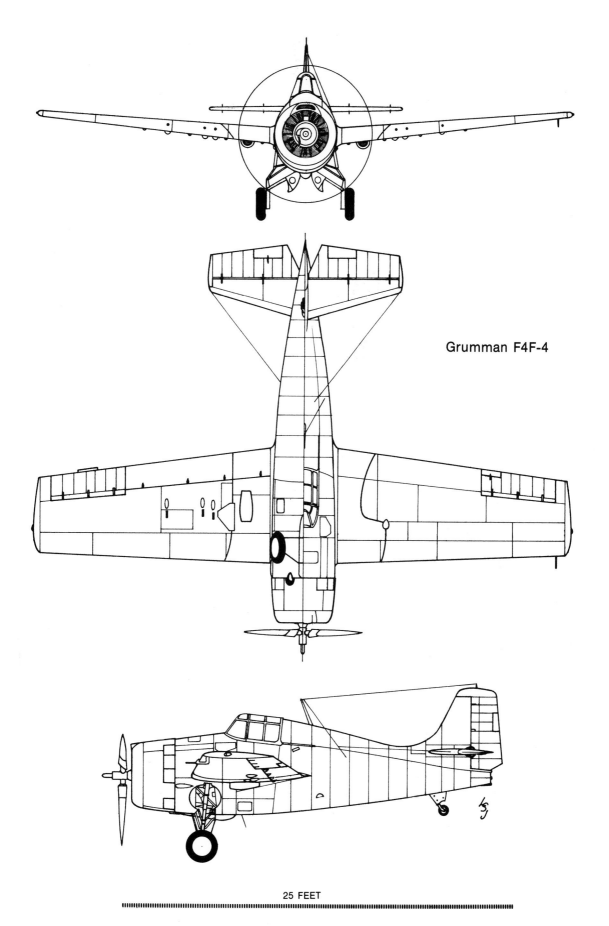

Grumman F4F-4

25 FEET

BELL XFL-1
AIRABONITA

The Bell Airabonita was based on the Airacobra design, but not a conversion of the Army fighter. Navy pilots did not like the car-like door for cockpit access.   *Bell*

The Airabonita was another attempt to modify an Air Corps fighter into a carrier plane. It was patterned after Bell's XP-39 Airacobra which had flown on April 6, 1938, and had reached 390 mph during tests. Air Corps trials were encouraging, so Bell offered a suitably altered version of the fighter to the Navy. On November 8, 1938, an agreement was signed identifying the Bell proposal as the XFL-1, recalling the unused Loening designation code.

The Airabonita, as Bell called the XFL-1, displayed some rather novel features for a carrier plane which were viewed with concern by its pilots. A liquid-cooled Allison XV-1710-16, twelve cylinder inline engine was a deviation from the standard air-cooled types in the first place. But Bell engineers had installed this power unit in the middle of the airplane, driving the nose-mounted propeller by means of an extension shaft passing between the pilot's feet.

From a design point of view, this location places the heavy engine right on the center of gravity, an ideal position for good maneuverability. The drive shaft was 8 feet long and connected with a reduction gear which turned the propeller. During operations, the long shaft vibrated and gave rise to fear that it would either break loose and flail the pilot or lead to the premature fatiguing of the aircraft.

Another feature that was met with some apprehension was the design of the cockpit with its automobile-type doors. Indeed, if it became necessary to ditch the XFL-1, it would be very difficult to push the doors outward against the water pressure. In its favor, however, was the proposed armament of two .30 cal. machine guns in the nose and a .50 cal. machine gun or a 37 mm cannon firing through the hollow propeller shaft.

The Airabonita was first flown on May 13, 1940, with a conventional tailwheel landing gear instead of the tricycle arrangement on the P-39. For a better view of the carrier deck during approaches, the XFL-1 cockpit was slightly higher than that of the Airacobra; and a clear-view panel was installed between the pilot's feet. It arrived at Anacostia on February 27, 1941, for its service trials.

The 1,150 hp Allison supplied enough power to pull the XFL-1 to a speed of 336 mph at 10,000 feet—substantially slower than the P-39. In addition to the vibration,

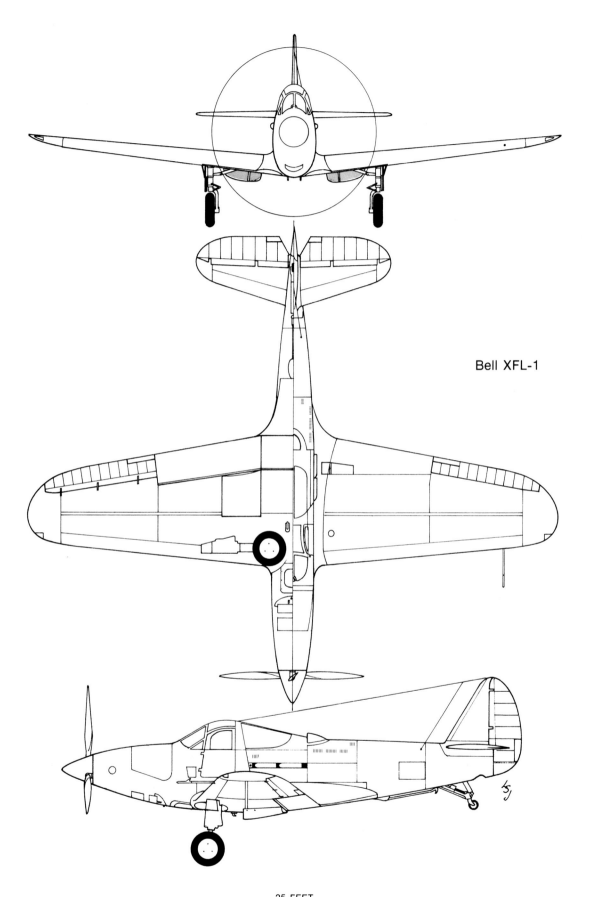

Bell XFL-1

25 FEET

Vibration in the drive-shaft of the rear-mounted engine contributed to the rejection of the XFL-1 as a Navy fighter.
Bell

the Airabonita suffered from longitudinal instability. A wind tunnel analysis of the design was undertaken using a scale model. It was found to be necessary to increase the vertical stabilizer area.

Although the XFL-1 had been strengthened to withstand the rigors of carrier service, the plane was beset with landing gear failures and was unable to pass its carrier qualification trials. At this point, it became apparent that the Bell fighter was simply not suited for carrier service, was summarily rejected, and ended its existence

in an earth fill for a runway extension.

The XFL-1 was not a converted P-39. In addition to the differences previously noted, it had a larger wing, spanning 35 feet with an area of 232 square feet. It was 29 feet 9 inches long and 12 feet 9 inches high. Empty weight was 5,161 pounds, maximum weight was 7,212 pounds. Fuel capacity was 126 gallons which gave a range of 965 miles. Service ceiling was 30,900 feet with an initial climb rate of 2,630 fpm. No armament was installed in the Airabonita prototype.

GRUMMAN XF5F-1
SKYROCKET

The Grumman Skyrocket represented a bold step for Grumman. It was the first twin-engine carrier fighter.
Wayne Morris

Probably the most ambitious project undertaken for a carrier fighter during the late 'thirties was Grumman's Skyrocket. At a time when the Navy was embroiled in the selection of a monoplane fighter for the fleet, the planners at Grumman were busy devising a twin-engined shipboard machine. Since such a concept had never been attempted before, the big fighter was bound to be distinctive in appearance—and so it was! So distinctive, in fact, that it became the super weapon of "Black Hawk," a fictional comic strip hero of the day.

Grumman's boldness was rewarded with a development contract for one prototype as the XF5F-1 on June 30, 1938. Two 1,200 hp Wright XR-1820 engines, each rotating in opposite directions, were selected to power the big craft. The first flight was made on April 1, 1940. No doubt, its radical shape made it the butt of many jokes of the day, but its performance proved as revolutionary as its appearance. It had a top speed of 358 mph at 17,300 feet and could climb 10,000 feet in just over four minutes. Service ceiling was 34,500 feet.

Once again, the problem of cooling the

engines interrupted the test program. Additional air inlets were added to the cowlings, and ducts were revised. Other shortcomings relating to the boldness of the concept began to crop up, interfering with the testing. It wasn't until February 1941, that a comprehensive analysis of the XF5F-1 was ready.

Grumman took the Skyrocket back in March 1941, and subjected the fighter to an extensive redesign program. There was no doubt that they were on the right track with a promising design, but it clearly needed refining. The distinctive truncated nose was replaced by a more angular structure extending beyond the wing. Originally, the nose had been abbreviated to permit a virtually unobstructed forward view, but aerodynamics became a factor in the extension. Additionally, the engine nacelles were extended behind the wing and the landing gear doors redesigned to completely enclose the wheels. To further smooth the airflow around the nacelles, a pair of spinners were attached to the propellers. Completing the most apparent changes was a lowered cockpit canopy.

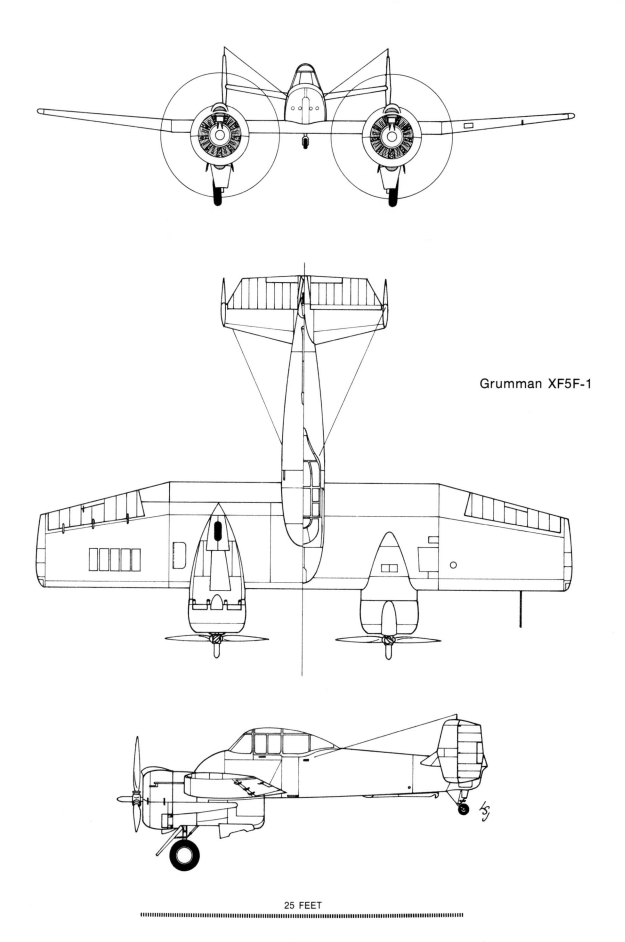

Grumman XF5F-1

25 FEET

During trials it was found necessary to extend the nose and lengthen the engine nacelles.   *Grumman*

The Skyrocket was returned to the Navy in July 1941, and more revisions were indicated as the testing resumed. One major problem was the location of the large engine nacelles which effectively blocked the pilot's view of the deck landing officer. Taking this, and the other factors which had led to the redesign, into account, Grumman abandoned further development of the Skyrocket as a fighter and directed their efforts toward perfecting another twin engine fighter. To this end, the XF5F-1 became a test bed.

On February 3, 1942, the Skyrocket lost its main gear during landing tests at the Naval Aircraft Factory and suffered severe damage. Still considered a useful test vehicle, the XF5F-1 was repaired; but four months later the gear was again torn off. Apparently these two accidents weakened the landing gear assembly and the aircraft was continually subject to gear failure, both in the air and on the ground. On December 11, 1944, this problem led to a final belly landing and the Skyrocket was written off, being disassembled at NAS, New York.

The boldness of the Skyrocket's design was also reflected in the proposed armament for the craft. It was intended to install two Danish-built 23 mm Madsen cannons in the nose. Before these weapons could be obtained, however, Denmark had fallen to the Germans so four .50 cal. machine guns with 400 rpg served as replacements. Two 165 pound bombs could be mounted under the wings. Another feature of the Skyrocket design was a set of ten tiny weapon bays in the outer wing panels which could hold a total of 40 anti-aircraft bombs.

The Skyrocket was the largest Navy fighter to date and had a wingspan of 42 feet which was reduced to 21 feet 2 inches when the wings were folded. Wing area was 303 square feet. Overall length of the twin-engined fighter was 28 feet 11 inches, and it measured 11 feet 11 inches high. The Skyrocket's empty weight was 7,990 pounds; and its normal gross was just over 5 tons at 10,021 pounds. Fuel capacity was 178 gallons for a range of 780 miles. In spite of its proportions, the XF5F-1 could land at 72 mph. On one occasion during dive tests, the Skyrocket reached a speed of 485 mph. However, speed attained in such a manner is not considered as part of the normal performance envelope of the aircraft.

The XF5F-1 was very distinctive with its huge nacelles and twin rudders.   *Wayne Morris*

The XF5F-1 lived up to its name. The Skyrocket could climb 10,000 feet in four minutes, quite remarkable in 1940.
                                                                              Grumman

CHANCE VOUGHT
F4U CORSAIR

The XF4U-1 was the first American fighter to exceed 400 mph. This plane was finally delivered to the Navy after the first 100 production F4U-1's had been received.   *Vought*

The fourth Navy fighter to carry the Vought designation was the eminently successful F4U Corsair. Preliminary plans for the F4U began in 1936, and a prototye was ordered two years later, on June 30, 1938—at the same time as Grumman's Skyrocket.

Pratt & Whitney had been working on an 18 cylinder air-cooled engine of 2,800 cubic inches. It was called the Double Wasp and had been putting out nearly 2,000 hp on the test stand. It was around this powerful engine that Vought engineers formed their new machine. The selection of this powerplant brought with it a unique set of problems, though. In order to absorb the tremendous power output of the new engine, a huge propeller would have to be mounted to its shaft. Even with three blades, the diameter of the required propeller was 13 feet 4 inches. Using conventional methods, this could lead to a landing gear strut of some 6 feet in length and, most certainly, many complications. The design team took an ingenious approach and canted the wing center section downward, creating an inverted-gull configuration. Now, with the landing strut a reasonable length, it was geared to revolve 90 degrees

as it folded to the rear with the wheel lying flat within the wing. An added benefit was the fact that the tilted center section met the fuselage at the optimum angle for minimum drag. To further enhance the performance of the XF4U, the aluminum skin was spot-welded to the metal frame. This eliminated the air-disturbing bumps of raised rivets and was smoother, even, than flush riveting while creating a hardy structure. Much of the wing was metal-covered—the exception was the fabric-covered center section of the outboard panels. The wings were designed to fold, as were those of all subsequent carrier fighters used by the Navy.

In February 1939, a wind tunnel model verified the designers' theories and work was begun on the first of what was to be known as the Corsair. (The name Corsair had graced many Vought aircraft preceding the F4U, but the gull-winged fighter was the first to be officially designated as such by the Navy.)

The XF4U-1 prototype first entered its intended environment on May 29, 1940. Thus began a prolonged evaluation which eventually led to its acceptance by the Navy after the first 100 production planes had been delivered! The prototype carried an

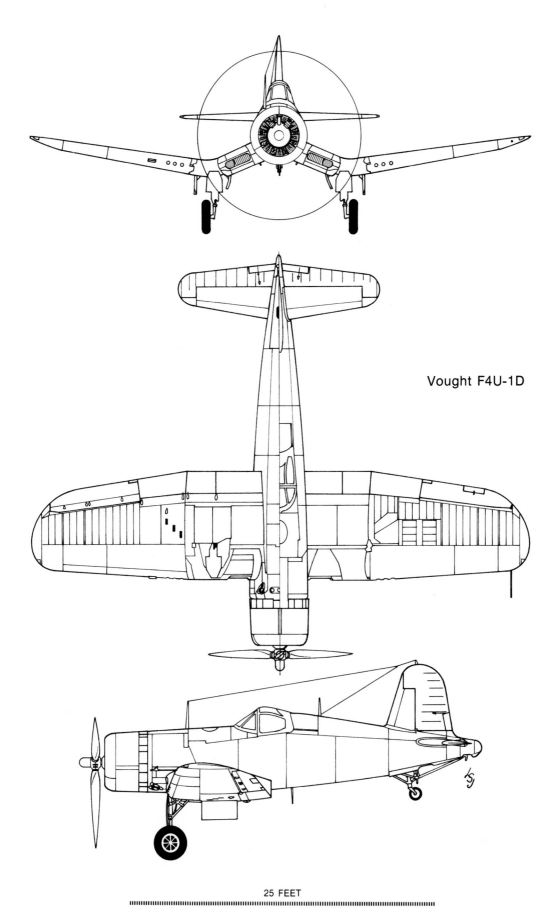

Vought F4U-1D

25 FEET

XR-2800-4 Double Wasp at the beginning of the tests. On July 12, the XF4U-1 was forced to land on a golf course during stormy weather, damaging the prototype. When the Corsair resumed flying, it was powered by a production model of the engine.

The results of the trials were more than encouraging, they were astounding! On October 1, the XF4U-1 reached the speed of 404 mph to become the first American fighter to exceed 400 mph. With the Corsair, Navy fighter design took a quantum leap forward. This remarkable plane represented a significant turning point in both engineering and performance.

The advanced concept of the Corsair was not without its drawbacks, however. In the first place, the landing speed was considered too high for carrier use. Production types, with combat gear, were slamming down at 87 mph. The long nose made observation of the carrier deck difficult, and the big fighter tended to bounce and swing on touchdown. Although it did pass its carrier qualification tests, the Navy considered the F4U-1 a land-based fighter.

The F4U-1 was ordered into production on June 30, 1941, when a contract for 584 machines was signed. The Navy had complained about the location of the cockpit over the wing, obscuring the downward view, so the F4U-1 cockpit was moved behind the wing. The span and length was increased slightly; otherwise the production Corsairs appeared much the same as the prototype.

Initially, the two-gun armament was mounted in the nose, as was usual. By the time production began, combat reports from Europe clearly showed the inadequacy of this arrangement, and four .50 cal. machine guns were placed in the wings. Very soon, this was increased to six wing-mounted .50's.

Complaints about the Corsair's poor forward visibility persisted; and on the 689th plane, a bubble-like canopy replaced the "birdcage" structure enabling the seat to be elevated seven inches. This became the first F4U-1A. Even though a great deal of attention had been directed toward improving the carrier landing characteristics of the big fighter, the Navy still refused to assign them to carrier duty. It would appear that the Navy was being overly cautious in this respect. One entire squadron, VF-17, had successfully landed their F4U-1A's on board the Essex and Bunker Hill when they ran low on fuel following an intercept mission in which they had destroyed 18 attacking bombers. Not only this, but the British Royal Navy was routinely operating

To improve pilot visibility the cockpit of the production F4U-1 was moved aft of the wing. This has the "birdcage" canopy, so called because of the framing. Note the extended landing light under the wing. Vought

their Lend-Lease Corsairs from their smaller escort carriers. In April 1944, the Navy finally approved the F4U for carrier use.

Four 20 mm cannons, in place of the machine guns, distinguished 200 F4U-1C's. The cannons proved especially effective for ground attack; but Navy pilots preferred their machine guns for dogfighting so no further orders were placed for -1C's. The F4U-1B designation had been given to the British Lend-Lease Corsairs.

The F4U-1D was substantially improved to increase the Corsair's versatility. A pair of bomb racks, each with a 1,000 pound capacity, were installed under the wings, and eight attachment points on the outer panels could carry five-inch rockets. The uprated Pratt & Whitney R-2800-8W had water injection giving the big engine a 2,250 hp kick. This Corsair could reach 425 mph at 20,000 feet and could carry 2,000 pounds of bombs for 500 miles.

As in the case of the Wildcat, the demand for the Corsair far exceeded the production ability of the Vought Company and supplemental assembly lines were set up at the Goodyear and Brewster plants. Goodyear produced the FG-1D, while Brewster's version was labeled F3A-1D. In all, the parent company built 7,830 of their superb fighters, while Goodyear made 4,-017, and Brewster added 735 to the total of 12,582 of the bent-winged birds. This accounted for all of the total production, from the F4U-1 through the F4U-7 built for the French Aeronavale after the war.

The F4U remained in production longer than any other American fighter. The first Corsair was assembled at Stratford, Connecticut; the last one rolled from the factory at Dallas, Texas, after the company had moved west. As a result of this longevity, a considerable number of variants were produced. Seven major subtypes were made with many additional classifications within them. Throughout its life, the Corsair was subjected to nearly 1,000 major modifications and over 20,000 minor ones.

War-time Corsairs included radar-

These night-fighting Corsairs carry radar in the pod on their wingtips. These F4U-2's prepare for a mission from the carrier USS Intrepid. Twelve of these were modified from F4U-1's and used by VNF-75 and VFN-101.
Vought

equipped night fighters and camera-filled reconnaissance planes. These were based on the F4U-4 and designated F4U-4N and F4U-4P respectively. The F4U-4 was powered by the R-2800-18W giving 2,450 hp for a speed of 446 mph with a four-bladed propeller.

In combat against the Japanese, 189 Corsairs were lost; but in exchange, the F4U's extracted a toll of 2,140 from their foes for a kill ratio of 11.3 to 1. The wing-mounted intercoolers made a distinctive whine as the Corsair hurtled through the air, leading to the Japanese nickname "Whistling Death." But to the Americans, she was the "Sweetheart of Okinawa."

The F4U was responsible for many American aces, and four of its pilots were recipients of the Congressional Medal of Honor. Charles A. Lindbergh was assigned to evaluate the Corsair in combat, but was prohibited from flying any missions. Somehow, he managed to be in a position where the "testing" of his guns and bombs often caused damage to the Japanese forces. On one occasion, he flew over Rabaul for a "test." Another time, he left Roi Island on a test with three 1,000 pound bombs—quite a load for a fighter. A few days later, with a 2,000 pound bomb on the center pylon and two 1,000 pounders under the wings, he ferried his load to Watje Atoll where he "tested" a Japanese gun emplacement into

oblivion. This is believed to be the heaviest load ever carried by a single-engine prop-driven fighter during the war.

With the end of WWII, remaining Corsair contracts were severely cut. The Vought factory had moved from Connecticut to Dallas shortly before North Korea began their invasion of the South. There was an immediate need for low-level close support aircraft in this new war, and Vought received an order for 110 attack Corsairs, designated AU-1, which were delivered to Marine squadrons in Korea. The AU-1 was similar to the earlier F4U-5 which was being built when World War II ended. It had an R-2800-83W supercharged engine for superior low altitude performance. Four 20 mm cannons peered from the wing gun ports and it could equal the load-carrying ability of Lindbergh's "test" plane with a 4,000 pound bomb load or ten 5 inch rockets.

The low-level operations of the Corsair in Korea brought about some new tactics. The night-fighting F4U-5N brought some surprises to the Communist forces. With a bulbous radar pod mounted on the tip of the right wing, the fighter could locate and attack an enemy in pitch darkness. One pilot became a night-fighting ace by downing five enemy aircraft in only 18 days. Another pilot created some havoc with a Communist communications center by dragging his ex-

The F4U-1D introduced a raised canopy. This model was the most widely used Corsair in World War II.   *Vought*

175

These F4U-1D's show the distinctive three-color camouflage scheme used by the Navy midway through WW II. The bottoms of the outer wing panels were painted dark blue because they were visible from above when the wings were folded on the carrier deck. *Vought*

tended tail hook through their telephone lines. Even though the Corsair was obsolete by the time it went to Korea, one of the gull-winged fighters from VMA-312 was credited with destroying a MiG-15 jet fighter.

The Goodyear F2G-1 was devised as an interceptor to counter the threat of the Japanese Kamikaze planes. This model had a huge twenty-eight cylinder Pratt & Whitney R-4360-4 with an incredible 3,000 hp. This plane also featured a full bubble-type canopy. Only 5 of an order for 418 units were built due to lateral instability and a lower than anticipated speed of 431 mph. These planes were intended for land-based operations and did not have folding wings. Ten of the type with hinged wings were ordered as the F2G-2, but none were built. One XF4U-4 even tried its wings behind an Aeroproducts contraprop.

Corsairs surviving both World War II and Korea have found another arena for combat as they are common sights at the various air races held throughout the country.

The F4U-1D, the type most widely used in World War II, had a wingspan of 40 feet 11 inches. Wing area was 314 square feet. Length was 33 feet 4 inches, height was 15 feet 1 inch. Empty weight was 8,694 pounds. Normally loaded, this Corsair weighed 12,039 pounds. Fuel capacity was 178 gallons internal plus 185 gallons in drop tanks. Service ceiling was 33,900 feet.

This Corsair is an AU-1 of the type used by the Marines for ground attack operations in Korea.   Vought

An F4U-4B of VMF-214, "Pappy" Boyington's famous Black Sheep squadron, lining up on the catapult for a launch prior to a mission in the Korean war.   *Vought*

The nearest F4U-1 is carrying a pair of 1,000 pound bombs.   *Vought*

A large air scoop identifies this rocket-armed F4U-4C, the second greatest production version of the Corsair. A total of 2,356 -4's were built. *Vought*

This F4U-5N carries bright yellow markings for tests. The F4U-5N was used effectively for night fighting in Korea. *Vought*

An F4U-5NL preparing for a night mission over Korea.   *Vought*

The most radical change in the appearance of the Corsair came when a 3,000 hp Wasp Major engine and tear-drop canopy were installed. This modification created the Goodyear F2G-1D shown here. Note also the increased vertical tail to handle the extra torque.
Gordon S. Williams

The big Curtiss XF14C-2 was not able to meet the Navy's requirements. Excess weight and vibration problems led to its demise.
Gordon S. Williams

On June 30, 1941, the Navy placed development contracts for three new fighters; one destined for immortality; one to pioneer a new class of fighting plane; and the third to vanish into obscurity. These contracts were for Grumman's F6F and F7F, and the Curtiss XF14C. Whereas the first two of these fighter prototypes were based upon an established powerplant, the Curtiss was to use an untried Lycoming XH-2470-4—a 24 cylinder liquid-cooled creation of unconventional layout. The cylinders were arranged in four banks of six in an "H" formation with each pair of six operating in opposition to the other. This machine was to produce 2,200 hp at sea level and 2,000 hp at 4,500 feet. However, in light of the availability of an established 2,000 hp radial engine, it is strange that the Navy would consider a liquid-cooled type at this point.

Some foresight had been shown, however, when the Navy specified that the XF14C-1 was to be armed initially with four or six .50 cal. machine guns. These were to be replaced with four 20 mm cannons at a later date.

The Curtiss designers proceeded with the engineering of their new ship with the authorization for two XF14C-1 prototypes. In October, 1942, a wind tunnel model of the fighter was evaluated at the Navy's Aeronautical Laboratory in Washington, D.C. These tests indicated that the Curtiss performance estimates for the XF14C-1 were highly optimistic, even unrealistic. Added to this was the fact that the development of the Lycoming engine was faltering; so in December 1943, the Navy cancelled the original contract for the liquid-cooled fighter.

There was still a need for a high-altitude carrier fighter, so Curtiss was directed to revamp the design to accept a turbo-supercharged Wright XR-3350-16 with 2,300 hp and a pair of contra-rotating propellers. Thus, as the XF14C-2, the big Curtiss fighter made its appearance and began flight testing in July 1944.

Once again, the Curtiss estimates were beyond the capabilities of the large fighter. A maximum speed of 424 mph at 32,000 feet had been promised, but the airspeed indicator would not go beyond 398 mph at the specified altitude. The XF14C-2 did come close to the targeted service ceiling, however, by reaching 39,500 feet. The dual-rotating contra-props set up an undesirable

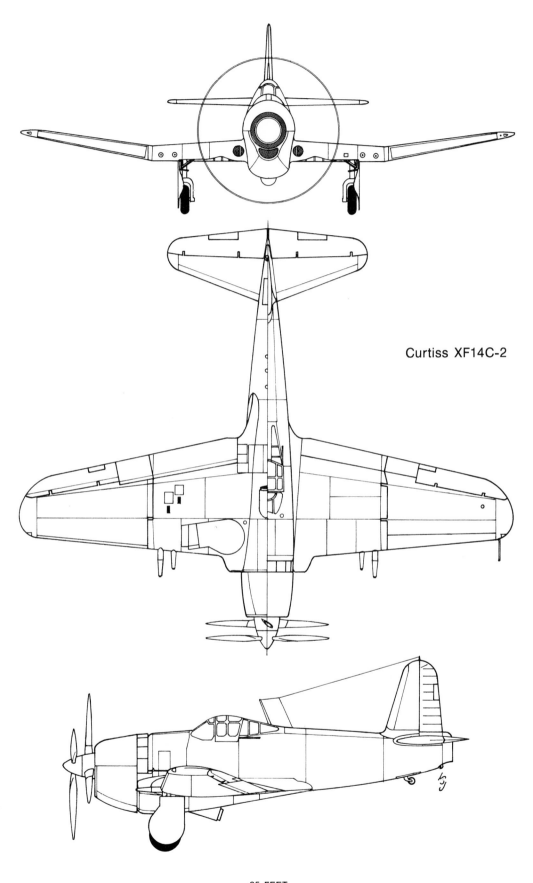

Curtiss XF14C-2

25 FEET

vibration; so, once again, the XF14C was cancelled.

In a parallel development, Curtiss was also building a high altitude interceptor for the Air Force, the XP-62. A great deal of engineering had gone into the design of a pressurized cockpit for this fighter, and it was felt that the XF14C could benefit from such a feature. Hopeful that the defects in the existing prototype could eventually be ironed out, Curtiss again approached the Navy, this time with a plan to pressurize the cabin of their fighter. Still in need of a high altitude carrier-based interceptor, the Navy reinstated the development contract for two of the pressurized machines as XF14C-3's, but no prototype contract was let and the project was finally dropped.

Even if the high altitude capabilities of the XF14C-3 had been perfected, it is unlikely that the fighter would have been suitable for carrier duty. Without the heavy pressurization gear, the plane had an empty weight of 10,582 pounds and grossed at 13,405 pounds. Its wingspan was 46 feet with an area of 375 square feet. Length was 37 feet 9 inches and it was 12 feet 4 inches high. The armament of four 20 mm cannons was installed in the wings.

The exhaust for the turbo-supercharger extends below the fuselage of the XF14C-2. Even the supercharger was unable to provide enough power to reach the design speed.
                                                                    Gordon S. Williams

GRUMMAN F6F
HELLCAT

BuNo 02981. A sire of champions, this is the prototype Hellcat. The skin lines show the typical Grumman construction used on the fuselage. The spinner and wheel fairings were subject to changes, but the production Hellcats were virtually unchanged in appearance.
Grumman

With the combat debut of the F6F Hellcat over Marcus Island on August 31, 1943, the Navy at last had a fighter that was superior to the Japanese Zero-Sen in nearly every respect. Here was a machine that could dictate the terms of combat, and American pilots immediately set about showing the enemy how the battles would be fought in the future. By the time World War II was over, Hellcats were credited with 5,156 of a total of 6,477 Japanese planes downed by American Navy pilots.

Conceptual planning for the Hellcat began on June 30, 1941, when the Navy ordered one prototype XF6F-1. With the attack on Pearl Harbor and the awareness of the Zero-Sen threat, Grumman reassessed their fighter in the light of combat experience. A proposal was made to install a turbo-supercharger as the XF6F-2, but this idea was short-lived and the upgraded design became the XF6F-3, under which label the prototype appeared.

To keep the wing at the lowest drag angle, the big Pratt & Whitney R-2800-10 Double Wasp was tilted downward 3 degrees which also benefitted the pilot by improving his visibility over the nose. The

Hellcat was constructed of, and entirely covered with, metal and large areas were flush riveted for the least air resistance.

The XF6F-3 thundered off the runway on June 26, 1942; but a month earlier, the Hellcat had been ordered into full-scale production. The Navy was quite pleased with the prototype's 380 mph top speed and the outstanding maneuverability afforded by its low wing loading. Just a month later, the first F6F-3 joined its progenitor on the flight line.

Differences between the prototype and production articles were minimal. The changes were confined to a redesign of the landing gear fairings, elimination of the spinner, and a Hamilton Standard Hydromatic replacing the Curtiss Electric propeller.

By January 16, 1943, enough Hellcats had been delivered to outfit squadron VF-9 on board the USS Essex. Within eighteen months of the Hellcat's first flight, it was presenting its credentials to the Imperial Japanese Navy. By the end of the year, Grumman had delivered 2,545 of their new fighters to the U.S. fleet.

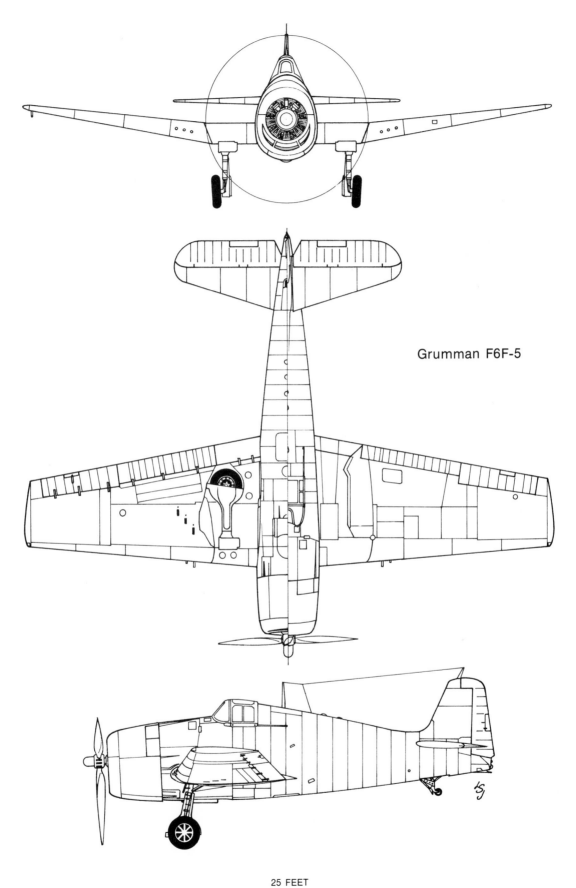

Grumman F6F-5

25 FEET

The XF6F-2 had a four-bladed propeller driven by a turbo-supercharged R-2800-21. The name Fuzzy Wuzzy *appears in yellow script on both sides of the cowl.*
Grumman

The Hellcat began replacing the Wildcat on the decks of the fast carriers, while the F4F's were transferred to the smaller escort vessels. The F6F's supplemented the land-based Corsairs and gave the Navy an added versatility.

The six .50 cal. machine guns, with 400 rpg, had a devastating effect on the Zero-Sen. As the Hellcat pilots gained familiarity with their mounts, they became more aggressive and this led to some very interesting encounters. On one evening, a group of Hellcat pilots joined in the landing circle with 49 Japanese carrier planes approaching Orote Field on Guam. Picking them off one by one, the Hellcats shot down thirty of the enemy planes; and the remaining 19 were so badly shattered that they crashed on landing. Another Hellcat pilot unknowingly jettisoned his drop tank onto a pride of the Rising Sun, sending his Zero spinning into the ocean.

In combat, the Hellcat was only slightly less maneuverable than the Zero-Sen, but it possessed superior speed in the areas of climb, level flight and diving. It was rugged enough to withstand the Zero's 7.7 mm guns, and armor plate protected the pilot and oil system.

The 4,403rd Hellcat was the first F6F-5. It used a water-injected R-2800-10W with 2,200 hp and, with combat gear, could reach 380 mph. Aside from a flatter windshield and some rework around the exhaust outlet, the -5 was virtually identical to the -3. (The -4 version of the Hellcat was built from the original XF6F-2, but used an R-2800-27. Only the single experimental model was built.) As production of the F6F-5 increased, provision was made to arm the Hellcat with either the six .50 cal. machine guns or four 20 mm cannons. Two 1,000 pound bombs could be carried under the wings between the landing gear, and launching posts for six 5 inch rockets were installed outboard.

The Royal Navy also availed itself of the Hellcat's capabilities, operating both the F6F-3 and -5 types and calling them Hellcat I's and II's.

Night fighter and photo reconnaissance Hellcats existed—the F6F-3N and -3E carrying radar under the right wing for night interceptions. The F6F-3E carried additional electronic devices and totaled 18 examples. The success of the radar-guided night fighters was such that of the 7,625 F6F-5's built, over 1,000 were night fighters. The F6F-5P's were camera-equipped; but unlike most other reconnaissance machines, these also carried guns.

The fastest Hellcats were the two XF6F-6's using uprated R-2800-18W's of 2,100 hp normally but boosted to 2,450 hp with water injection. This engine turned a four-bladed Hamilton Standard propeller and pushed the needle to 417 mph at 22,000 feet. No production order was received for this type, however, as the final tests were completed after the end of the war. Hellcat production terminated after 12,275 units had been built.

F6F-5's from a reserve unit fly in echelon during maneuvers. *Navy*

Although no Hellcats were produced after the war, the big fighter continued to serve in reserve squadrons. Hence, when the Korean War broke out, many of the F6F's were still serviceable. Though not used in a fighting role, Hellcats did participate in the Korean War as radio-guided flying bombs. Six F6F-5K's, assigned to Guided Missile Unit 90, were loaded with high-explosives and directed against North Korean ground targets. The first of these sorties was launched from the USS Boxer on August 28, 1952.

An F6F-5K was launched from the carrier and guided by radio toward Hungnam, where the target was a railroad bridge. Controlling radio signals were sent from Skyraiders of VC-35.

Other Hellcats were used as targets themselves to help develop the next generation of airborne weapons—the air-to-air missiles. These planes were identified by their brilliant red or yellow paint schemes.

The F6F-5, the major production type of the series, had a wingspan of 42 feet 10

The F6F-5 gave improved performance, was cannon-armed and could carry six rockets under its wings. Navy

The F6F-5N served well as a night fighter with APS-6 radar in a streamlined radome on the starboard wing. *Navy*

The first production model of the Hellcat was the F6F-3. *Grumman*

inches with an area of 334 square feet. Length was 33 feet 7 inches and the height was 13 feet 1 inch. The -5 had an empty weight of 9,238 pounds and grossed out at 12,740 pounds. Maximum speed was 380 mph at 23,400 feet; landing speed was 88 mph. Service ceiling was 37,300 feet. With an internal fuel capacity, this model of the Hellcat had a range of 945 miles.

GRUMMAN F7F
TIGERCAT

The prototype XF7F-1 Tigercat. The experience gained on the Skyrocket project was useful in designing the
Navy's first operational twin-engined fighter.   *Grumman*

Grumman's F7F brought to the Navy two features that were to have a significant influence on future ship-based fighter design. It successfully combined twin engine performance with tricycle landing gear, both firsts for an operational carrier fighter. The third of the three new planes ordered for evaluation on June 30, 1941, the XF7F-1 was loosely patterned after the unsuccessful XF5F-1 Skyrocket and its Air Corps twin, the XP-50. With a maximum gross weight of 22,560 pounds, the twin-engined Tigercat weighed less than the top gross of two Hellcats. Yet it carried four .50 cal. machine guns in its nose, PLUS four 20 mm cannons in its wing roots, 2,000 rounds of ammunition, and two 1,000 pound bombs. With 426 gallons of fuel, the F7F could carry this load for a range of 1,170 miles, then return to its base at a speed of 427 mph at 19,200 feet! Or it could carry a standard torpedo instead of the bomb load—the first time such a weapon could be carried by an operational fighter.

The first of two prototype Tigercats rose from Grumman's runway in December 1943, under the pull of two Wright R-2600-14 engines of 1,500 hp. Since the big plane was intended for carrier operations, it had been given a set of short-span broad-chord wings to facilitate ground handling yet provide adequate area for short takeoffs. In addition, the folding mechanism for the outer panels was power-operated.

Official flight trials were interrupted on May 1, 1944, with the crash of the first prototype. However, testing was satisfactorily completed after the second plane arrived; and Grumman was awarded a production contract for 500 F7F-1's. The Tigercat's phenomenal firepower made it ideal for ground support and the first production machines were earmarked for delivery to Marine squadrons in the Pacific. The first F7F-1's were similar to the XF7F-1's except for the use of a pair of Pratt & Whitney R-2800-22W powerplants of 2,100 hp each. The initial production Tigercats included huge spinners of the type seen on the prototypes, but continued cooling difficulties soon led to their abandonment.

The size of the Tigercat made it a candidate for the role of a two-place night fighter, and the thirty-fifth unit was experimentally fitted with a second seat to become the XF7F-2N. The four nose-mounted machine guns were replaced by the radar scanner and the fuselage-mounted

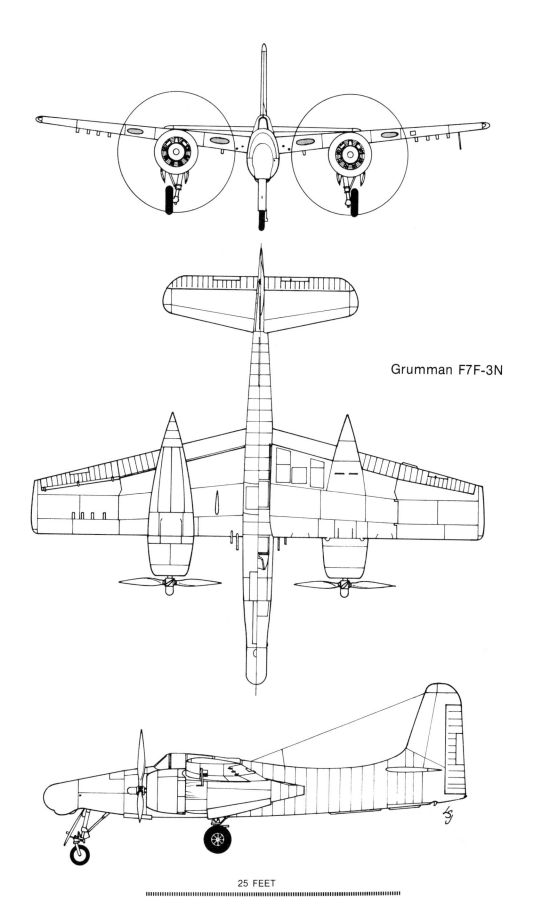

Grumman F7F-3N

25 FEET

An early production F7F-1 Tigercat. *Grumman*

fuel tanks reduced in size to allow accommodations of the radar operator. This conversion proved quite suitable to the Navy's requirements and a further sixty-four F7F-2N's were accepted.

By March 1945, a more powerful single-seater was on the lines, the F7F-3 — last of the one-place Tigercats. The nose battery of four machine guns was reinstated and two R-2800-34W engines, with an additional 250 hp each, gave the -3 a top speed of 435 mph at 22,000 feet.

By the time of the Japanese surrender ending World War II, the Tigercat had not been used in combat. Post-war cancellations restricted production of the F7F-3 to 189 planes, but sixty F7F-3N biplace radar-directed night fighters were delivered in 1946. Up to this point, all the Tigercats were made for land operations. The final model of this fighter, the F7F-4N, was the sole version with carrier gear actually installed. Only thirteen of these were built.

The basic F7F-3 underwent several latent changes after it went into service. In its original form, it was a day fighter with the nose-mounted machine guns. As the F7F-3N, the nose housed an SCR-720 radar set—relying on the four wing-mounted 20

mm cannons for armament. A bank of cameras in the nose created the F7F-3P for photo reconnasissance duty; a proposed F7F-3E with electronic gear was cancelled. The Tigercat also served in both the roles of drone controller and the drone itself as F7F-3D and F7F-3K respectively.

The Korean War finally presented the Tigercat with it's first opportunity for combat. On September 18, 1951, United Nations troops captured Kimpo Airfield and within hours, three Marine squadrons began operations from the field. One squadron was equipped with F7F-3N night fighters. Its effectiveness in the close support role is indicated by the following event.

During the fighting in Seoul, advancing Marines were held up by a particularly heavy concentration of Communist troops. Many of these troops had been noticed running toward two buildings, which it was learned, was the Communist Command Post. A forward air controller with the Marines quickly radioed for an air strike and was surprised when he coincidentally recognized the voice of the pilot as an old squadron buddy. The pilot then directed his Tigercat toward the buildings and fired a short burst at the target for identification.

The nose-mounted machine guns can be seen in this shot of the third F7F-1. Its phenomenal firepower of four .50 cal. machine guns and four 20mm cannons made the Tigercat an ideal ground-support weapon.

Wayne Morris

The F7F-3N carried a radar operator in a second seat over the wing. Sixty of these were built. These also had wider fins than previous models.

Wayne Morris

This F7F-3N has been converted from an F7F-3.   *Wayne Morris*

Assured he had the right target, he swung the F7F around and dropped to treetop level. The first building had three windows facing the approaching plane and the pilot fired one of his rockets squarely through the center window, the missile exploding well inside the building. A second pass wiped out the remaining structure.

The night fighting F7F-3N had a wingspan of 51 feet 6 inches, and the shoulder-mounted wing had an area of 455 square feet. With a length of 45 feet 4 inches, the -3 version was a half-inch short-er than the -2, but the height of 16 feet 7 inches was 16 inches taller. With radar gear replacing the nose guns and a second seat added, the night fighter weighed 16,400 pounds and grossed at 21,476 pounds with a maximum takeoff weight of 25,846 pounds. Maximum speed was 423 mph at 21,900 feet. Service ceiling was 40,800 feet. The ability to deliver a full-size torpedo gave the Tigercat the added distinction of being the world's fastest torpedo bomber.

Including the two prototypes, production of the Tigercat amounted to 363 aircraft.

BOEING
XF8B-1

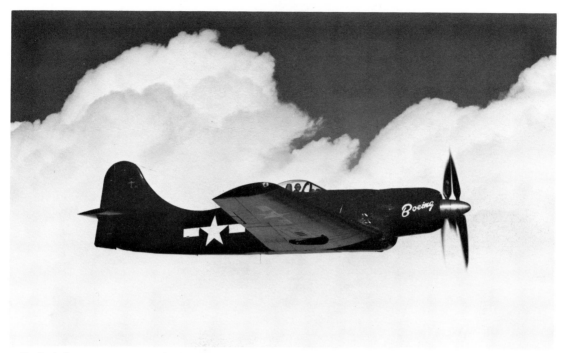

Boeing's long range XF8B-1 had an internal weapons bay that could carry two 1,600 pound bombs. Boeing

After nearly a decade of absence from the Navy register, the name Boeing reappeared when a contract was awarded for their mammoth XF8B-1. The proportions of this machine had been dictated by the Navy's need for a far-ranging carrier fighter capable of delivering a bomb load directly to the Japanese home islands. The requirements indicated that something more than just a fighter would be needed to fit this bill, so provision was made to include a bomber-type internal weapons bay. Two 1,600 pound bombs could be loaded into this compartment, and two more could be carried beneath the wings for a total of **6,400 pounds. Alternately, a pair of 2,000** pound torpedoes could be loaded on the wing racks. Six gun ports in the wings revealed the location of the .50 cal. machine guns on the prototype; but production fighters could use a sextet of 20 mm cannons as alternate armament.

The contract for three prototype XF8B-1's was handed to Boeing on May 4, 1943, but commitments for B-29 Superfortress bombers held development of the fighter to a slow pace. The power source selected was the Pratt & Whitney XR-4360-10 Wasp Major, the world's most powerful piston engine with over 3,000 hp. This engine was connected to a six-bladed contra-rotating Aeroproducts propeller with a thirteen-and-a-half foot diameter. The landing gear rotated and folded flat against the bottom of the wing.

November 27, 1944, was the day the big Boeing fighter first tested the atmosphere; and the XF8B-1 demonstrated a maximum speed of 432 mph at 26,900 feet. With a cruising speed of 162 mph, the bomber-fighter could deliver its load to a target 1,305 miles away in about eight hours. Fortunately, the end of the war precluded the need to consider a mission of such duration for the pilot of a single-seat airplane.

The second and third prototype XF8B-1's were the subject of minor refinements such as raising the height of the bubble canopy. The second machine was fitted with a jump-seat to permit a passenger for in-flight evaluations of the big ship. The capabilities of the XF8B-1 were such that the Air Force showed some interest in the design and the final prototype was sent to them for their consideration.

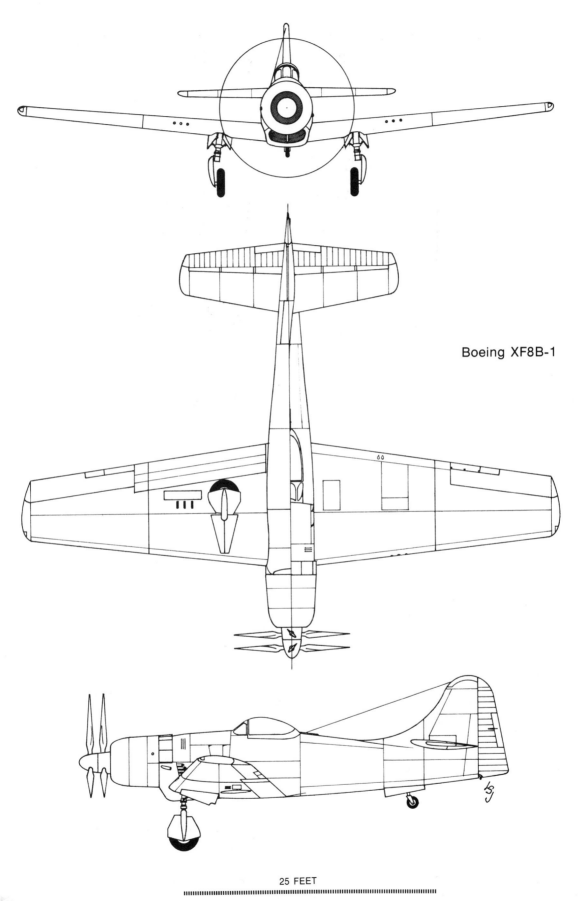

Boeing XF8B-1

25 FEET

The XF8B-1 was powered by a 3,000 Pratt & Whitney R-4360 Wasp Major, the largest piston engine ever put in a fighter.
Boeing

Boeing's big bombers had a noticeable influence on the design of the tail surfaces. The fin shape is similar to that of the B-17 and B-29.
Boeing

Commitments to the Air Corps for B-29's delayed development of the XF8B-1 until the end of the war, by which time it was no longer needed.
Boeing

Although the performance of the XF8B-1 was up to the Navy's expectations, the end of the piston era was at hand and the military was again on the threshold of a revolution in aircraft design. The turbojet engine was showing great promise and piston-powered fighters were already falling behind in the performance race, so the three XF8B-1's were finally discarded.

The wings of the XF8B-1 stretched 54 feet tip to tip, and encompassed an area of 489 square feet. Overall length was 43 feet 3 inches, and the height was 15 feet 11 inches. Empty weight of the hulking fighter was 13,519 pounds, gross weight was 20,508 pounds, and the XF8B-1 could lift off with a maximum of 21,691 pounds. Internal fuel capacity was 384 gallons; external tanks increased the capacity to 954 gallons providing a maximum range of 2,780 miles. The XF8B-1's rate of climb was 2,800 fpm and its service ceiling was 37,500 feet.

GRUMMAN
F8F BEARCAT

This F8F-1 is shown carrying two 11.75 inch Tiny Tim rockets.   *Grumman*

While Grumman's Hellcat was wresting air superiority from the Japanese at high altitudes, its low-level performance was still somewhat behind that of the lighter Japanese types. To fill this gap in Navy fighter ranks, Grumman undertook the design of a scrappy, light-weight fighter that would combine nimble maneuverability with rapid climb characteristics. The Navy expressed its interest in the project by awarding a development contract for two XF8F-1's on November 27, 1943. Their faith in Grumman's engineering capabilities is reflected in the fact that no full-scale mock-up was required—just the engine mounting and a detailed cockpit. Grumman set about their task with such rapidity that the Bearcat was in the air on August 21, 1944—just ten months after the contract was approved.

The Bearcat made an immediate hit with the pilots and required only moderate revisions to become fully acceptable to the Navy. The second prototype, delivered in November, already embodied many of the changes. Most notable among these was the addition of a dorsal fin to improve its directional stability. Within five months of the XF8F-1's initial flight, the first produc-

tion Bearcats were rolling out of the Grumman plant. Though a few of these planes had reached the Navy before the war had ended, none were used in combat.

The original contract called for 23 Bearcats, but this was upped to 2,023 before the first one was completed. This was followed by another increase of 4,000 planes. General Motors received a contract for 1,876 F2M-1 and F3M-1 Bearcats, but these became victims of the postwar cutback and none were built. Grumman also suffered a severe reduction in orders on VJ Day, with the result that only 765 of the F8F-1 Bearcats were completed.

Grumman engineers included a novel feature into the design of the Bearcat's wings. In the event of excessively high "G" loads during maneuvering, the wingtips would break away to allow the shortened wings to safely withstand a higher "G" factor. The folding portion of the wing was designed to fail at half the distance to the tip if the plane exceeded 9 "G's." Problems with this system led to the addition of explosive bolts along the separation line. If only one tip separated, the explosive bolts would assure that the opposite side was ejected also. This would allow half of the

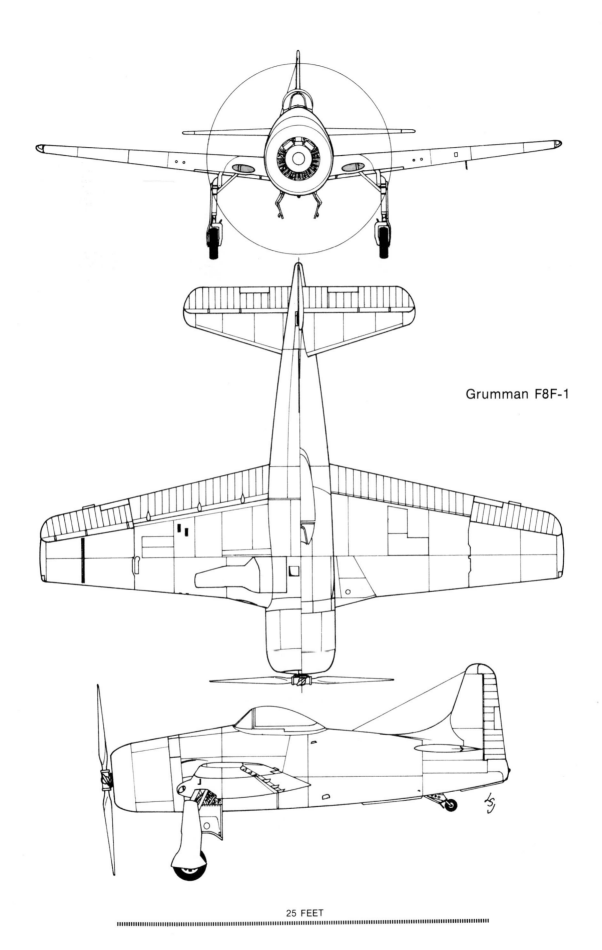

Grumman F8F-1

25 FEET

An F8F-2 on display after the war. Bearcats have become favorites for air race pilots.   *Air Museum*

The large white number on the nose of the F8F-2 is the factory delivery number. It is the last three digits of the bureau number. The vertical tail was enlarged on the F8F-2 models.   *Gordon S. Williams*

aileron area to remain, but greatly reduced the stress on the balance of the wing structure permitting it to withstand even higher forces.

After the war, Bearcat production continued with the F8F-1B. One hundred of these appeared with four 20 mm cannons replacing the original Bearcat armament of four .50 cal. machine guns. Thirty-six F8F-1N's, with radar pods suspended from a pylon on the right wing, were ordered as night fighters. Upgrading the design and increasing the height of the tail brought about the F8F-2 and an order for 293 copies. The order also included 60 camera-bearing F8F-2P's with only two 20 mm cannons.

The Bearcat did not see combat in the colors of the U.S. Navy; but many of the planes, declared obsolete by the U.S. government, were delivered to the French for use in Indochina. These were in use by the Thais and Vietnamese during the conflict in that area.

Power for the nimble F8F came from a Pratt & Whitney R-2800-34W. With 2,100 hp for take off and 1,850 hp for maneuver-ing, the Bearcat had a maximum speed of 447 mph in the -2 version—26 mph faster than the first model. The F8F-1 had a wingspan of 35 feet 10 inches with an area of 244 square feet. It was 28 feet 3 inches long and stood 13 feet 10 inches high. By comparison, the F8F-2 was 27 feet 8 inches long and 12 feet 2 inches high.

Respective weights of the two were: F8F-1—empty, 7,070 pounds; gross, 9,386 pounds; maximum, 12,947 pounds. F8F-2—empty, 7,690 pounds; gross, 10,426 pounds; maximum, 13,494 pounds. Fuel capacities were 183 gallons for the -1 and 185 for the -2. The earlier model had a service ceiling of 38,700 feet and a range of 1,105 miles, compared to a 40,700 foot ceiling and 865 mile range for the -2. The rate of climb was rather exciting at some 4,500 fpm for the Bearcat.

Had the war continued, there is little doubt that the Bearcat would have been recorded as one of the combat greats along with its larger relative, the Hellcat, and the Vought Corsair. Fortunately, these latter two went a long way to eliminate the need for their nimble successor.

121703 is one of the F8F-2's built after the war. It differed from the -1 mainly in the height of the fin and the mounting of four 20mm cannons in the wings.
Gordon S. Williams

VOUGHT
XF5U-1

The "Flying Flapjack" ready for a flight that never took place. The broad-chord propellers were articulated and could perform as rotors for vertical flight. The emblem on the nose is Bugs Bunny on a flying carpet.

Vought

Call it what you may, "Flapjack," "Saucer," "Pancake;" it had no official name, but Vought's last propeller-driven fighter would certainly answer to "weird." Initial planning for the odd craft actually began in 1938, when a patent was obtained for an airplane of generally circular planform. The designer was Charles H. Zimmerman, an engineer for NACA. Tests of scale models indicated that an airplane using large-diameter propellers and Zimmerman's circular wing would have the ability to take-off and land vertically as well as hover in the air, yet be able to flash away at a speed of over 500 mph.

In 1939, plans for full-size flying model were presented to the Navy by Vought, who now employed Zimmerman. Interested in the concept, the Navy submitted the idea to NACA and requested wind tunnel data on the radical proposal. These tests also indicated a remarkable performance potential so the Navy authorized the construction of the full-scale flying model to further evaluate the unique characteristics of the

proposed aircraft. This model was designated V-173, assigned BuNo 029781, and was constructed of wood covered with fabric. Two 80 hp Continental A-80 engines were used to drive a pair of 16 foot 6 inch wooden propellers. The V-173 weighed 2,-258 pounds; and in keeping with the Navy colors of the day, was painted chrome yellow on top and silver on the bottom.

The V-173 made a rather hairy first flight on November 23, 1942. The low-powered engines could barely keep the craft in the air and the stick forces were extremely heavy and performance sluggish; but it took off in about 50 feet and landed in an equally short distance. Flying of the V-173 continued with the shortcomings being corrected as the tests proceeded. In the meantime, Vought engineers were drawing up the plans for the definitive combat weapon which received the official designation XF5U-1 from the Navy.

The V-173 proved to be virtually stall-proof. At no time would the plane ever stall or spin during the tests, no matter how tight

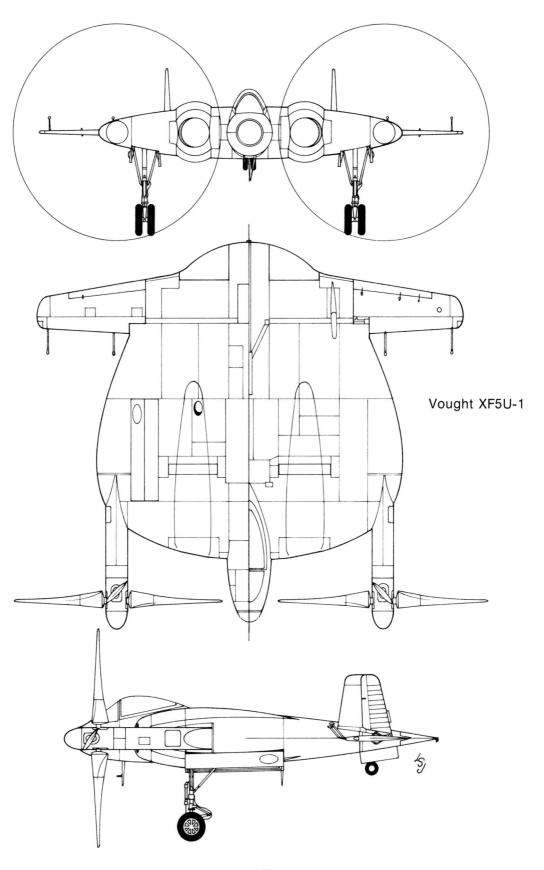

Vought XF5U-1

25 FEET

The XF5U-1 was painted glossy sea blue overall. The dark patches in this photo are protective covers to keep the paint from being damaged during servicing.   *Vought*

the turn. Maximum speed of the craft was 138 mph and it could climb 5,000 feet in 7 minutes.

The specifications for the XF5U-1 fighter were truly exciting considering the performances being achieved by the typical 1942 fighter. With a pair of 1,600 hp Pratt & Whitney R-2000-7 air-cooled water-injected engines, the maximum speed was to be 460 mph while the landing speed was to be as low as 20 mph. Projecting even further, a pair of gas turbines could provide a speed of 550 mph while landing at near zero ground speed. With the turbine powerplant, the XF5U-1 would actually hover motionless in the air, hanging under its props like a helicopter.

The Navy ordered two XF5U-1's as the V-173 flights proceeded. One was to be used for static testing while the second would be used for flight evaluation. Even the construction of the strange fighter was unconventional. To keep the weight as low as possible, the skin was formed of aluminum laminated to a balsa core, a material called Metalite and developed by Vought.

The two engines were located on either side of the cockpit with fans drawing air from the inlets and forcing it over the powerplants. Drive shafts extended outward at right angles toward the propeller shafts on each side, where a second gear box directed the power forward to the props. The blades were specially constructed of wood and mounted in two vertical planes. Each propeller blade was articulated and

could tilt fore and aft of its connections on the shaft. This is similar to the movements of the rotors on a helicopter, to which the XF5U-1 seemed a second cousin.

The control system of the XF5U-1 consisted of a pair of conventional vertical stabilizers on the symmetrical airfoil. Between these were two stability flaps. Pitch and roll were achieved with a pair of ailavators—combination ailerons and elevators located on the edges of the wing-like body.

The cockpit featured an ejection seat, and access was by means of a series of steps built into the right top of the body. The arresting gear was also on top of the body. An actuator pushed the forward edge of the assembly upward and slid the hook to the rear and below the trailing edge of the body.

The proposed armament was six .50 cal. machine guns or four 20 mm cannons. Two 1,000 pound bombs could be suspended under the body.

The lifting surface had a span of 23 feet 4 inches with an area of 475 square feet. The ailavator span was 32 feet 6 inches, but the overall width of the machine, measured to the tips of the propellers, was 36 feet 5 inches. Length of the strange fighter was 28 feet 1 inch and height was 16 feet 8 inches. Empty weight was 13,107 pounds, gross was 16,722 pounds. It was anticipated that the XF5U-1 would have a climb rate of 3,590 fpm with a service ceiling of 34,500 feet. With 300 gallons of fuel, the range was to be 710 miles.

Ailevators extending from the side of the body served as ailerons and elevators on the XF5U-1.   *Vought*

Not only the design of the XF5U-1 was unique. The skin was formed of a metal and wood sandwich material called "Metalite" devised by Vought.
Vought

The prototype of the unique fighter was completed and prepared for engine testing on August 20, 1945. For the initial run-ups, a pair of Corsair propellers were installed; but they were not satisfactory for flight. The articulated propellers were not available until 1947, when taxiing tests were finally undertaken. During one of these tests, the big blue "flapjack" actually lifted off the runway. Full flight tests were scheduled for December 1948, and Vought had decided

that the safest place to fly their radical machine was at the Air Force Flight Test Center, now known as Edwards Air Force Base. Because of its shape, it would be necessary to transport the plane by boat from Connecticut through the Panama Canal to California.

Before this event could take place, the Navy had reconsidered its position in the development of a piston-powered airplane at a time when jet propulsion was showing

The V-173 which proved the feasibility of the circular-wing concept has been preserved at the Smithsonian Institution.   Vought

A flying mock-up of the XF5U-1 was built to test the flying characteristics of the novel fighter. It was designated V-173 by Vought.   Vought

its greater potential as a power unit.

On March 17, 1949, the contract was cancelled with orders to destroy the sole prototype—the static test vehicle had already gone that route. The XF5U-1 was so sturdy that even a steel ball dropped from a crane only bounced off the body. Finally, the ball was dropped between the spars, falling through the structure to the ground; then blowtorches were used to reduce the bold experiment to rubble.

AIR FORCE TYPES WITH NAVY
DESIGNATIONS
LOCKHEED FO-1, BELL F2L-1K,
NORTHROP F2T-1

This Shooting Star, BuNo 29668, was fitted with arresting and catapult hooks for carrier trials. It is listed by Lockheed as "FO-1" but official records carry it as a P-80A.   *Warren Bodie*

Often the Navy and the Army Air Corps would evaluate each other's machines for comparison with the types in their own ranks—a practice still used today. This was helpful in establishing new specifications, and it allowed the evaluation of new equipment without the extra cost of duplication. Occasionally, such comparisons would lead to the direct development of a new type, such as the Army B-24 providing the basis for the Navy's PB4Y-2 Privateer patrol bomber, or the Navy's A3D paving the way for the B-66. In other cases, the planes could be used as transitional trainers for more advanced types just entering production.

Four Air Force fighter types were acquired and given Bureau Numbers and Navy designations. These planes are mentioned here since they complete the "F" series described in this history; otherwise, their significance is minimal. Engineering and development details for these planes are outlined in the companion volume "U.S. Fighters, Army-Air Force, 1925 to 1980's."

The operational records of these four types is relatively obscure. Since the planes were purchased, or otherwise obtained, directly from the Air Force, there was no

manufacturer involvement in the transaction—hence, no company records. The accounting of these planes is based on personal inquiries to persons who in one way or another were concerned with their use by the Navy.

LOCKHEED FO-1

Four Lockheed P-38 Lightnings were purchased in 1943 and designated FO-1, BuNos 01209-01212. Some sources indicate they were used for photographic work in North Africa. Another more likely use was as twin-engine trainers for experience in preparation for the F7F Tigercat. One source reports that they were based at Hawaii for a time, were left in bare metal, and carried their Bureau Numbers on the tail in the Air Corps manner.

LOCKHEED FO-1 SHOOTING STAR

This strange duplication of designation seems to be due to the fact that the Navy obtained their Lightnings directly from the Army. Apparently Lockheed was unaware that the FO-1 classification had already been assigned and, in company records, lists three P-80A's as FO-1's. However, these planes, BuNos 29667, 29668 and 29689, are

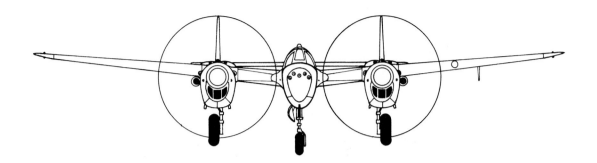

Lockheed FO-1

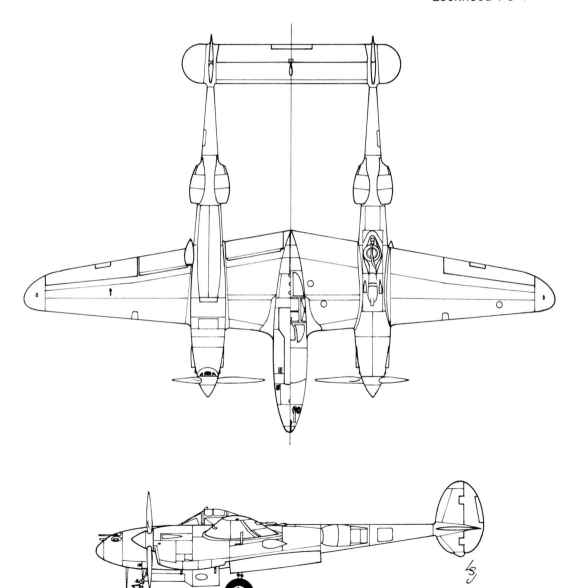

25 FEET

Four Lightnings of this type were acquired from the Air Force and designated FO-1.   *Lockheed*

listed on official Navy documents under their Air Force designations as P-80A's. Number 29668 was outfitted with catapult hooks and arresting gear for carrier trials aboard the USS Franklin D. Roosevelt. Although fifty of the single-seat Shooting Stars were ordered by the Navy, they were of the F-80C types and classed as TO-1 trainers. (Later, Lockheed's identification letter became "V" and the planes were relabeled TV-1's.)

In 1948, Marine squadron VMF-311 received 16 TO-1's and operated them as fighters, but no carrier equipment was installed.

BELL F2L-1K AIRACOBRA

In 1946, the Navy purchased two P-39Q Airacobras, AF serial nos. 42-20807 and 42-19976, assigning BuNos 91102 and 91103

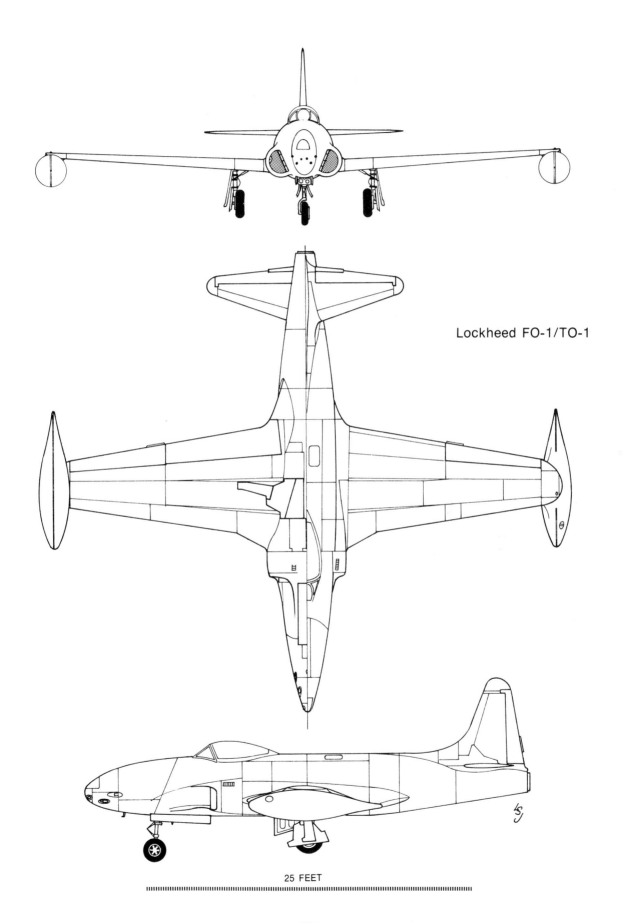

Lockheed FO-1/TO-1

25 FEET

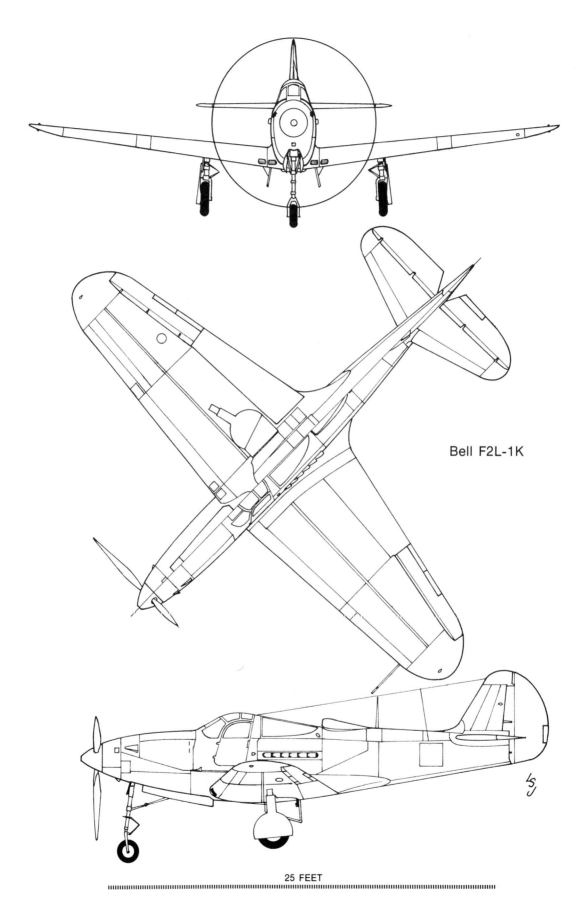

Bell F2L-1K

25 FEET

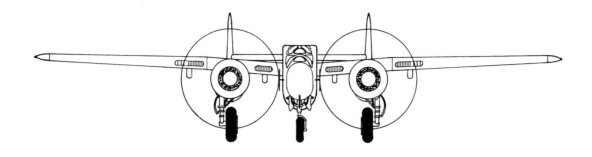

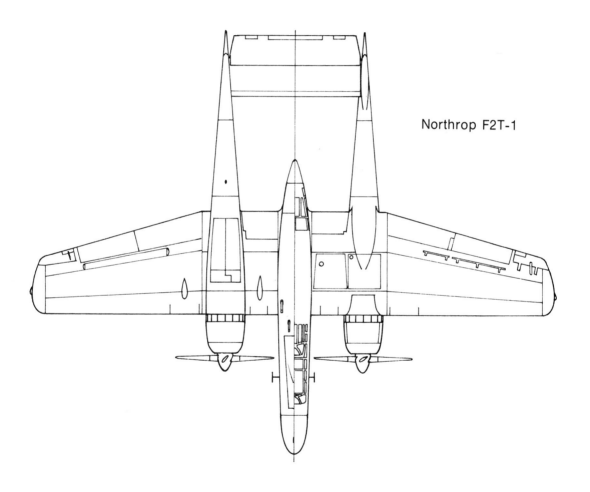

Northrop F2T-1

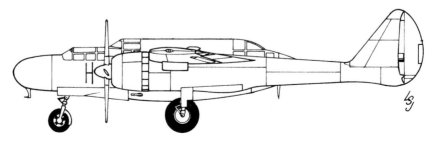

25 FEET

Two Airacobras were used by the Navy for research and targets. These were called F2L-1K's.　　　*Bell*

respectively. These were classed as F2L-1K's and used as unarmed drones. In 1946, one was fitted with swept wings for evaluation of their use on future high performance fighters.

NORTHROP F2T-1 BLACK WIDOW

In late 1945, twelve P-61A's were given the Navy Bureau Numbers 52750 through 52761. These were used for radar operator training in the use of the SCR-720 airborne intercept radar—the type used in the F7F Tigercat. In 1946, four of these planes were assigned to Headquarters Squadron MAG-31, Marine Corps at NAS Miramar. They remained on the Navy roster until 1948. The F2T-1's retained their distinctive all-black color scheme throughout their Naval service.

The Marines used several P-61A Black Widows to train crews on the use of radar. They were designated F2T-1. Three F2T-1's are seen in this photo taken at NAS Miramar.　　　*Clay Jannson*

212

RYAN FR FIREBALL, XF2R DARK SHARK

Fireballs of VF-66 cruising on their jets alone. The squadron called themselves "The Firebirds."   *Ryan*

The first gas turbine-powered flight had been made before World War II in Germany. The Air Corps began flying their first jet, the Bell XP-59, on October 2, 1942. The Navy was quite interested in the new powerplant, but the slow acceleration of the jet made normal carrier takeoffs virtually impossible. This factor also would have a direct bearing on the landing characteristics since rapid acceleration is a requirement in the event of a wave-off during the approach. The obvious solution was to devise an aircraft with the best features of both power systems; and, in the meantime, design a fleet of carriers capable of launching and recovering the pure-jet types of the future. The British had already perfected the steam catapult and this would become a fixture on the next generation of American carriers as well. But for the moment, the composite fighter appeared to be the most practical solution to the needs of

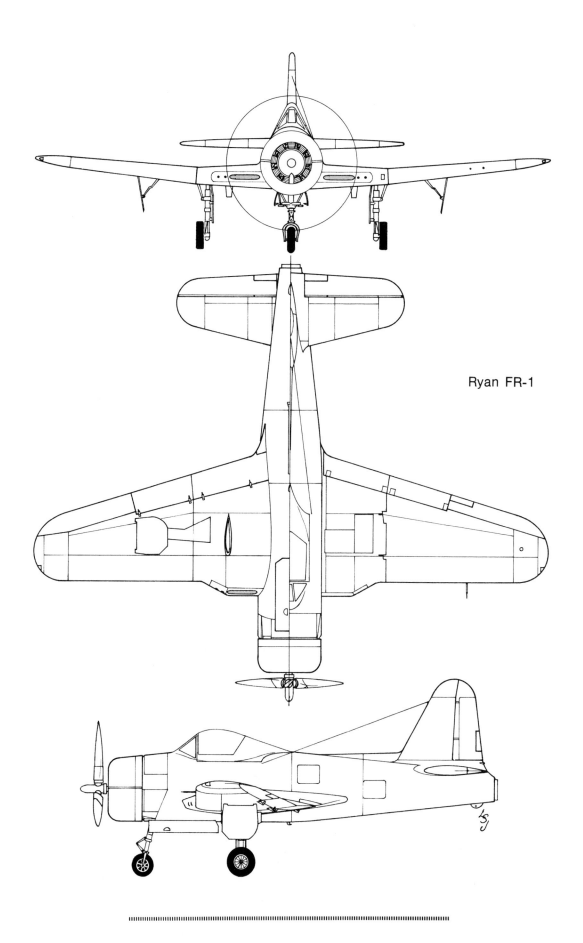

Ryan FR-1

The XFR-1 in its original form. Wind tunnel studies advised a change in the tail surfaces.　　　*Ryan*

It was startling to see a Fireball cruising along with its propeller feathered.　　　*Ryan*

the Navy.

Nine airframe manufacturers were asked to submit proposals for the prop-jet fighter. Among the responses was one from the Ryan Company whose main contribution to the aeronautical world was the famous "Spirit of St. Louis" and a line of popular sport planes. Their only military experience had been in the design and construction of primary trainers during the war.

The Fireball was the first Navy plane to be completely flush-riveted and use a laminar airfoil. Here VF-66 prepares for a mission.   *Ryan*

Ryan presented their proposal to the Navy and a development contract for three XFR-1 prototypes was awarded in January 1943. As the design progressed, the Navy awarded a full production contract for 100 FR-1's on December 2, 1943. The Ryan fighter, dubbed Fireball, a name given by its builder and retained by the Navy, was mainly a state-of-the-art machine. It was conventional in appearance, except for the fairly new tricycle landing gear, and gave only a hint of its composite design. The air inlets for the jet engine were inconspicuous in the wing roots, and the only indication of the second power unit was an 18 inch hole where a tail cone might be expected. The Fireball was the first carrier plane to utilize the new high-speed laminar-flow wing, though this also was not apparent to the casual observer. Its smooth exterior was due to the use of flush riveting over the entire aircraft—the first Navy plane completely finished in this manner. In addition, all control surfaces were metal-covered—another exclusive.

The first two flights of the Fireball were made on June 25, 1944, before the General Electric jet engine was installed. The XFR-1 performed well and the jet was mounted a few days later. The two types of engines gave the Ryan fighter a remarkable versatility. The Wright R-1820-72W Cyclone had 1,350 hp and imparted good low altitude performance, while the GE I-16 with 1,600 lbs. of thrust, performed best at higher altitudes. Initial studies showed the Fireball had a maximum speed of 430 mph, and the new airfoil gave the fighter better maneuverability than existing Navy fighters. But, the inevitable bugs began to appear and a modification program was established to eliminate the undesirable features.

Overheating of the piston engine required some rework around the cowling, and the empennage was completely revised. The horizontal stabilizer had been mounted to a rather small vertical fin. Wind tunnel studies advised a relocation of the stabilizer onto the fuselage and a substantial increase in fin area. On one occasion, the wing assembly failed during a high-speed demonstration causing the plane to plummet into a new Navy patrol bomber at the end of the runway. The pilot, who was thrown free, stated that the plane had become uncontrollable after his canopy blew off. Examination showed that the sharp edges of the metal at the bottom of the counter-sunk rivet holes rubbed against the rivets on the wing leading edge as the wing normally flexed. This action eventually weakened the rivets, causing the leading edges to separate, forcing air through the wing into the fuselage, and blowing the canopy off moments before the wing disintegrated. This flaw was to follow the Fireball throughout its service life. It was found that as long as the wings were not stressed beyond 7.5 "G's", there was no

The jet intakes were moved to the fuselage on the XFR-4 shown here. This Fireball had a more powerful jet, but performance was restricted by the drag of the piston engine. **Ryan**

A sharp pull-up forms vapor trail at the wingtips as the Dark Shark goes through its maneuvers. **Ryan**

danger. To add a safety factor, operational pilots were prohibited from exceeding 5 "G's"; but the Fireball was so maneuverable it was sometimes accidently overstressed leading to structural failure.

VF-66 was the only squadron to operate the Ryan Fireball, the first plane being delivered in March 1945. Training began immediately to prepare the squadron for combat against the Japanese Ohka suicide bombs—the FR-1 was the only Navy plane with the performance to catch the rocket planes. However, before the Fireball squadron was fully qualified, the Japanese surrender cancelled their need.

For those privileged to see a Fireball in operation, it was a startling sight. The pilots seldom failed to take advantage of the composite fighter's unique ability to seemingly fly without any power. Often, the pilot of the FR-1 would cruise up beside a contemporary piston-powered fighter and casually feather the propeller on his piston engine. Before the wide eyes and gaping mouth of the unsuspecting aviator, the Fireball would then outdistance the older fighter on its jet alone.

Although the Fireball was not designed

The XF2R-1 had a General Electric turboprop engine turning an eleven foot propeller. Top speed of the Dark Shark was over 500 mph.
Ryan

for pure-jet operation, the General Electric engine provided adequate power for sustained flight. On one occasion this trait proved most valuable. On November 6, 1945, Ensign J. C. West took off from the USS Wake Island and soon the Wright engine began faltering. Before the piston engine failed completely, West started the jet and returned to the carrier; thus, making the first landing by jet power alone on a carrier.

Ryan's composite fighter had a 275 square foot wing with a span of 40 feet. Overall length was 32 feet 4 inches, height was 13 feet 7 inches. Maximum speed of the production Fireball was 404 mph at 17,800 feet with both engines operating. On the prop alone, the best speed was 295 mph at 16,500 feet. Service ceiling was 43,100 feet. The FR-1 had an empty weight of 7,689 pounds, a gross of 9,958 pounds, a maximum of 11,652 pounds. Four .50 cal. Browning MG 53-2 machine guns, with 300 rpg, were carried in the wings next to the jet air inlet, and fittings for two 1,000 pound bombs were underneath the wings.

The end of the war brought cancellations of orders for the Fireballs. Over 1,000 units had been on order, but ultimately only sixty-six of the jet/prop fighters were completed. One of these, BuNo 39661, was reworked to utilize a 1,700 hp turboprop engine in place of the piston type. This ship was redesignated XF2R-1 and carried the

nickname "Dark Shark." The new engine installation increased the gross weight to 11,000 pounds but also brought the maximum speed to over 500 mph.

The turboprop engine offered several advantages over the piston type. Since the turboprop normally operates at full rpm, the power is controlled by propeller pitch; thus, acceleration and deceleration are almost instantaneous. The thrust of the propeller could be reversed in flight to abruptly slow the fighter or increase its glide angle for landing, thereby reducing its landing roll. This would be a very desirable feature for a carrier fighter.

The "Dark Shark" was first flown in November 1946, and became the first Navy turboprop plane to fly. The engine was built by General Electric as the XT-31-GE-2. In addition to the 1,700 hp delivered to the 11 foot propeller, a residual-thrust benefit of 550 lbs. was received from the exhaust. The rear engine was the same as that used by the Fireball, but now it was designated J31-GE-3. Except for its length of 36 feet, the proportions of the XF2R-1 were the same as those of the Fireball.

Two altered Fireball designs were proposed, but not built. The XFR-2 was to use a Wright R-1820-74W of 1,500 hp. Six hundred had been ordered before VJ Day cancellations eliminated them. The XFR-3 was to add a 2,000 lb. thrust GE jet to the uprated Wright.

The XF2R-1 was the first Navy plane to fly with a turboprop engine.   *Ryan*

This photo shows the mock-up of the proposed XF2R-2 with a Westinghouse jet engine.   *Ryan*

The XFR-4 faired somewhat better. The single example used a 3,400 lb. thrust Westinghouse J34-WE-22 jet engine fed via flush air inlets on the fuselage. This Fireball was tested at the end of 1944. It was found that, whereas the greater jet power increased the performance at higher altitudes, the piston engine caused so much drag that neither unit could operate effectively. This, then, led to the design of the XF2R-2 which would combine the more powerful jet with the "Dark Shark" turboprop. The XF2R-2 had reached the mock-up stage before the entire program was dropped.

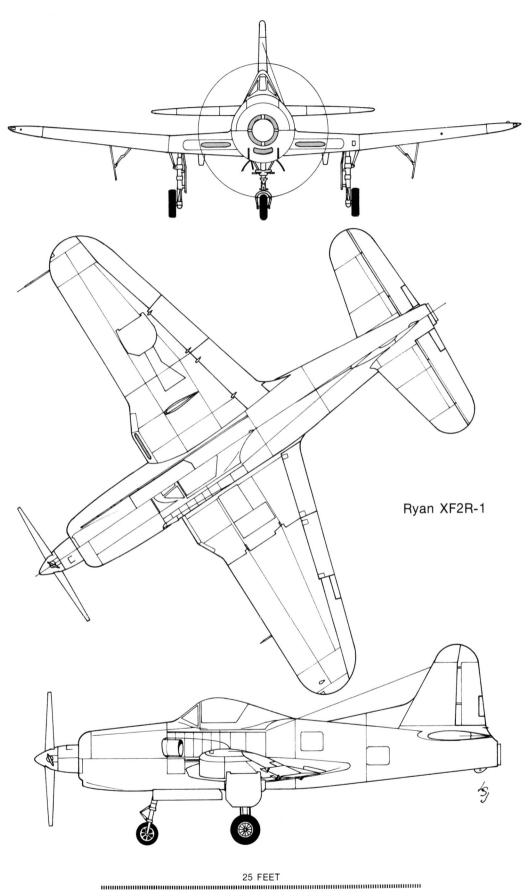

Ryan XF2R-1

25 FEET

In its original form, the Curtiss XF15C-1 stabilizer was mounted on the fuselage. The company nickname was "Stingaree."
Warren Bodie

With the cancellation of the Curtiss XF14C-1 imminent, the Navy and Curtiss agreed to concentrate on a large composite jet piston-powered machine with an eye toward greater high altitude performance than that offered by the Ryan Fireball.

Curtiss submitted its preliminary studies to the Navy in December 1943, and plans were made to use a British engine to be built in the U.S. A laminar-flow low drag airfoil was specified for the wings, and the jet unit would be located amidships, exhausting just aft of the wing under a boom-mounted tail. This arrangement had been adapted to reduce thrust loss from an extended jet tailpipe. Also, the Curtiss fighter was to use a stronger new aluminum alloy than that generally in use.

Authorization was given for the construction of three XF15C-1 prototypes on April 7, 1944, but Curtiss had already been working on the project and told the Navy the mock-up would be available for inspection the next day!

Curtiss desperately needed to win another production contract if it hoped to survive. Following the success of the P-40, the pioneer airframe builders had been beset

with one failure after another. To add insult to injury, Curtiss was even then building Republic P-47 Thunderbolts for the Air Corps instead of one of their own planes designed for the same role. To ensure the success of the XF15C-1, the design was subjected to intensive wind tunnel analysis. It featured a cockpit layout patterned after the Navy's own desires and used the new tear-drop canopy for greater visibility. To gain experience in the operation of the new jet engine, Curtiss borrowed a Grumman Avenger torpedo bomber and mounted the unit in the weapons bay.

By the end of February 1945, the XF15C-1 was ready to fly. As in the case of the Fireball, the jet engine was not yet in place, but on February 28, the big Curtiss fighter was airborne. Tests with the jet engine began in May, but on the 8th of that month, the plane was destroyed in a crash. The second XF15C-1 took over the testing chores on July 9, 1944; but by this time it had been decided to redesign the entire tail assembly. This consisted of moving the horizontal stabilizer to the tip of a greatly broadened fin. This configuration was first used on the third prototype shortly after its first flights.

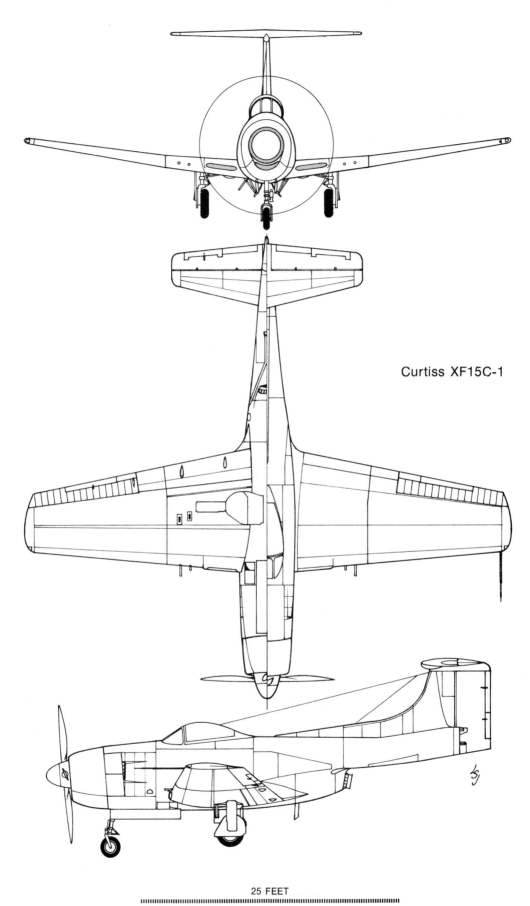

Curtiss XF15C-1

25 FEET

The third Curtiss XF15C-1 after installation of the T tail.　　　　　　　　　*Gordon S. Williams*

The last Curtiss fighter, as it appeared at the end of its test program. This plane still survives at the CAHA's Bradley Air Museum.
Gordon S. Williams

The Curtiss composite fighter used a British-designed engine for added thrust during combat.
Gordon S. Williams

In spite of the efforts to perfect the big fighter, many serious defects, including excessive vibration, were present when the two XF15C-1's were finally delivered to the Navy and the project ended. Unfortunately for Curtiss, the company whose name had once been synonymous with great military fighting machines, they were soon out of the airframe business. Regrettably, a great deal of the reason for the failures of the later Curtiss designs was in the extremely advanced concepts of many of the original requirements presented for development which were no fault of the builder.

The third XF15C-1, which had received the unofficial company name "Stingaree," survived and is now a part of the Connecticut Aviation Historical Association's Bradley Air Museum. It has a wingspan of 48 feet with an area of 400 square feet. Length is 44 feet, height is 15 feet 3 inches. Empty weight is 12,648 pounds, normal gross is 16,630 pounds. Fuel capacity is 376 to 526 gallons for a range of up to 1,385 miles.

The powerplant for the XF15C-1 was comprised of a 2,100 hp Pratt & Whitney R-2800-34W eighteen cylinder piston engine in the nose and an Allis-Chalmers J36 (license-built Halford H-1B) jet in the fuselage delivering 2,700 lbs. of thrust. Maximum speed achieved during evaluation was 469 mph at 25,000 feet. Service ceiling was 41,800 feet. Four 20 mm cannons were installed in the wings.

McDONNELL
FH-1 PHANTOM

The McDonnell XFD-1 Phantom prototype. The Designation was later changed to FH-1 to avoid confusion with Douglas products.   *Navy*

The distinction of being the first American jet fighter designed expressly for carrier operations has earned for the McDonnell FH-1 Phantom a permanent place in the Smithsonian's National Air and Space Museum at Washington, D.C.

The McDonnell Company had been formed in 1939, and their first product was a single experimental twin-engined fighter built for the Air Corps. Designated XP-67, it was noted more for its bold design concepts than for its influence on mass production methods. On August 30, 1943, this St. Louis-based company was given a contract to develop the next significant step in the evolution of Naval fighters.

Once again, a virtually unknown manufacturer was given the responsibility of designing a machine that would become the foundation for a new generation of fighters. However, it was actually a logical selection in view of the overworked production lines which were, at that time, turning out thousands of fighting machines for the war. Not only that, but the new company had already shown some imaginative engineering concepts which could prove valuable in approaching the task.

The original studies were imaginative indeed. At one time, they envisioned the use of six or eight tiny 9½ inch diameter jet engines of some 340 lbs. of thrust each. This, of course, led to some very strange shapes for the airframe. These were design studies only, which represent a necessary step in the creation of any advance design. In fact, when the final decision was made to use only two 19 inch diameter Westinghouse WE-19XB-2B power units, the final appearance was still quite distinctive. It is no surprise that the prototype Phantom has a general resemblance to the XP-67, the wing and tail shapes being very similar. The new jet was designated XFD-1. McDonnell was issued the "D" code since Douglas had produced no fighters for more than ten years; but on Douglas' reentry into the field, the Phantom became the XFH-1.

The two Westinghouse turbojets were mounted next to the fuselage with the wing roots flaring over them to form blended nacelles. This arrangement allowed very short inlet ducts and exhaust pipes for the greatest efficiency. By the time the Phantom airframe was completed, only one of the Westinghouse engines had been delivered.

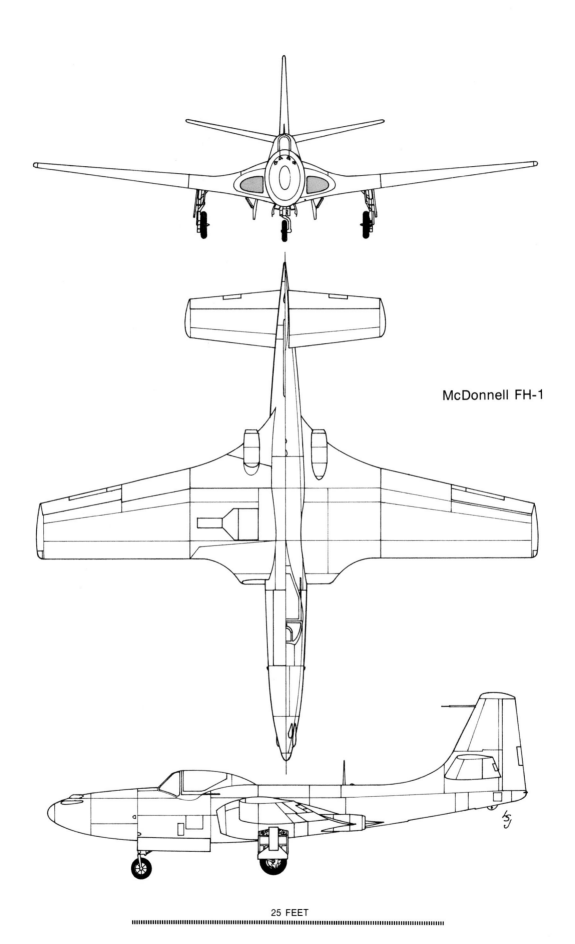

McDonnell FH-1

25 FEET

This is one of the first production Phantoms at the Naval Air Test Center, BuNo 111760. Gordon S. Williams

The Marines also used the Phantom. Here is Marine squadron VMF-122 with their FH-1's.   *McDonnell*

227

The FH-1 Phantom was the first Navy pure-jet to land on an aircraft carrier, and was the first operational carrier jet in the world.   *Gordon S. Williams*

This was placed into the plane and taxi runs were made early in January 1945. On January 26, the XFD-1 was ready to commence full flight tests, but the one engine was still absent. Fully confident of the abilities of their creation, McDonnell then decided to fly the plane with only the single engine installed! The single-engine flight was completely successful and McDonnell proceeded with the test program while waiting for the second engine.

Pleased with the wisdom of their choice of contractor, the Navy placed an order for 100 more FH-1's (with two engines) on March 7, 1945. But again, the end of the war reduced the order and only 60 were delivered. Six months before the first FH-1 was delivered, on July 21, 1946, the Phantom made its historic first carrier landing and takeoff from the USS Franklin D. Roosevelt.

The rounded tips of the flying surfaces on the XFH-1 were squared off on production models, but the other physical characteristics remained. The cockpit was located well forward of the wing providing excellent all-around visibility. Fairings over four .50 cal. machine guns disturbed the slim nose contours, but the Phantom displayed an aesthetic elegance that gave a hint of future aeronautical trends.

The FH-1's were first assigned to VF-17A, which became qualified on the USS Saipan as the first carrier-based jet fighter squadron in the world. Marine squadrons VMF-122 and VMF-311 were the first of that service to complete jet transition. The Phantom also became the first jet fighter to perform with a flight demonstration team - the "Marine Phantoms," also known as "The Flying Leathernecks."

The Navy's first jet fighter had a wingspan of 40 feet 9 inches, a wing area of 276 square feet, a length of 38 feet 9 inches, and height of 14 feet 2 inches. The Phantom weighed 6,683 pounds empty and grossed 10,035 pounds. Extra fuel could be carried in a huge tub-like tank faired into the fuselage between the wings. This tank could hold another 295 gallons of fuel to give a maximum range of 1,400 miles. With the two Westinghouse engines, ultimately designated J30-WE-20, the FH-1 had a top speed of 505 mph at 40,000 feet. Service ceiling was 43,000 feet.

Although the Phantom was only in use a short while, it was the first of an un-interrupted line of outstanding McDonnell jet fighters that has been in continuous service with the Navy since 1947.

VOUGHT
F6U-1 PIRATE

This shows the third XF6U-1 after the dorsal fin was added.   *Vought*

While the Second World War was still raging in early 1944, Navy planners were looking for powerful twin engined fighters with great range for far-reaching strikes against the Japanese home islands. Grumman's F7F-1 Tigercat was already in the air and showing considerable promise. The Chance Vought Company undertook a design program for a similar fighter with a pair of Pratt & Whitney R-2800-E supercharged engines. This proposal was originally assigned the designation XF6U-1. In September 1944, the Navy Bureau of Aeronautics indicated that a review of these requirements showed the need for the twin-engined piston fighter no longer existed and requested instead a jet fighter powered by one of Westinghouse's new 3,000 lb. thrust axial-flow engines.

Responding to the Navy's request, Vought devised a single-seat carrier fighter which would utilize their new Metalite laminated skin. This material consisted of a thin piece of aluminum alloy bonded to each side of a balsa sheet. The resulting material was ¼ inch thick and highly resistant to wrinkling. The inherent stiffness of the Metalite allowed the simplification of

the internal structure and promised a lightweight airframe. The proposal was submitted and the Navy issued an order for three prototypes on December 29, 1944. The new jet fighter was now designated XF6U-1 by the Navy.

The XF6U-1 was named Pirate in keeping with the trend of the Vought Company to give their products titles reminiscent of buccaneer days. Upon completion of the first prototype, it was loaded into a C-119 and flown to the flight test center situated on Muroc Dry Lake in California where it underwent its preliminary trials. The first flight occurred on October 2, 1946. Although somewhat pudgy in appearance due to its blunt nose, the XF6U-1 had simple lines; but as the program progressed, these lines were subject to at least five major configuration changes. These mainly centered around the empennage, whose surfaces were progressively enlarged to correct inadequate lateral stability.

Part of the stability problem came with the installation of a Solar afterburner which had been adapted to increase the amount of thrust from the J34 engines.

While Vought engineers tackled the dif-

229

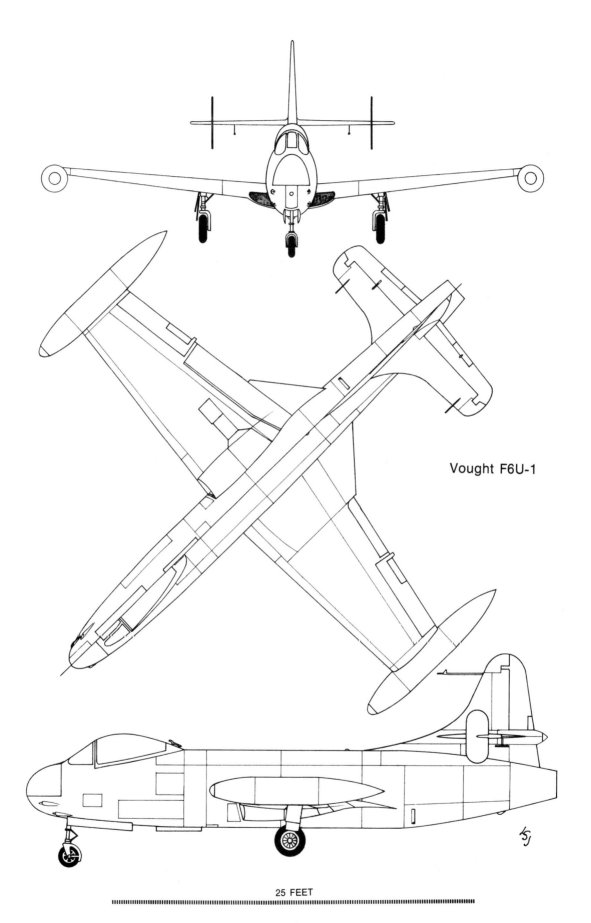

Vought F6U-1

25 FEET

33532 is the first Pirate, shown here in the original configuration with the small fin and undercut fuselage.

Vought

ficulties encountered in the prototypes, the Navy ordered 30 production F6U-1 Pirates. These were to use a 3,200 lb. thrust Westinghouse J32-WE-30A engine with the afterburner boosting the thrust to 4,225 lbs. To house the afterburner, the first ever used on a Navy plane, a stainless steel shroud was added to the fuselage. Even though the power had increased on the production Pirates, so had the weight. From the outset, the F6U had suffered from insufficient power, and the weight growth was not offset by the extra thrust obtained by the afterburner. The anticipated speed had been in excess of 600 mph, but Vought's figures show that the speed was 478 mph. No other actual performance figures have been announced.

The thirty production machines were delivered to the Navy; but their poor perfor-

mance precluded their use by fleet squadrons and they were relegated to ground training units.

The F6U-1 Pirate had a span of 36 feet 8 inches with tip tanks and an area of 203.5 square feet. Length, with the afterburner extension, was 37 feet 8 inches; and the rudder topped out at 12 feet 11 inches.

The nose held four 20 mm cannons with 150 rpg, the barrels of which were blended into the fuselage with streamlined fairings.

Empty weight of the Pirate was 7,320 pounds, gross weight was 11,060 pounds, maximum takeoff weight was 12,900 pounds. Fuel capacity with tip tanks was 700 gallons.

Estimated performance figures gave the Pirate a service ceiling of 46,300 feet and a range of 1,150 miles.

The number-two prototype with tip tanks and fin "bullet" fairing.   *Vought*

The final shape of the Pirate with the enlarged fin, afterburner and stabilizer finlets.   *Vought*

A Phantom and Banshee fly wing on Vought's Pirate.　　　　　　　　　　　　　　*Vought*

NORTH AMERICAN
FJ-1 FURY

The white crosses on this Fury are for reference during flight tests. *Rockwell*

As a producer of fighting machines, the North American Aviation Company was no stranger. To this the exploits of their P-51 Mustang could attest. And, although they had never produced a carrier-based fighter, their name was familiar to the Navy as the builder of the SNJ series of advanced trainers. Since the future of aviation rested now on the development of jet-powered types, any progressive company would have to become involved in the new concepts as quickly as possible if it was to remain competitive. One of the major advantages of the jet was that it could be used with current design technology. It did not require a radical departure from existing aircraft engineering to build a jet fighter with noticeably better performance than the piston types then in use. This was seen when the Russians successfully adapted their piston-powered Yak-3 into the jet-engined Yak-15, substantially increasing its performance. The characteristics of the powerplant itself were largely responsible for this since the jet generally had less frontal area and a higher power-to-weight ratio; and its location in the middle of the

fuselage permitted more efficient streamlining. For this reason, the first generation of American Navy jet fighters looked very much like conventional airplanes, but without the propellers.

Not wishing to lose the lead they already held in contemporary fighter design, North American began development of a single-engine jet fighter which it offered to the Navy on January 1, 1945. It looked typically North American, with straight wings and angular lines, and the Navy was impressed enough to order three prototypes as XFJ-1's. But not only the Navy liked the design, the Air Force, too, ordered the tubby fighter, designating it XP-86; and development began on both types simultaneously.

Before engineering had reached an advanced stage, material concerning German studies of swept-back wings became available, and North American felt their design could benefit from such a feature and suggested redesigning the XP-86 to incorporate swept surfaces. On November 1, 1945, the Air Force agreed to this recommendation. However, the Navy's three XFJ-1's were nearing completion; and since

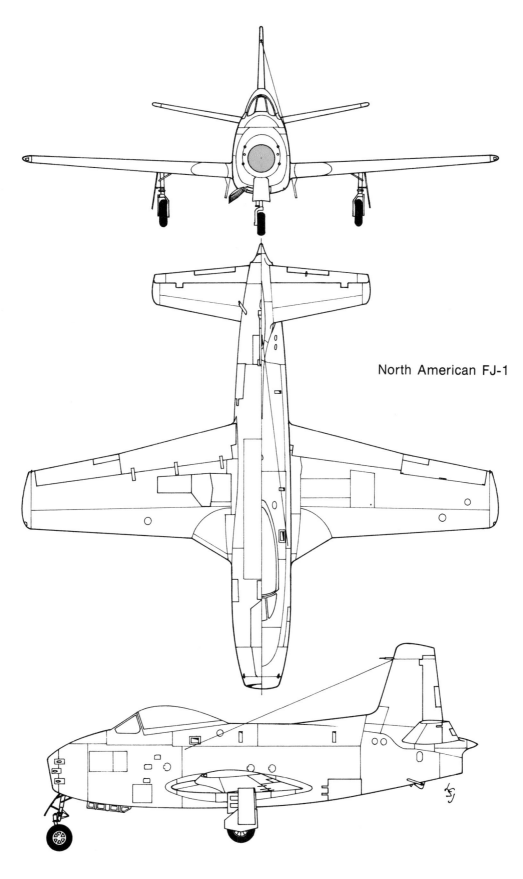

North American FJ-1

25 FEET

The view inside. Cockpit of the XFJ-1 Fury.   *Rockwell*

The Fury was operated by only one squadron, VF-5A. Although it was the second operational Navy jet, it was the first to go to sea under operational conditions.
                                                                 Rockwell

One of VF-5A's Furys coming up the elevator to the flight deck.   *Rockwell*

the effect of swept wings on a carrier fighter was an unkown factor, the Navy elected to retain the original concept.

The prototype XFJ-1 flew on September 12, 1946, using a General Electric J35-GE-2 engine with 3,820 lbs. of thrust. The engine was located amidships with the air being fed directly through a nose inlet. The placement of the cockpit above the duct gave the XFJ-1 a fat profile, but the high fuselage also provided space for the fuel tanks which had a content of 465 gallons.

The original contract called for 100 FJ-1 Furys, as the type was now named; but by the time the first of these was delivered, the order had been cut to 30 units. The production Fury obtained its power from an Allison-built J35-A-2 which upped the available thrust to 4,000 lbs. It also carried a small wing leading edge extension to increase its wing area.

A novel feature of the Fury was its ability to kneel on the carrier deck by retracting the nose gear and resting on a tiny wheel. This would allow the planes to be parked with the nose of one under the tail of another in lieu of folding wings.

The performance of the Fury was a decided step beyond existing Navy types. For a short time, it was touted as the fastest American fighter when it reached Mach .87 in a dive. More realistically, it could reach 547 mph at 9,000 feet and had a rate of climb of nearly a mile a minute. The FJ-1 had a service ceiling of 32,000 feet; and with droppable fuel tanks on the wingtips, had a maximum range of 1,500 miles.

The only fighter squadron to operate the FJ-1 was VF-5A aboard the USS Boxer. On March 10, 1948, the North American fighter became the first jet of its type to serve at sea under operational conditions. However, technology and exciting new concepts in naval fighter design were rapidly overtaking the Fury, and their operational life lasted only fourteen months before they were transferred to Naval Reserve squadrons.

The FJ-1 weighed 8,843 pounds empty and grossed 15,115 pounds. Maximum takeoff weight was 15,600 pounds. Wing area was 221 square feet, span was 38 feet 2

Within fourteen months of their introduction to the fleet, the FJ-1's were transferred to Naval Reserve squadrons. Notice the orange band around the fuselage, denoting the reserve status. Navy

inches without tanks, and 40 feet 11 inches with the tip tanks in place. Overall length was 34 feet 6 inches and the rudder tip stood 14 feet 6 inches above the deck. Six .50 cal. machine guns with 250 rpg were located in the nose beside the jet intake. The FJ-1 was the last Navy fighter to carry .50 cal. machine guns as the 20mm cannon was becoming the favored armament.

McDONNELL
F2H BANSHEE

An F2H-2P photo Banshee in the background is escorted by an F2H-3.   Hughes

The second generation of Navy jet fighters began when McDonnell received an order for an enlarged model of their Phantom. Two prototypes of the XF2H-1 (at first called XF2D-1) were ordered on March 2, 1945 — two days before ordering the Phantom into production. The Banshee, as the new fighter was called, was essentially a scaled-up Phantom and represented a relatively safe approach to increased performance. The prime mover for the Banshee was to be a pair of Westinghouse J34-WE-22's whose 3,000 lbs. of thrust was nearly twice that of the units in the Phantoms.

Development and assembly time was such that the first Banshee howled into the air on January 11, 1947, just two years after the Phantom's maiden flight. By this time, the Navy had cut its teeth on jets and was ready to absorb the new fighter into its ranks. Because of the direct relationship between the two types, flight testing proceeded rapidly with a minimum of changes required. Production began in May 1947, after 56 F2H-1's were ordered. Surprisingly, the production models were slightly faster than the prototypes. By March, 1949, F2H-1's were being delivered to VF-171.

As the jet powerplants were becoming more refined, fuel economy improved; but the Navy was looking for an even greater range increase for its carrier fighters. To achieve this, a 13 inch section was added to the fuselage to hold an extra 176 gallons of fuel, and two 200 gallon tanks were permanently secured to the tips of the wings. A simultaneous increase in engine power compensated for the added weight. This became the F2H-2, production of which was well under way when the invasion of South Korea began. Production of the long-range Banshee was increased and the F2H-2 was prepared for war. Bomb pylons were added as standard gear on the -2 so that up to 3,000 pounds of offensive weapons could be delivered. These planes were produced throughout most of the Korean War, and the last of 364 F2H-2's was completed in September 1952. The need for a night fighter brought about the experimental mounting of a radar pod under one of the wings; but by moving the four 20 mm cannons slightly aft, an APS-6 radar scanner could be mounted in the nose. Fourteen of these were built as F2H-2N, and 58 long-nosed photo-reconnaissance F2H-2P's were

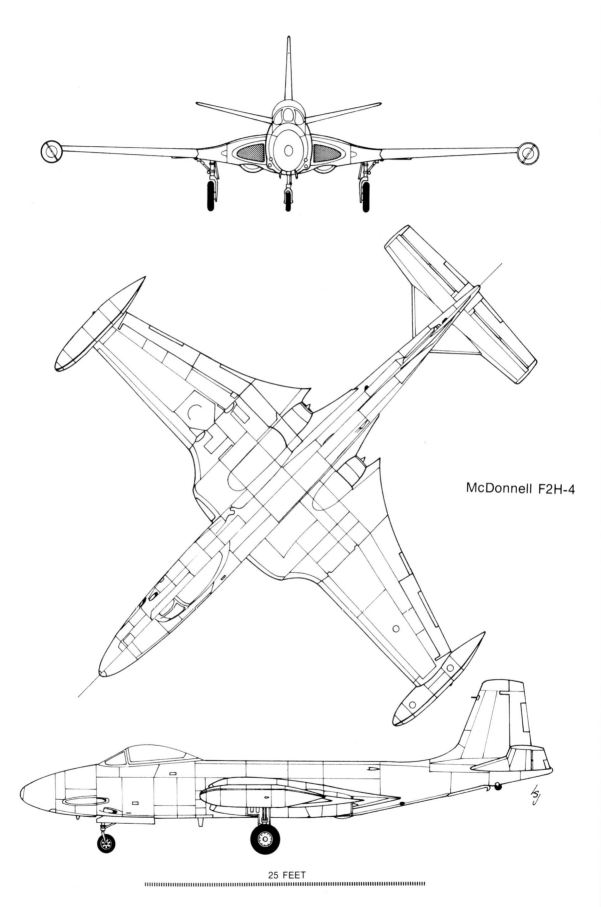

McDonnell F2H-4

25 FEET

The F2H-4 was the final production model of the Banshee.   *McDonnell Douglas*

Banshees played an important part in Naval operations during the Korean war. This is an F2H-1.   *Navy*

The prototype Banshee, originally designated XF2D-1.   *McDonnell Douglas*

The F2H-1 Banshee was an enlarged development of the FH-1 Phantom. It was the first McDonnell aircraft used in combat.   *McDonnell Douglas*

also delivered to the Navy.

The Banshee's extremely low wing loading permitted a further lengthening of the fuselage, so an additional 7 feet 4 inches was added to the overall length of the F2H-3 to hold two more fuel tanks. One hundred seventy-five of this model were built. Fifty-five F2H-4's, similar in appearance to the -3, were built with inflight refueling gear. At last, the Banshee's seemingly insatiable thirst was quenched. The remaining F2H-2's and -3's were retrofitted with these refueling booms providing a range limited only by human endurance.

The F2H-3 received a more powerful air intercept radar which gave it all-weather capabilities. The larger size of the antenna required moving the guns aft again, and the weapons pylons were increased to eight. Now the Banshee could be equipped with air-to-air missiles for its missions.

The basic design philosophy that began with the Phantom proved to be amazingly versatile. In Korea, Banshees were used with great success as bombers and ground support weapons. The plane was well behaved and looked upon kindly by its crews, earning the nickname "Banjo." By the early 'sixties, most of the Banshees had been retired. Those that remained were reclassified as F-2's under the Defense Department ruling of 1962, in which the Navy was compelled to drop its more descriptive aircraft classification codes.

The F2H-4 had a wingspan of 44 feet 11 inches with an area of 294 square feet. Fuselage length was 47 feet 6 inches—9 feet 5 inches longer than the F2H-1. Height was 14 feet 5 inches. The -3 and -4 had slightly longer gear struts to avoid dragging the lengthened tail during rotation. The Westinghouse J34-WE-38 used in the F2H-4 had 3,600 lbs. of thrust to produce a maximum speed of 610 mph at sea level. Service ceiling was 56,000 feet. Maximum take-off weight was 29,000 pounds.

GRUMMAN
F9F PANTHER

The Panther became the first jet mount of the famed Blue Angels flight team. Here the team shows off their F9F-5's.
Grumman

Grumman, too, was looking toward the future when they began a design study for a four engined jet-powered night fighter in the early part of 1946. Although the Bearcat production line was still operating, Grumman was hoping to have a new breed of cat waiting in the wings when the F8F commitments were finished.

In order to obtain the desired performance for their new fighter, Grumman's designers had determined that a thrust of some 6,000 lbs. would be required. The Westinghouse J30 engine which was available at the time had a rating of only 1,500 lbs. − one-quarter of the requirement. Therefore, it was determined that four of these units be fitted into the wings. On April 22, 1946, the Navy gave its support to the project and it was tagged XF9F-1. As Grumman delved further into the design, serious doubts arose regarding the use of four engines, and they turned instead to the 5,000 lb. thrust British Rolls-Royce Nene.

A new proposal was drawn up around a single Nene as a day fighter and this won approval of the Navy Bureau of Aeronautics as the XF9F-2. As an alternative to the Nene, the similar sized, but lower powered, Allison J33-A-8 was specified for the XF9F-3. At the same time, studies were to be made on a swept wing version for it was already obvious that straight wings were being pushed to their limits. The XF9F-1 contract was amended in September to produce two XF9F-2's and one Allison-powered -3. In the meantime, arrangements were being made for the licensed production of the Nene as the Pratt & Whitney J42.

The first XF9F-2, bearing a black panther silhouette on its nose, flew on November 24, 1947. The Allison-equipped XF9F-3 flew the following August. Both versions were ordered in quantity simultaneously, and the first production models of each type flew only a few days apart. The order called for 43 examples of the F9F-2 and 54 of the -3. Not surprisingly, the higher-powered F9F-2 was the better performer, and subsequently the -3's were re-engined with the Pratt & Whitney version of the Nene. New contracts brought the total F9F-2 Panther orders to 437, including the re-engined models. Fuel tanks were permanently mounted to the wingtips of all the production models.

The second F9F-3 Panther. The -3 used an Allison engine instead of the Pratt & Whitney in the F9F-2.
Grumman

This F9F-3 shows how to lighten its load by rapidly dumping fuel from its tanks.   *Grumman*

The F9F-5 had a taller, more pointed fin tip than its predecessors. This one has a refueling probe mounted in the nose.   *Grumman*

The Allison J33 was again specified for 73 F9F-4's, but continuing bearing failures caused considerable problems with this series. Engine troubles also plagued the F9F-5 with the Pratt & Whitney-built Rolls-Royce Tay, designated J48, and delivering 6,250 lbs. of thrust. Eventually, the problems were overcome and the Panther proved worthy of membership in Grumman's kennel of cats.

On July 3, 1950, the Panther became the fourth Grumman Navy fighter type to fire its guns in anger when F9F's of CAG 5 from the USS Valley Forge attacked targets in North Korea. On this occasion, two Russian-built Yak 5's felt the claws of the Panther, becoming their first victims. On November 9, 1950, an F9F-2 of VF-111 became the first carrier-based jet to score against the MiG-15. Near the end of the Korean War, Panthers operated by the Navy and Marines were used almost exclusively as fighter-bombers.

As the Panthers were supplanted by newer fighters, several were converted to drones and drone controllers with the sub designation F9F-2KD or F9F-2D. The -KD's could be used as both drone or controller. These planes were used during the development of the Regulus guided missiles. Camera-laden photo reconnaissance F9F-5P's were used by both the Navy and Marines.

The last combat-ready Panthers were flown by Marine Squadron VMF(AW)-314 in December 1957; and a few F9F-5KD's survived long enough to be classed DF-9E under the new DOD ruling.

Grumman's F9F-2 Panther had a wingspan of 38 feet with an area of 250 square feet. The length was 37 feet 3 inches and height was 11 feet 4 inches. The Pratt & Whitney J42-P-8 developed 5,750 lbs. of thrust for a speed of 526 mph at 22,000 feet. The F9F-5 had a Pratt & Whitney J48-P-6 with 7,000 lbs. of thrust and provided a speed of 579 mph at 5,000 feet. The -5 was 1 foot 7 inches longer, had an empty weight of 10,147 pounds, and a gross of 17,766 pounds with 1,003 gallons of fuel. Service ceiling was 42,800 feet and range was 1,300 miles. The streamlined nose held the armament of four 20 mm cannons.

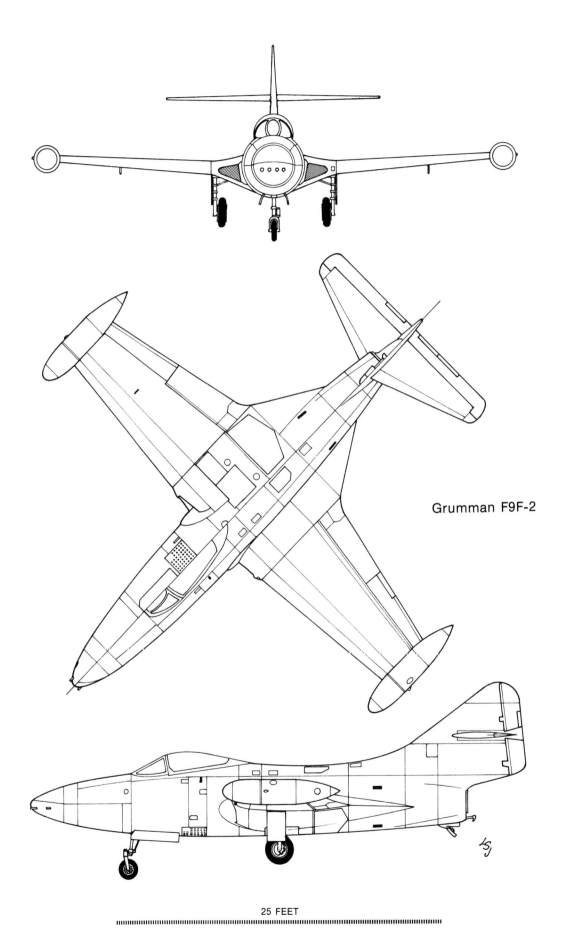

Grumman F9F-2

25 FEET

An F9F-4 Panther displays its folding wings.   *Grumman*

VOUGHT
F7U CUTLASS

The distinctive shape of the Cutlass was unmistakable. This is the first production F7U-1, 124415. Vought

The German aircraft industry had built up a remarkable technical background of extremely advanced aerodynamic concepts during World War Two. Not only had they perfected the jet fighter to a degree of reasonable reliability, they were operating them in squadron strength. These planes were so advanced that the speeds at which they operated brought them onto the threshold of compressibility. This is a phenomenon which, expressed in its simplest terms, means that the aircraft moves so fast that the air molecules cannot move out of the way fast enough and become "compressed" around the airframe, often causing destructive results.

The highly imaginative German engineers had already begun to attack the compressibility problems by designing aircraft with their flying surfaces angled sharply rearward. With the fall of Germany this research material became available to American designers toward the end of 1945. Among the material was found some data on tailless aircraft being studied by the German Arado Company. Guided by this data, Vought engineers devised an unorthodox twin jet carrier fighter which was proposed

to the Navy during a design competition in 1946. Though radical in appearance, the tailless configuration promised a substantial performance advancement coupled with carrier compatibility. On June 25, 1946, three XF7U-1 prototypes were ordered, and the raked-wing shape inspired the name Cutlass.

Such a bold departure from the conventional obviously had to produce some new devices for control, and the Cutlass displayed several of these. Since there was no horizontal stabilizing surface, the function of the elevators was taken over by large surfaces built into the wing trailing edges. Called "ailevators," they served the dual function of inducing roll as would conventional ailerons and pitch as elevators. The entire leading-edge of the wing was hinged to slide forward and down to alter the camber of the airfoil for slow speeds. Aerodynamic braking was achieved with a pair of split flaps between the vertical fins and the fuselage side. Operation of the controls from the cockpit was quite normal, however, and the pilot was provided with the conventional stick and rudder pedals for his part in the flight. The Cutlass was the

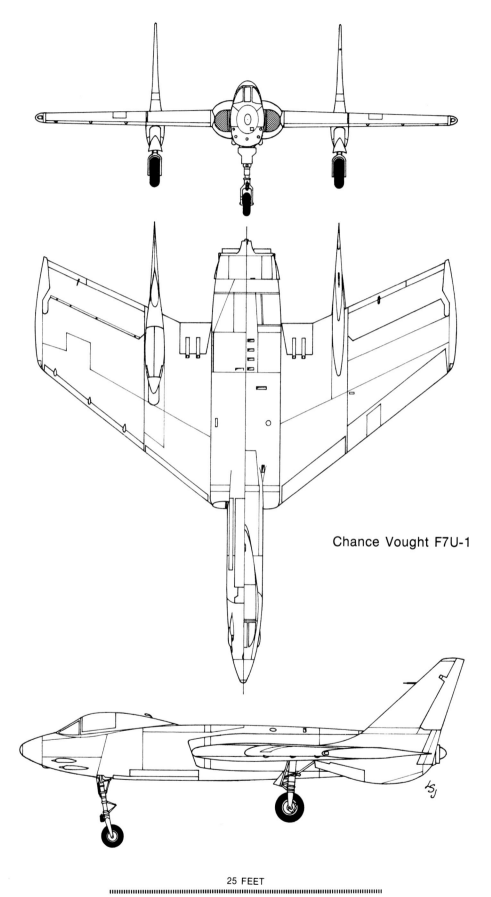

Chance Vought F7U-1

25 FEET

A Cutlass is catapulted from the USS Midway during carrier trials. Note the catapult launching bridal whipping along the deck behind the plane. *Vought*

The two F7U-1's used by the Blue Angels. These were flown by the solo pilots while the rest of the team flew F9F Panthers. *Vought*

The third prototype XF7U-1 with short vertical stabilizers.　　　　　　　　*Vought*

first jet to be designed from the outset to incorporate afterburners. The first flight was made on September 29, 1948, from the Naval Air Test Center, now located at Patuxent River, Maryland. Although the second prototype Cutlass was lost on March 14, 1949, the plane had shown sufficient promise, and 14 F7U-1's had already been ordered for assembly at Vought's new Texas plant.

The teething problems that accompany a new prototype were found in abundance; and alterations were recommended for inclusion in 88 F7U-2's. But a vastly modified version was now available, and the -2 stayed on paper while production turned instead to the F7U-3.

With the F7U-3, only the general arrangement of the original design remained. The XF7U-1 had an elongated nose strut to elevate the ground angle to increase the wing's angle of attack for catapult launching. On the prototypes, this angle was 9 degrees. To further improve the launch characteristics, this angle was increased to 20 degrees on the F7U-3. The four 20 mm cannons were moved from the nose on the F7U-1 to over the air inlets on

the later type. This led to some problems of smoke ingestion into the engines when the guns were fired, but this was solved by cutting vents into the skin behind the muzzles. Cockpit visiblity was improved by enlarging the canopy and cutting the nose sharply down in front of the windshield.

In operations, the Cutlass proved to be structurally sound, and on occasion withstood up to 16 "G's" and -9 "G's" without damage. Its spinning characteristics were looked upon with considerable apprehension, however. Just before entering a stall, the Cutlass tended to flip end over. At that point, the pilot usually parted company with the ship. It was found, however, that by simply releasing the controls, the inherent stability of the design would assert itself and the Cutlass recovered by itself.

The first 16 F7U-3's were constructed with Allison J35-A-29's without afterburners when development problems slowed delivery of the power-booster. Subsequent F7U-3's were equipped with afterburning Westinghouse J46-WE-8 units of 4,000 lbs. of thrust normal, but boosted to 5,725 lbs. with afterburning.

The long, box-like fairing on nose of the F7U-1, seen here just below the insignia, was to deflect spent cannon shells away from the engine inlets.   *Vought*

Cutlasses were assigned to four Navy squadrons—VF-81, VF-83, VF-122 and VF-124. Two of the tailless fighters were given to the Marines for high-speed mine-laying tests. In service, the Cutlass proved to be a problem child. Maintenance time was high and the fighter was subject to an excessive accident rate during carrier operations.

Two of the original F7U-1 Cutlasses were used by the Navy's Blue Angels demonstration team, their unique shape presenting a startling contrast to the rest of the team's F9F Panthers.

The F7U-1 had two 3,000 lb. thrust Westinghouse J34-WE-32 engines and a wingspan of 38 feet 8 inches. Wing area was 496 square feet. Length was 39 feet 7 inches and height was 9 feet 10 inches. Empty and gross weights were 9,565 pounds and 14,-505 pounds respectively. Maximum permissible weight was 16,840 pounds, which included 971 gallons of fuel. This provided a ferry range of 1,170 miles. Maximum speed of the F7U-1 with afterburning was 672 mph at 20,000 feet. Service ceiling was 41,400 feet.

The F7U-3 was somewhat larger than the -1 models. A total of 290 of this type were built, including 98 F7U-3M's armed with four Sparrow missiles on underwing pylons to supplement the four cannons. Also included in the total are 12 F7U-3P reconnaissance machines. The F7U-3 used a pair of Westinghouse J46-WE-8A powerplants with 4,600 lbs. of thrust normally and 6,100 lbs. with afterburning. With this power, the maximum speed was 680 mph at 10,000 feet with a rate of climb of 13,000 fpm. Service ceiling was over 40,000 feet.

The F7U-3 wingspan was 39 feet 8 inches, length was 43 feet 1 inch, and height was 14 feet 7 inches.

The Cutlass was not the Navy's first tailless aircraft. That distinction goes to the Burgess-Dunne AH-7 tailless biplane of 1916.

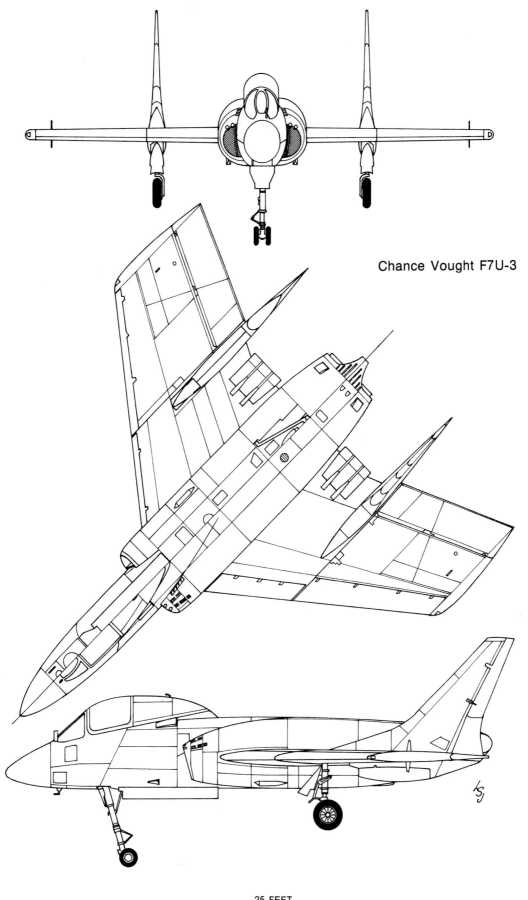

Chance Vought F7U-3

25 FEET

The F7U-3 reflected extensive design changes.   *Vought*

An F7U-3P photo-reconnaissance version of the Cutlass.   *Vought*

The F7U-3 had pylons for additional weapons.   *Vought*

This F7U-3M, preparing for a catapult launch, was equipped to carry Sparrow missiles on underwing pylons. The vents over the air inlets were to bleed off gasses when the 20 mm cannons were fired. Vought

The Burgess-Dunne AH-7 was the Navy's first tailless airplane, in 1916. Navy

DOUGLAS
F3D SKYKNIGHT

Marine-operated Skyknights were credited with more enemy planes destroyed in Korea than all other Navy types. This one is an F3D-2M, one of sixteen built. *Douglas*

The first major use of a night interceptor by the Navy was during the Korean War, where the Douglas F3D Skyknight was responsible for destroying more enemy aircraft than any other Navy types. This includes the first nighttime jet interception of another jet, culminating in the destruction of a MiG-15.

The Navy's first jet designed expressly for night fighting was conceived after Douglas was given a contract for three planes on April 3, 1946. It required two seats, two engines, and provisions for air intercept radar. The resultant design was uncomplicated, with a mid-wing and a plump fuselage straddling a pair of 3,000 lb. thrust Westinghouse J34-WE-22's. The crew was placed side by side in a pressurized cockpit and this arrangement necessitated a wide fuselage. However, the large amount of radar required for night interception was easily accommodated in the bulbous nose that resulted from the fuselage width. Four 20 mm cannons lay alongside the nose gear and fired beneath the radome.

The development of a reliable ejection seat was still in the future, so Douglas engineers provided an escape tunnel for the crew, leading from the cockpit to a hatch between the engines. In the event of an emergency exit, the pilot and radar operator would simply slide down the chute and drop from the bottom of the plane. This system was proven safe even at high speeds.

The Skyknight prototype first flew on March 23, 1948, and preceded 28 F3D-1's A larger engine was scheduled for installation in the F3D-2, and this necessitated the redesign of the nacelles. The new Westinghouse J46-WE-3 powerplants were to give 4,600 lbs. of thrust; and an order for seventy F3D-2's was placed. Continued troubles led to the abandonment of the engine and the F3D-2's received two 3,400 lb. J34-WE-6 units instead. Production orders for the -2 resulted in deliveries of 237 of this model.

Squadron deliveries of the F3D-1 began late in 1950. Most of these were sent to Marine squadrons, and were used for training when the more powerful F3D-2's were issued. It was, therefore, the Marines who were called upon to bring their Skyknights into the black skies over Korea. The F3D's were rigged for carrier operations, but all Skyknights used for the night interception

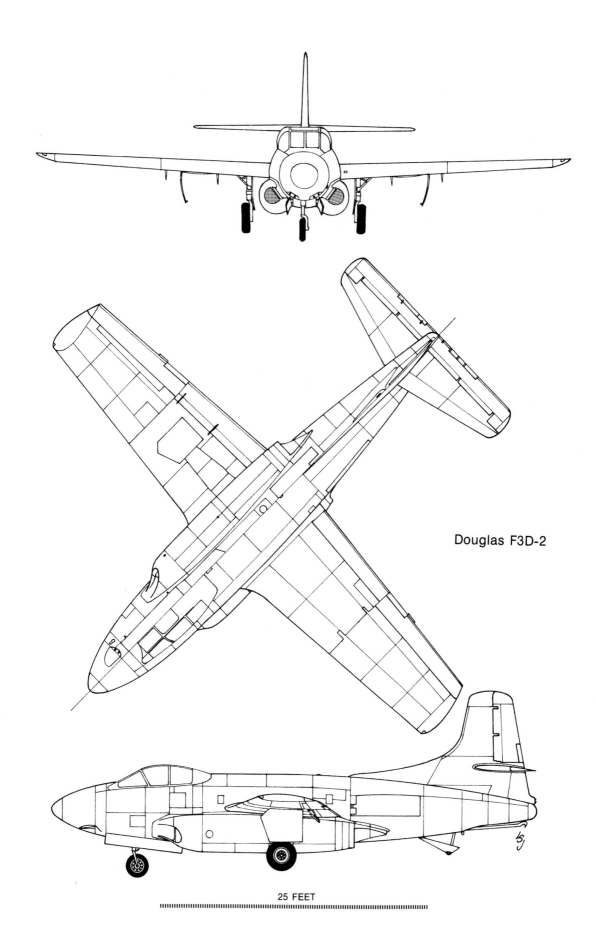

Douglas F3D-2

25 FEET

The marks on the fin of this F3D-1 are to aid the landing officer by showing him the attitude of the plane during approach to the carrier.
Douglas

The XF3D-1 Skyknight prototype. The large nose was ideal to hold the great amount of radar gear needed for night interception.
Douglas

missions in Korea were land-based.

The Skyknight proved to be a valuable tool due to its basic design layout. The F3D was the Navy's first two-place jet, and as such became candidate for training as the F3D-2T. Sixteen became F3D-2M missile launchers armed with four Sparrow AAM's; and thirty F3D-2Q's carried electronic countermeasures. All of these were modified from the original production F3D-2 batch.

The Skyknight's dimensions were: wingspan of 50 feet; length of 45 feet 6 inches; height of 16 feet 6 inches; and wing area of 400 square feet. The F3D-2 weighed 18,160 pounds empty and grossed at 26,850 pounds. Maximum speed was 560 mph at 20,000 feet. Service ceiling was 42,800 feet. Fuel capacity was 1,290 gallons for a maximum range of 1,120 miles.

The one main objection to the Skyknight's performance was its poor climb rate of 1,960 fpm. To overcome this and increase the all-around performance of the design, Douglas suggested a swept-winged version, the F3D-3. After examination of the new proposal, the Navy placed an order for 102 examples and construction was begun.

However, new developments had already obsoleted the basic Skyknight design. Since the swept-wing version would only result in moderate improvement, and availability of the engine was in doubt, the project was cancelled before the first prototype was built.

Engineering drawings for the F3D-3 swept-wing Skyknight indicate that it would have had a wingspan of 50 feet, length of 48 feet 1 inch, and a height of 16 feet 1 inch. It was to have a gross weight of 34,000 pounds, and use two Westinghouse J46 engines of 4,600 lbs. thrust. This was to provide a maximum speed of 515 mph at 40,000 feet.

The designation F2D, the logical classification for the second Douglas fighter, was not assigned since the Skyknight appeared at the same period as the McDonnell Banshee. The original Banshee designation was XF2D-1; this was changed to XF2H-1, but to avoid further confusion, the F2D label was dropped altogether. Those Skyknights remaining in service after September 1962 were classed as F-10's.

The F3D-2 had larger engine nacelles than the -1. Although clumsy looking, the Skyknight was an effective fighting machine.
                                                                                    Douglas

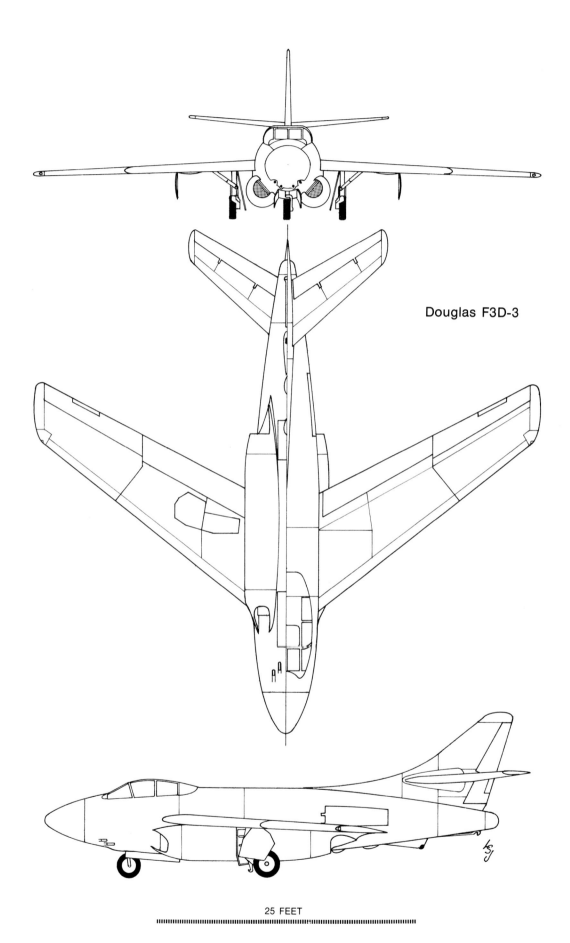

Douglas F3D-3

25 FEET

The underwing tanks on this Skyknight from VMF(N)-513 gave it a range of 1,120 miles.   *Harry Gann*

DOUGLAS
F4D-1 SKYRAY

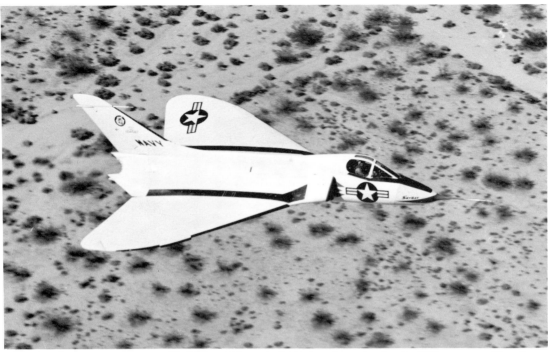

This XF4D-1 Skyray set a new World Speed Record of 743.4 mph on October 3, 1953.   Douglas

When the Navy received their first production F4D-1 Skyray, they had in their hands the first Navy fighter capable of exceeding the speed of sound in level flight. But this achievement was accomplished in a somewhat roundabout way, for when the bat-like plane first appeared, there were serious challenges to its future.

The Skyray's inception was the result of research done on the delta wing by Dr. Alexander Lippisch in Germany during World War II. The Navy's Bureau of Aeronautics had become intrigued with the possible application of such a wing on a fighter. In 1947, the Bureau came to Douglas with a request for a short-range interceptor with a high climb rate and a wing to be based on the delta form. At this point, the delta wing had never been flight tested.

At the same time, the Air Force was undertaking a similar project. Convair had been selected to design a rocket-propelled delta fighter, the XF-92. To expedite their studies of the new wing, Convair constructed a full-size jet-powered model of their planned fighter. Their approach was about as straight forward as one could get—a tube carrying the cockpit and engine with a triangular wing on each side and

topped by a fin of similar shape. On June 8, 1948, it became the first airplane to fly with a delta wing.

Meanwhile, the Douglas fighter had evolved into a manta-like form with a low aspect ratio swept wing with rounded tips. All horizontal flying controls were mounted on the wing trailing edge, thus classifying the fighter as "tailless."

The results of the Douglas studies met with the Navy's approval and an order for two XF4D-1's was issued. The plane was to be built around a Westinghouse J40 engine with 7,000 lbs. thrust. However, the engine was still under development and the first two of the new Skyrays were completed before the powerplants were available. To expedite flight testing, a lower powered Allison J35-A-17 with only 5,000 lbs. was placed into the fuselage. Thus powered, the XF4D-1 was flown on January 23, 1951; and at the same time, the first of its problems developed. Because of insufficient power, the design characteristics of the new fighter could not be properly investigated.

With the arrival of the 7,000 lb. Westinghouse XJ40-WE-6, there was encouraging improvement in the Skyray's performance. But even this engine was con-

The prototype XF4D-1 Skyray looked like this when it made its first flight, January 23, 1951.   Douglas

Skyray's were also operated by Marine squadrons such as VMF-115.   *Douglas*

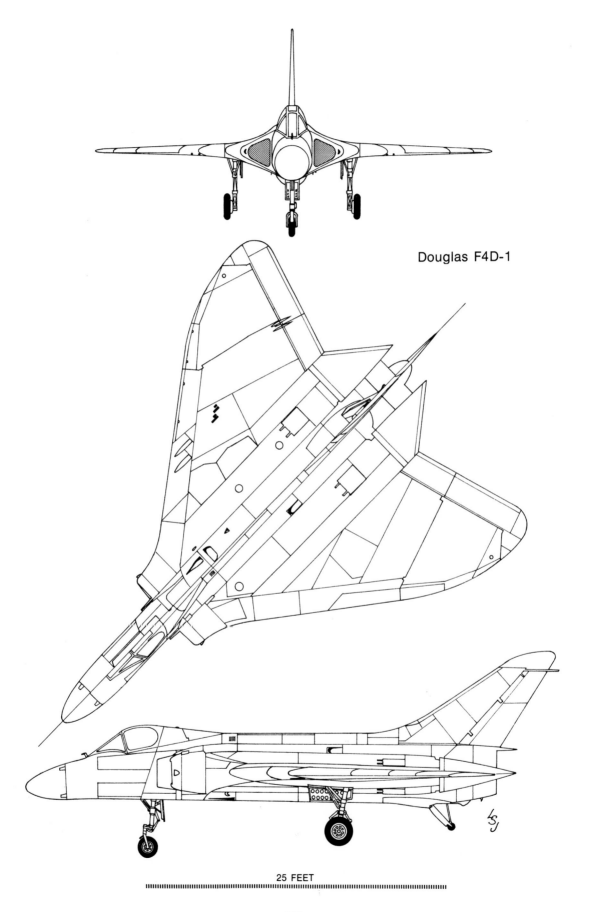

Douglas F4D-1

25 FEET

The Skyray was liked by its pilots and gave the Navy a supersonic muscle. *Douglas*

sidered temporary until the 11,600 afterburning XJ40-WE-8 would be available in mid-1953. Before the uprated Westinghouse was ready, though, the Navy decided to change the powerplant to the Pratt & Whitney J57-P-2 for the production Skyrays.

The decision to change the engines was to have a profound effect on both the performance of the Skyray and its production schedule. The larger size of the J57 required an almost total redesign of the airframe. To save time, the redesign was done while assembly was beginning on the first production planes.

Testing of the Skyray continued with the afterburning Westinghouse engine; and on October 3, 1953, the second prototype set a new world's speed record of 753.4 mph. This was the first time a carrier plane had ever held that honor. Thus, even though the

Skyray was still considered underpowered, it foretold the great possibilities of the new fighter. In all, the Skyray was to establish seven official world records.

The J57-powered F4D-1 lifted off on its maiden flight on June 5, 1954, and startled even the pilot with its fantastic acceleration. On this first flight, the Skyray easily passed Mach 1. One more delay was encountered while the inlet duct was altered to correct an air flow deficiency, then the F4D-1 was ready for the Navy. Production was completed with the 420th F4D-1.

The Skyray had all the requirements of its interceptor role. It carried four 20 mm cannons in its wings, and hardpoints under the wings could carry four rocket canisters with a total of seventy-six 2.75 inch rockets. It could reach its operational altitude of 49,-212 feet in two-and-a-half minutes and its maneuverability was considered outstand-

This Skyray of VFAW-3 was part of the squadron assigned to the Tactical Air Command. This gave the squadron the unique distinction of operating as an arm of both the Navy and Air Force. *Douglas*

The Manta-like wing is apparent in this view of an F4D-1. The wing was quite thick for a supersonic airplane.
Douglas

One of the XF4D-1's during carrier qualifications.
Navy

ing. The Skyray was also found to be effective as a general-purpose fighter and could handle ground support duties too, if necessary.

The Skyray's wing spanned 33 feet 6 inches and had the greatest area yet seen on a Navy fighter—557 square feet, which accounts for some of its flashing performance. Overall length was 45 feet 8 inches, and the tip of the fin was 13 feet from the deck.

Empty weight was 16,024 pounds; maximum takeoff weight was 27,000 pounds including 1,240 gallons of fuel, both internally and externally.

Maximum speed of the F4D-1 was 695 mph at 36,000 feet. The Pratt & Whitney J57-P-8B generated 10,500 lbs. of thrust with the afterburner. Service ceiling was 55,000 feet. Combat duration on intercept missions was 45 minutes.

McDONNELL
F3H DEMON

The large proportions of the F3H-2N are apparent by the size of the figures in this picture. Gordon S. Williams

McDonnell's first swept-winged aircraft was the tiny XF-85 parasite fighter the Air Force had studied as a defensive means for the giant B-36 bomber. This was followed by the big twin-jet XF-88 Voodoo, also swept-winged and also unsuccessful. At this point, McDonnell was singularly unlucky with its proposals to the Air Force so the opportunity to move forward with its Navy programs with a swept-winged carrier fighter was welcomed. But even this project seemed jinxed when a good design was nearly cancelled due to a tragic flaw.

The Navy requirement that spawned the F3H-1 Demon was seeking a high-performance carrier-based interceptor comparable to the latest Air Force types. In response, McDonnell showed the Navy their plans for a large single-engined machine loosely patterned after the XF-88 design. The major difference was in the selection of a single-engine layout—a deviation from their established pattern for Navy fighters.

On the basis of past performance, McDonnell had already received orders for 150 F3H-1N night fighters when the prototype XF3H-1 was flown on August 7,

1951. An order increasing the amount to 528 Demons came through following this flight; and McDonnell's future seemed secure in the light of these contracts. The estimated performance indicated the new interceptor could easily meet the Navy's requirements. This performance was kept secret from the public, however, as these characteristics are usually classified on new aircraft. In order to mislead anyone who tried to determine the engine power by measuring the air intakes, the censors carefully retouched the publicity photos to imply that the air was admitted through two small rectangular openings in the fuselage sides. Ironically, it was this very power, or lack thereof, that brought a tragic interlude into the history of the Demon.

Shortly after flight testing started, the prototype Demon crashed, thus beginning the series of mishaps which clouded the development of the F3H. Even as the production tempo increased, it was determined that, with the J40 engine, the Demon was critically underpowered. A more powerful J40 engine was promised; but since it was still in development,

267

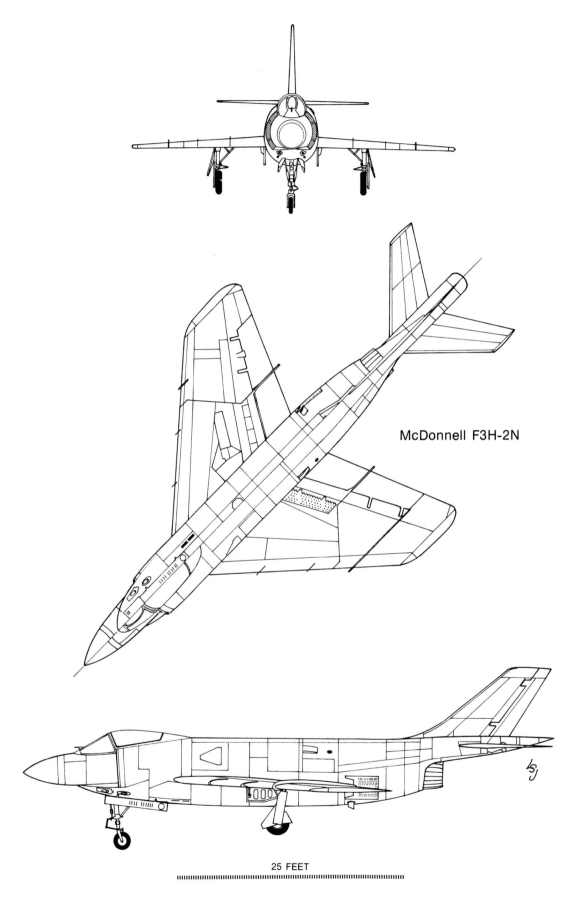

McDonnell F3H-2N

25 FEET

Four Sparrows added to the bite of the F3H-2M. The broad-chord wing is typical of the Allison-powered Demons.

Navy

McDonnell recommended replacing the powerplant with an Allison J71-A-2. This engine offered 14,250 lbs. with afterburning — more than twice the power of the faltering J40. But the Navy decided to complete the first 60 Demons with the J40; the Allison would power number 61 and those that followed.

The first of the J40-powered F3H-1N's began leaving the factory in January 1954, and the underpowered J40 began exacting its toll in airplanes and pilots. The Demon became a political football as the Navy and the government argued over the reasons for the crashes. Following eleven crashes and four fatalities, the F3H-1N's were grounded while 29 were re-engined with the Allisons. The remaining 21 planes, worth nearly $30,000,000 were permanently relegated to ground training duties.

The redesigned F3H-2N received a larger wing in addition to the Allison J71 engine, and finally the Navy had the plane they wanted. In November 1959, the last of 519 Demons left the McDonnell factory. The

design had been fully vindicated and the Demon proved a successful front line fighter, remaining operational into 1965.

The F3H-2N interceptor was a large aircraft with a wingspan of 35 feet 4 inches, an area of 519 square feet, and a length of 58 feet 11 inches. The swept-back fin was 14 feet 7 inches high. Empty weight was 22,133 pounds, gross weight was 33,900 pounds with 1,500 gallons of fuel. The maximum speed of the Demon was 647 mph at 30,000 feet. Service ceiling was 42,650 feet. The F3H-2N was fitted with a probe to enable aerial refueling for extended range. Its unrefueled range was 1,370 miles.

Four 20 mm cannons were located in the fuselage, and underwing pylons held four air-to-air missiles. To guide the interceptor to its target, the Demon carried a Hughes APG-51 radar behind its pointed fiberglass nose. On reaching its objective, the Demon could unleash its missile load which could include either beam-riding Sparrow I's, radar-guided Sparrow III's, or infrared-aimed Sidewinders.

One of the ill-fated F3H-1N Demons with the Westinghouse J40 engine.   *Gordon S. Williams*

Progenitor of the Demons. This depicts the prototype XF3H-1 during takeoff. The black wedge is actually an auxiliary intake to provide more air to the engine. This is normally closed in flight. *McDonnell Douglas*

The F3H-2N was equipped with radar for use as a night fighter and all weather interceptor.
McDonnell Douglas

These F3H-2M's are assigned to VF-112. After receiving more powerful engines, the Demons proved to be efficient machines and remained operational for over five years.
Gordon S. Williams

GRUMMAN
F9F COUGAR

This F9F-8, from China Lake, was used to test the infrared homing Sidewinder missile. For high visibility during the tests, it was painted dayglo orange on the wings, nose and tail. The fuselage was the standard Navy blue.

Navy

The Navy's first operational carrier fighter to utilize the new high-speed swept-back wing configuration was Grumman's F9F-6 Cougar. Obviously a derivation of the Panther series, the Cougar was ordered on March 2, 1951, to provide the Navy with a weapon to combat the swept-winged MiG-15's being encountered in Korea. During the original planning of the Panther, Grumman had studied the effects of the raked wing and it was determined that they could be easily incorporated into the basic design. As a result, the prototype Cougar was completed in six months, first flying on September 20, 1951. Even less time was required for the initial production plane, this making its debut only five months later.

Accompanying the Cougar's wing change was an increase of 1,000 lbs. of thrust from a Pratt & Whitney J48-P-8 rated at 7,250 lbs. These factors gave the 706 F9F-6 Cougars an 85 mph increase over the Panther series. The second Cougar order gave the fighter a 6,350 lb. thrust Allison J33-A-16A, but water injection increased the rate to 7,000 lbs. One hundred sixty-eight of these F9F-7's were delivered.

The Cougar lived up to its expectations and its advancement over the Panther was obvious. But it was felt that the swept-wing design was still at the low end of its development cycle. One area needing improvement was the low speed handling characteristics. This directed attention to the wings which were given wider outer panels and a cambered leading edge eliminating the slats. An increase to the trailing edge gave a thinner wing section raising the critical Mach number. Reworking the wing had the added benefit of increasing the fuel capacity. Lengthening the fuselage improved the fineness ratio and also allowed for another fuel tank, adding a total of 140 more gallons to the Cougar's capacity. As the F9F-8, the first of the revised fighters flew on December 18, 1953, and displayed a high speed of 714 mph — a difference of 24 mph over the F9F-7. This merited an order for 711 more F9F-8 Cougars making the type the most prevalent jet fighter in the Navy at the time.

Extension of the fuselage by 2 feet 10 inches and the addition of a second seat gave the Navy the F9F-8T, its first swept-

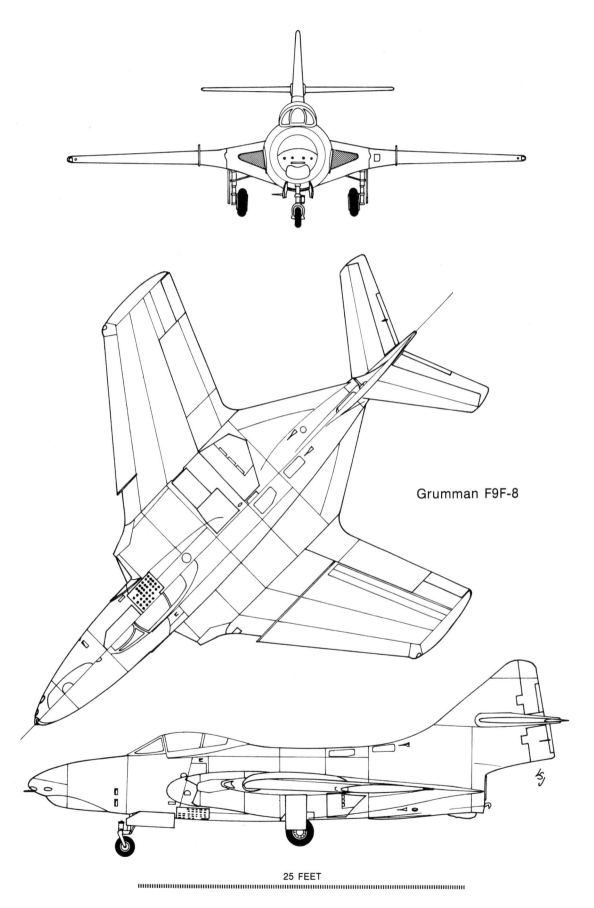

Grumman F9F-8

25 FEET

The Cougar was the Navy's first swept-wing fighter. This is a late F9F-8 with enlarged wing surfaces. U.S. Navy

An F9F-6 lugging a pair of bombs during a practic mission. The nose probe was for special instrumentation.
Grumman

One hundred and eight of these F9F-8P's were built. A refueling probe points the way on this plane. Grumman

winged trainer. Grumman built 399 of this model which had a maximum speed of 705 mph.

Other versions of the F9F-8 were the camera-equipped F9F-8P's and the F9F-8B missile platform capable of launching four air-to-air missiles. Many cougars were fitted with refueling probes to extend their range to the requirements of their specific missions. On their retirement from front line duty, the Cougars continued serving as radio-controlled drones and drone con-trollers. These were usually redesignated QF-9's in keeping with the new classification.

The definitive F9F-8 Cougar had a wingspan of 34 feet 6 inches, length of 40 feet 10 inches and a height of 15 feet. Maximum launch weight was 20,000 pounds, service ceiling was 50,000 feet. Fixed armament was four 20 mm M3 cannons, and up to 3,000 pounds of bombs could be hauled on the underwing racks.

NORTH AMERICAN
FJ-2/4 FURY

The FJ-3 shared many features with the Air Force's F-86 Sabre.   *Rockwell*

With the Korean War focusing attention on the advancements made in Russian aircraft technology through the appearance of the MiG-15, the Navy looked for a rapid means of acquiring a fighter with even better performance. The logical subject was the F-86 Sabre, which was developed from the original Fury and had proved easily capable of besting the Russian fighter. Converting the Sabre into a carrier fighter should take a relatively short development time, the Navy reasoned, and ordered three XFJ-2's on March 8, 1951. North American had already done some design work on a navalized Sabre which helped reduce the time even more.

The XFJ-2's were essentially F-86E's with folding wings, catapult launching and arresting hooks, and a lengthened nose strut to increase the launch angle for carrier take-offs. The first XFJ-2 to fly was actually the third constructed and differed from the others in its armament. Whereas the F-86 carried six .50 cal. machine guns, this XFJ-2B sported the now preferred Navy armament of four 20 mm cannons, which were standard on all subsequent Furies. The first flight occurred on December 27, 1951, and was made by R. A. "Bob" Hoover, later to

become a popular aerobatic pilot on the air show circuit.

The first two XFJ-2 prototypes were delivered to the Navy's test center at Patuxent River for service trials early in 1952. In December, the new Fury passed qualification tests on the USS Coral Sea. North American had already received an order for 300 FJ-2's in February and had set up a production line at the former Curtiss plant in Columbus, Ohio.

FJ-2's were produced alongside Air Force Sabres, and the first production Fury was completed shortly before the end of 1952. Because of the added equipment, the Fury was 1,000 pounds heavier than the F-86. Although the FJ-2 was carrier qualified, this extra weight had a negative influence on carrier operations and most of the planes were assigned to the Marines for land-based duties. It is ironic that the weight of the very features added to make the Fury suitable for carrier work was a major factor in its poor carrier performance. As the direction of the Korean War became more favorable and the conclusion seemed imminent, the contract for 300 FJ-2's was cut and only 200 were delivered.

The similarity between the Sabre and

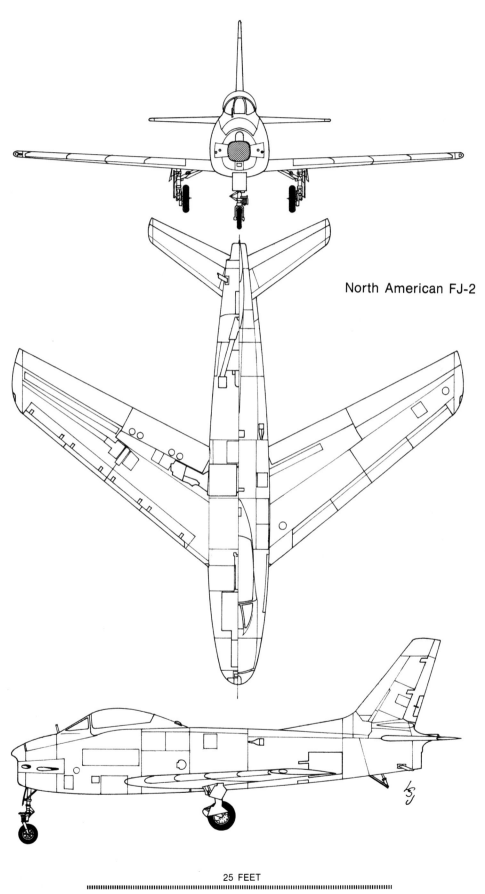

North American FJ-2

25 FEET

An FJ-3 coming aboard. Notice the arresting cable in the foreground. *Navy*

Fury offered advantages beside the conveniences of production. The Fury also benefitted from the Sabre's evolution. During the Sabre's operations in Korea, it was learned that leading edge slats greatly improved the maneuverability of the F-86. This feature, plus the use of a 7,700 lb. thrust Wright J65-W-2 engine, put the Fury back in the running as a first-line carrier fighter. Now designated FJ-3, the Fury was ordered into production on the basis of a contract for 389 examples on April 18, 1952. These new Furies passed their trials rapidly and were dispensed to the fleet where they became operational with both Navy and Marine squadrons.

During the production of the FJ-3, further improvements were made to the wing. The movable slats were replaced by a fixed, but extended, leading edge with air flow fences. Extra fuel tanks were also added. Initially, two external weapons pylons were fitted to the FJ-3; but it proved capable of hauling increased loads, so all aircraft were provided with a second pair. Philco's AAM-N-7 Sidewinders were part of the armament of 80 FJ-3M's.

On October 28, 1954, an all new Fury roared into the Ohio skies. Though it was obviously a member of the same clan, the newcomer was virtually a different machine. The desire to increase the operating range had fattened the fuselage lines to accept fifty percent more fuel. A much broader swept wing extended from the plumper fuselage. The ailerons were located inboard of the hinged wing panels with high-lift flaps separating them from the fuselage, and all flying surfaces were thinned down. The new FJ-4 could sweep through the sky at 680 mph. This Fury was roughly equivalent to the Air Force's F-86H. Its source of power was the 7,700 lb. Wright J65-W-16A. One hundred fifty-two of these Furies were built at the Columbus plant. Most of the FJ-4's were assigned to the Marine Corps who used them as day fighters.

The final version of the Fury took the form of the FJ-4B. This model was strengthened and carried six underwing hardpoints for ground-attack stores. It differed also from its predecessors in having a LABS installation to enable it to deliver tactical nuclear weapons. With the comple-

This heavily-laden FJ-4B is armed with Martin Bullpup missiles.   Rockwell

tion of 222 FJ-4B's, Fury production ended.

The FJ-2, powered by a 6,000 lb. General Electric J47-GE-2, had a wingspan of 37 feet 1 inch, a length of 37 feet 7 inches, and was 13 feet high. Wing area was 288 square feet. Empty, it weighed 11,802 pounds; gross weight was 16,482 pounds. Maximum speed was 676 mph at sea level; combat ceiling was 41,700 feet.

The proportions of the FJ-3 were similar, but the wing area increased to 302 square feet. It was 1,000 pounds heavier than the -2 and used a Wright J65-W-48 license-built Armstrong-Siddeley Sapphire with 7,650 lbs. thrust. With this engine, the Fury had a speed of 681 mph at sea level. Service ceiling was 49,000 feet.

The final Fury model, the FJ-4, had a wingspan of 39 feet 1 inch, wing area of 338½ square feet, was 36 feet 4 inches long, and stood 13 feet 11 inches high. Empty weight was 13,210 pounds; loaded it weighed 20,130 pounds. This version had a maximum speed of 680 mph at sea level and a ceiling of 46,800 feet.

All Furies used four 20 mm cannons in addition to the other loads mentioned.

The new DOD Fury classification was F-1.

The FJ-4B was strengthened to carry hardpoints for six external underwing stores.　　　**Rockwell**

A broad wing and deeper fuselage were distinguishing characteristics of the FJ-4 Fury.　　　**Rockwell**

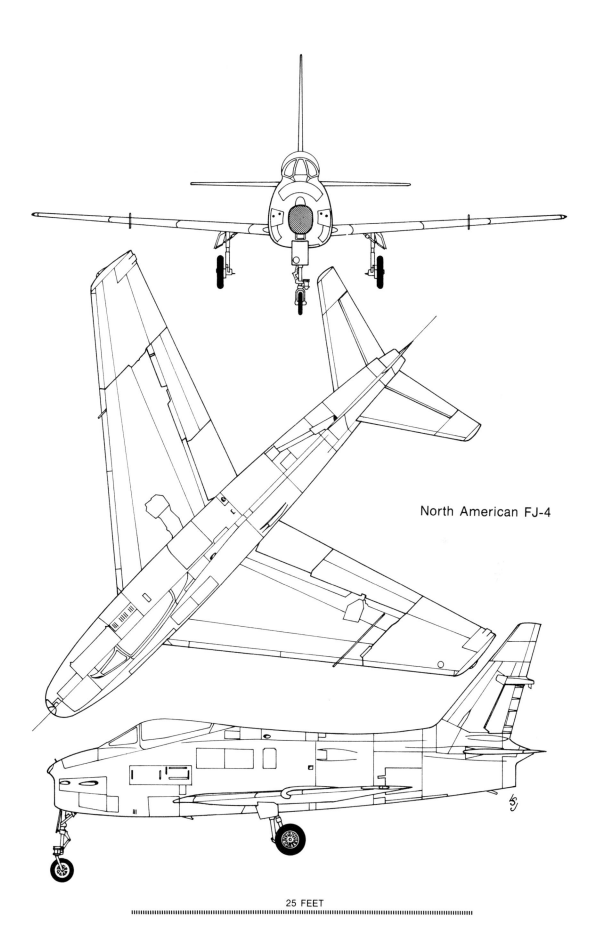

North American FJ-4

25 FEET

The wing-folding mechanism in detail. This is one of the Marine FJ-2's, operated from land bases because of its excessive weight.
                                                                                           Rockwell

A Marine Corps FJ-2 of VMF-122 from Cherry Point, N.C.   *U.S. Marine Corps*

A sky full of star-spangled Furies from VMF 235. These are FJ-2's.   *Rockwell*

DOUGLAS
F5D-1 SKYLANCER

The F5D-1 Skylancer was a refined version of the Skyray.   *Douglas*

The combination of jet fighters, radar, and guided missiles had substantially altered the principles of combat after the end of World War II. It used to be a simple case of, "If you see him, go get him; if the weather is bad, forget it." But super speed and the electronic eyeball had dictated a new set of rules. Now, radar told you he was coming and where you could find him regardless of the darkness of the night or the density of the cloud cover. The secret was to get up there fast and nail him—now! To do this required an interceptor having a rapid rate of climb, carrying sufficient radar search gear, and armed with target-tracking missiles to finish the job.

As the result of the Skyray's remarkable adaptability and outstanding performance, Douglas drew up plans to expand its all-weather abilities. This would include providing a more sophisticated electronic auto-pilot and radar systems to aim and fire four infrared homing missiles. The project originally was designated F4D-2N, but the modifications were so extensive it became the XF5D-1 and received the name Skylancer.

Although the power unit was the same as that in the Skyray, only the general configuration of the F4D remained. The wing retained the distinctive bat-like shape, but the thickness/chord ratio was reduced and the fineness ratio of the fuselage was increased. The Skyray's flat windshield was replaced with a sharp Vee-shaped affair on the F5D which further improved the streamlining of the new interceptor.

The projected performance of the Skylancer was promising enough to win approval for further studies. The original contract authorized nineteen F5D-1's, but these were gradually cut until only four Skylancers remained. The Skylancer went aloft on April 21, 1956; and, like the Skyray, slipped into the supersonic realm on its first flight.

Although the four Skylancers were consigned to the test role, their performance fully qualified them for their intended duties. Their climb rate exceeded that of the Skyray; at 40,000 feet, the F5D-1 could streak along at 1,098 mph (Mach 1.5).

As excellent as the Skylancer was, the Navy felt that it would soon be bypassed by more versatile all-weather types entering development. New fire control and

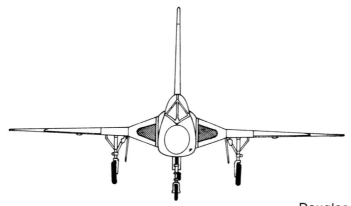

Douglas F5D-1

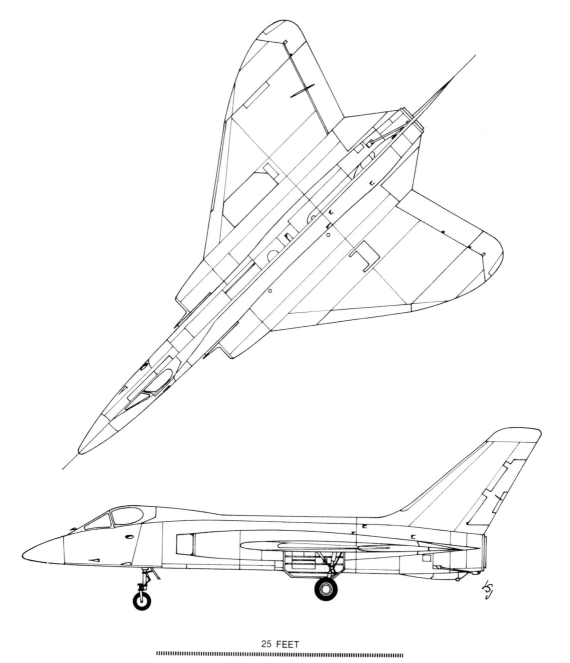

25 FEET

Similar in appearance to the Skyray, the F5D-1 could out-climb the earlier fighter.   *Douglas*

The size difference between the Skyray and Skylancer can be seen in this photo.   *Douglas*

Although the Skylancer had a top speed of 1,098 mph, the F5D-1 was outdistanced by technology and was obsolete before it could enter service.   *Douglas*

automatic navigational systems were being perfected. These would have to be integrated into the new aircraft as a part of the initial design. The Skylancer had become a victim of rapidly advancing technology.

Two Skylancers were delivered to NASA at Ames Research Laboratories for use as high-speed test machines. One of these received an ogee wing, similar to that on the Concorde SST, to study leading edge vortex airflow.

The F5D-1 was slightly larger than the Skyray with a wingspan of 33 feet 6 inches and an area of 560 square feet. Overall length was 50 feet, height was 15 feet. Gross weight of the F5D-1 was 25,000 pounds. Operational ceiling was 55,000 feet. Production Skylancers were to carry retractable missile launchers supplementing their four 20 mm cannons and external AAM's.

LOCKHEED
XFV-1

A lightweight landing gear was installed on the XFV-1 for flight testing.   *Lockheed*

In 1949, the Navy began exploring the potential of the gas turbine engine. Here was a powerplant that offered more than just a means of increasing speed in the new generation of military aircraft. The ratio of the available energy output compared to the weight of the machine was exceedingly high. Through careful design, it might even be possible to devise an aircraft in which the delivered power actually exceeded the weight of the loaded airframe. Such a plane could theoretically lift itself straight up from the ground, and level flight characteristics might be equally spectacular.

The exciting possibilities of a fighter capable of lifting itself vertically into the air brought Lockheed and Convair to the Navy with a pair of proposals for this novel concept in 1951. While Convair, already involved in delta-wing research, planned to use this shape for its flying surfaces, the Lockheed design favored the stubby straight wings of the type being used on their supersonic F-104. Both companies came away with development contracts for the unique vertical take-off(VTO) planes. Although the contract indicated that the new types would

be fighters, they were in fact, research vehicles for exploring this new aspect of flight.

Lockheed's VTO fighter design was designated XFV-1, since the Navy had replaced the letter "O" previously signifying Lockheed as the constructor with "V" to avoid confusion with the number zero. Progress was made on the radical plane in total secrecy. It was several years after the program had been instituted before the public was even aware of such an exotic craft. By this time, the XFV-1 was nearing its initial testing; and procedures nearly as unique as the aircraft itself were devised.

The specified powerplant was a pair of turbojet engines coupled to a set of 16 foot three-bladed contra-props. This device was designated XT40-A-6 and was built by Allison. Its 5,500 shaft hp provided some 20 percent more push than the gross weight of the entire airplane.

Even the engine had to be developed specifically for VTO operation. It had to be able to operate unfalteringly while in a vertical or horizontal position. Due to delays encountered while this engine was being perfected, Lockheed chose to use a

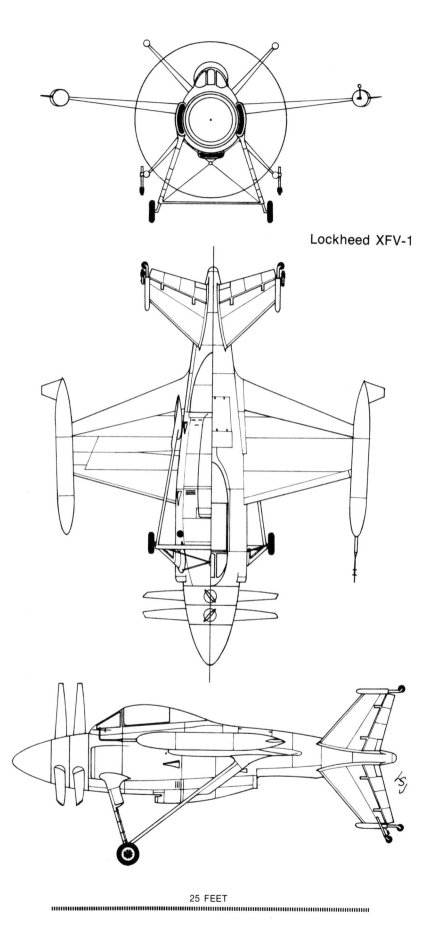

Lockheed XFV-1

25 FEET

The cruciform tail surfaces contained all of the flight controls. The four surfaces acted as ailerons, rudders, and elevators.   *Lockheed*

horizontal-running model of the engine for initial tests. Although it could not be used to lift the XFV-1 straight up from the ground, it did permit vertical operations in the air for a short time. This meant that the first flight would have to be made with a conventional takeoff run. Therefore, a lightweight fixed gear was attached to the XFV-1.

As may be presumed, a plane with enough power to rise vertically from the ground had a remarkable acceleration rate while horizontal. So rapid was this speed increase that on one taxi test, the plane accidentally exceeded liftoff speed and "unofficially" soared down the runway at Edwards AFB. The official first flight occured several months later, on June 16, 1954.

The XFV-1 made twenty-two flights during which it was flown into the vertical mode 32 times. While vertical, the XFV-1 performed as anticipated. It could hover motionless, climb straight upward, or descend downward. Its highest vertical ascent speed was 60 mph and its maximum controlled vertical descent speed was 8 mph. The XFV-1's hovering characteristics were quite similar to a helicopter.

Test pilot "Fish" Salmon pulls the XFV-1 into its first vertical test.   *Lockheed*

This rig was designed to lower the XFV-1 for servicing. Lockheed

The distinctive cruciform tail assembly, upon which the XFV-1 rested, contained all the flight controls. The four movable surfaces performed the functions of rudder, elevator and ailerons through differential movement of each surface. Apparently this system performed satisfactorily as there were no reported problems.

The Lockheed XFV-1 had an overall span of 30 feet 11 inches with an area of 246 square feet. Length, or height in takeoff attitude, was 37 feet 6 inches. The XFV-1's empty weight was 11,599 pounds and gross was 16,211 pounds. The Lockheed tail-sitter was never fully tested to determine its entire

flight envelope, so only the estimated performance can be provided. Maximum speed was expected to be 580 mph at 15,000 feet, initial climb rate (after takeoff and horizontal transition) 10,820 fpm. Service ceiling was to be 43,300 feet.

Two prototypes of the XFV-1 were built, but only one was flown. One of the two examples of this unusual experimental craft is on display at the entrance of the Los Alamitos Naval Air Station in California.

The VTO fighter concept did not intend for the aircraft to take off vertically and streak upward to intercept any hapless intruder. As noted before, the XFV-1 had a

Although the Lockheed VTOL fighter was designed to take off from this position, the lack of a suitable engine prevented such lift-offs.
Lockheed

maximum vertical climb of only 60 mph from a standing start. As originally envisioned, the XFV-1 would be able to lift straight up from a confined area, transition to level flight, then accelerate to some 500 mph and engage the enemy in a conventional manner. Each pod on the wingtips was intended to hold either two 20 mm cannons or 24 HVAR rockets.

CONVAIR
XFY-1 POGO

"Skeets" Coleman becomes the first man to take off vertically in the XFY-1 Pogo.   *Convair*

Convair's response to the Bureau of Aeronautics proposal for a vertical takeoff fighter took the shape of a stubby delta-winged machine with two vertical surfaces forming a cross with the wings. The development of both the Convair and Lockheed VTO's proceeded in unison. Although the Convair plane flew after the Lockheed ship, the XFY-1 made all of its flights from a vertical takeoff. The presence of the lower vertical fin precluded the use of any horizontal launching gear, so from the outset, all flight test data would have to come after a vertical lift-off. For this reason, Convair received the only engine unit available from Allison with the necessary components for sustained vertical operation.

Engine tests began in San Diego in March 1954, then the little delta was transported north to Moffet Field. There, a system of pulleys and cables was rigged inside a 195 foot high blimp hangar. The XFY-1 was attached by its spinner to the end of a cable

and the engine started. In the event of a failure by the powerplant, the cable would support the craft and prevent serious damage. As it happened, the Allison engine performed flawlessly throughout the test program; but the restraining rig, no doubt, provided some feeling of security to the pilot.

Several captive takeoffs and landings were made with the XFY-1 inside the hangar while the pilot familiarized himself with the handling characteristics. On August 1, 1954, the Pogo, as it became known, rose from the apron outside the hangar—free of its fetters for the first time. It was hovered first at 40 feet, then gently descended to the ground. Once more, it rose upwards, this time to 150 feet before easing tail-first onto the concrete.

Satisfied that true vertical takeoffs could be made, Convair returned the Pogo to San Diego where further exploration of its flight envelope could be made. On November 2,

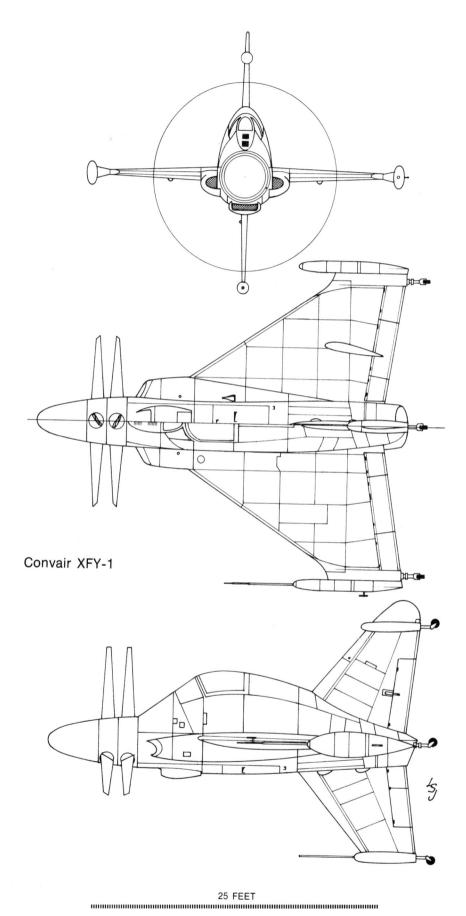

Convair XFY-1

25 FEET

1954, the XFY-1 became the first VTO airplane in the world to fly, in every aspect of the word. On this occasion, the Pogo rose off the field, nosed over and raced away like any new aircraft finally in its intended environment. Following a flight of some 20 minutes, the plump little fighter zoomed low over the airfield, pulled sharply upward and stopped in mid-air before settling gently tail-first onto the runway.

The armament was to be located outside the 16 foot arc of the contra-props in two streamlined pods. This was to consist of a total of four 20 mm cannons or forty-six 2.75 inch HVAR folding-fin rockets.

Several more of these spectacular flights were made before the program was drawn to a close. Like the Lockheed vertical-riser

The Pogo makes a low-level pass prior to climbing into the vertical attitude for landing. Convair

The pilot's seat was hinged to tilt forward during vertical operation. Convair

Convair's Pogo was considered by the Navy to be a test machine only. Although no production orders were received, the first tangible data on vertical flight was now available. Probably the most important material obtained from the tests concerned the tail-sitting attitude of the planes. It was very uncomfortable for the pilots and required a great amount of skill from the two highly experienced test pilots to achieve the desired goals.

Future pilots did derive a direct benefit from the VTO program, however. Because of the need to eject the pilot sideways in the event of an emergency, a rapidly opening parachute was devised. This laid the groundwork for today's zero-zero ejection seat from which a safe ejection can be made at ground level. With modern VTO types now in service, this is a very necessary part of the airplane's equipment.

Convair's history-making Pogo had a wingspan of 27 feet 8 inches. The delta wing had an area of 355 square feet. Fuselage length was 34 feet 11 inches, and the vertical stabilizers spanned 22 feet 8 inches. The Allison XT40-A-6 provided 5,500 shaft hp to pull the XFY-1's 16,250 pound gross weight straight up. Empty weight was 11,742 pounds.

As with the Lockheed XFV-1, the entire range of capabilities of the Pogo was not examined, but its estimated performance is given. Maximum speed: 610 mph at 15,000 feet, 592 mph at 35,000 feet. Initial climb rate from horizontal flight: 10,500 fpm. Service ceiling was 43,700 feet.

It took 5,500 shaft hp to pull the Pogo straight up from the ground. Wingtip pods were to house armament in fighter version.   *Convair*

In level flight, the XFY-1 handled like any other high performance aircraft.   *Convair*

CONVAIR
F2Y-1 SEA DART

With its hydro-skis retracted, the Sea Dart gave few clues to water-landing ability. The stripes gave reference lines for tracking cameras.
Convair

The Navy's past experience with water-based fighters had shown that such a plane could have some tactical advantages. The Japanese had used float fighters with some degree of success during World War II. Their most obvious disadvantage was the need of drag-producing floats to elevate the propeller above the water. Unlike wheels, which can be retracted into the airframe and out of the airflow, the floats must remain forever exposed.

The arrival of the jet engine brought the first practical solution to the float-drag dilemma. It was compact and did not have to be kept high out of the water as long as the air intake and exhaust were protected. The British had successfully flown the twin-jet Saunders-Roe SR. A/1 in July 1947. It was relatively conventional with a deep hull and semi-retracting wing floats. Other than its ability to operate from water, it offered no improvement over contemporary land planes.

Convair's approach to the jet seaplane fighter was much more dramatic. They proposed a sleek design with a swept wing blending smoothly into the body. The sealed fuselage became the hull and the plane would rest on its wings when in the water. Further streamlining was achieved by using a retractable step in the fuselage bottom. Convair gave the name "Skate" to their new fighter design and furthered its development by building a radio-controlled model to gather preliminary flight data.

Concurrent with Convair's work on the blended wing, NACA was deeply involved in studies on the use of skis as alighting gear for seaplanes. Several conventional water-based planes had been fitted with hydro-skis with encouraging results. The principal advantage to the skis was their ability to absorb the shock of slamming into the water, thus permitting the airframe structure to be lighter. Being essentially flat, the skis could easily be retracted and the seaplane would then have the same weight and drag as a land plane. By combining the hydro-skis with the blended hull and adding a pair of jets, perhaps the Navy would have their long-sought seaplane fighter.

On October 1, 1948, Convair entered the Navy's competition for the water-based interceptor and was chosen to make a comparison of the blended hull and hydro-ski approaches. During the study, it was

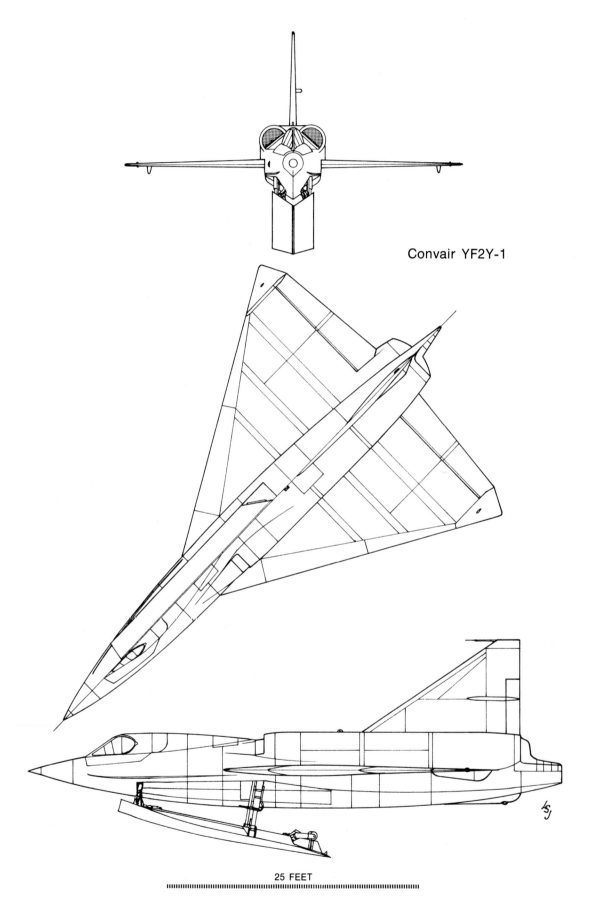

Convair YF2Y-1

25 FEET

While on the surface of the water, the Sea Dart has the appearance of a Jules Verne creation. B. J. Long

decided to combine the two concepts. By this time, Convair had considerable background in delta wing characteristics so this planform was chosen for the new fighter.

A contract for two prototypes of the XF2Y-1 was signed on January 19, 1951. Motive force was to come from a pair of 3,400 lb. thrust Westinghouse J34-WE-32 engines for initial flights. More powerful engines were to be used as soon as they became available. On August 28, 1952, the Navy ordered twelve more of the Sea Darts, and four months later they were able to look upon the first of the new breed.

A considerable amount of testing had to be done in the Sea Darts' water environment before actual flight studies could begin. This was prolonged when it was found that the skis tended to pound and vibrate the airframe when the planing speed exceeded 60 mph — far below the 140 mph take-off speed. The vibrations posed such a serious threat to the airframe that the skis were subjected to a study that would ultimately lead to the evaluation of over one hundred different configurations. During one of these tests, the prototype XF2Y-1 bounced into the air and skimmed over some 1,000 foot distance. By April 9, 1953, the ski pounding

had been reduced sufficiently to attempt the first flight, which was accomplished without difficulty on that date.

The original powerplant did not provide adequate thrust to reach the anticipated performance. Even the uprated afterburning Westinghouse XJ46-WE-2 engines could not attain the promised power output. But engine problems were not all that plagued the Sea Dart. A higher than anticipated transonic drag reduced the expected maximum speed from Mach 1.5 to an unsuitable Mach .99. The Sea Dart could attain Mach 1 in a shallow dive, but land-based fighters were reaching this mark in level flights.

To overcome the many shortcomings the Sea Dart now displayed would entail a complete redesign of the seaplane. Designated F2Y-2, the new Convair seaplane fighter would use a single 12,000 lb. thrust Wright J67 or 15,000 lb. Pratt & Whitney J75, both using afterburning. Since a single ski had proven the most efficient during tests, it would be used on the F2Y-2. In the face of the unexpected development problems, reconsideration raised the question about the feasibility of the seaplane concept in the first place. The final blow came when one of the Sea Darts disintegrated during a public showing on November 4, 1954. The Navy

Convair tested the blended-hull concept with this scale model of the Skate. The later studies added swept wings, then finally the delta was adopted.　　　　*Convair*

After testing over 100 ski designs, the single ski was found to be the most satisfactory.　　　　*Convair*

The afterburners required lengthening the engine nacelles and extended them beyond the vertical fin. Convair

During the early testing of the XF2Y-1, no afterburners were mounted.　　　　*Convair*

finally accepted the Sea Dart for evaluation in May, 1955, but continuing recurrence of the ski pounding finally brought the program to an end within a few months. Of the five Sea Darts built, all but the example destroyed in the accident remain on display in the U.S. Oddly, these were reclassed as F-7's by the DOD, even though they were no longer airworthy.

The triangular wing of the Sea Dart is 33 feet 8 inches in span, wing area is 563 square feet. Length is 52 feet 7 inches, and height is 16 feet 2 inches on its hydro-skis. Empty weight is 12,625 pounds. Gross weight is 16,527 pounds. Properly powered, it was estimated that the Sea Dart would reach 994 mph at 35,000 feet; however, the higher than expected drag would probably have prevented such speed.

A Sea Dart on final over San Diego Bay, just before splashdown.　　　　*Convair*

GRUMMAN
XF10F-1 JAGUAR

The small delta canard on the front of the stabilizer fairing actually operated the stabilator by using aerodynamic force. Unfortunately, control response was too slow for effective control on a fighter.Grumman

Experiments with a means of changing the flight characteristics of an aircraft by altering its wing shape while airborne had been tried many times before the Grumman Jaguar appeared. The first airplane to use variable wing-sweep was the Westland-Hill Pterodactyl IV, a tailless monoplane whose wing could be moved almost five degrees during flight. This plane was tested in 1931.

During the Second World War, the Germans also investigated the variable geometry principle. Bell Aircraft built their X-5, based on a German swept-wing fighter prototype captured after the war, and modified it to test the movable-wing principle.

To the Navy, the variable-geometry wing offered the best of two worlds. With the wings straight out, the takeoff and landing traits would be better suited for carrier operations, while the swept-back position would permit the sought-after high speed range. The first plane to introduce this feature to the Navy was Grumman's XF10F-1 Jaguar; and it also brought with it a bushel of engineering headaches.

At its inception, the XF10F-1 was no more than a progressive development of the F9F Panther with clipped delta wings and tail sufaces. No hint of its exotic future was visible in the original presentation. The XF10F-1 design went through an elaborate evolution, finally arriving at a point where it was to use a tilting, variable-incidence wing for takeoff and landing. At this stage, the construction of a mock-up was begun. Following examination of the mock-up, the intended role for the fighter was changed. Now its use was expanded to include patrol, interception, escort, and ground support. These new duties led to an increase in weight and the variable sweep wing entered the picture.

Essentially, the wing-sweep mechanism moved the root forward to adjust the aircraft's center of gravity as the surfaces swung aft. It was designed to remain at either the extreme forward position of 13.2 degrees of sweep, or fully raked at 42.5 degrees; but during the program, it was revised to stop at any position within the movable range.

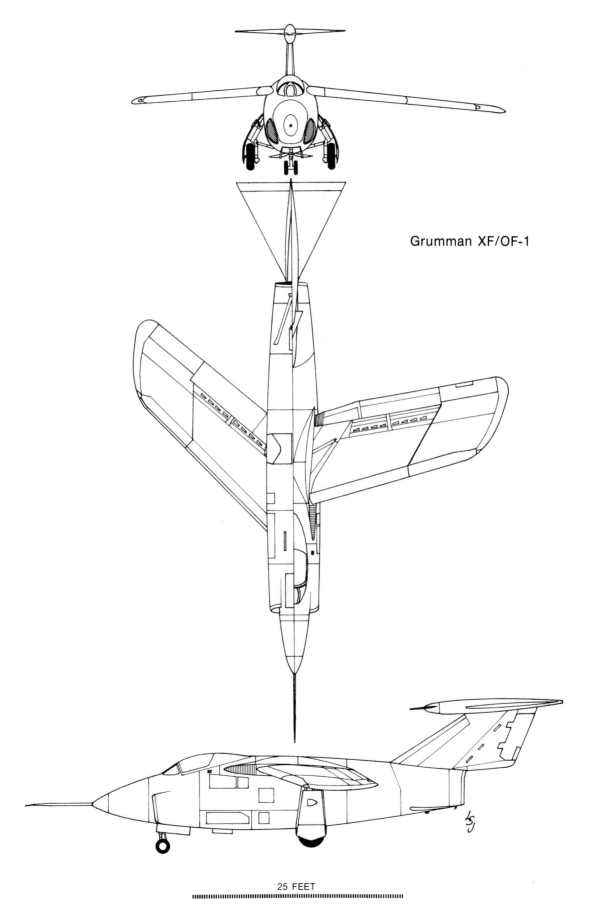

Grumman XF/OF-1

25 FEET

The XF10F-1 Jaguar, wings and leading edge slats extended, poses at the Grumman plant before flight testing begins. *Grumman*

The prototype XF10F-1 was completed and preliminary taxi tests were made at Grumman's plant early in 1952. The plane was transferred to Edwards AFB in April and readied for its first trials. Initial liftoff occurred on May 19, 1952. The wing-sweep mechanism proved very successful, but there were so many other innovative features on the big fighter that the Jaguar was constantly beset with problems.

Not the least of the difficulties centered around the novel delta-shaped stabilizer perched on the fin tip. This surface was actually controlled by the movement of a smaller delta canard attached at the front of the stabilizer bullet fairing. Movement of the control column activated the canard and the aerodynamic forces, in turn, moved the stabilizer. All this activity took time and the elevator response was excruciatingly slow. This was certainly no control system to use on a fighter, so it was abandoned in favor of a conventional power-boosted unit from a Cougar.

The engine also had its influence on the future of the Jaguar. The low output of the Westinghouse J40, coupled with the high operating weight of the aircraft, seriously restricted its performance.

To induce roll, the wings of the XF10F-1 were equipped with spoilers which extended vertically above and below the surface. Additional control came from a small set of ailerons at the wingtip. In use, however, the spoilers were so ineffiecient they were soon disconnected and the ailerons were the only roll controls used. The entire wing leading edge slid downward to become a slat.

The tribulations of the Jaguar were enough to fill a book of their own. There were so many innovative features incorporated into the bulky fighter that one engineer was prompted to remark that every flight was a first one. In all, the XF10F-1 was flown 32 times. Because of the innumerable problems and complexity of the machine, the entire program was ended on June 12, 1953.

The Navy assigned Bureau Numbers to 135 F10F-1 Jaguars and five F10F-1P reconnaissance machines. However, only two prototypes were assembled and of these, only the first one flew. Both were eventually destroyed—one in landing barrier tests, the other as a target for artillery shells.

The Jaguar was a large aircraft with an outspread wingspan of 50 feet 7 inches; swept span of 36 feet 8 inches; and a wing area ranging from 450 square feet to 467 square feet. Length was 54 feet 5 inches, height was 16 feet 3 inches. Empty weight was 20,426 pounds; combat weight, including proposed armament, was 27,451 pounds. Armament was to include four 20 mm cannons in the nose plus either forty-eight 2.75 inch FFAR's or twelve 5 inch rockets under the wings. Alternately, four thousand pounds of bombs were to be carried under the wings.

This picture shows the wing-fuselage junction with the wings in the forward position before painting.

Richard DeMeis

Estimated maximum performance gave the Jaguar a high speed of 710 mph at sea level with an afterburning 10,900 lb. Westinghouse J40-WE-8, which in fact was never installed. Combat ceiling was to be 45,800 feet. The actual engine used in the tests was a Westinghouse J40-WE-6, rated at 7,000 lbs. but consistently delivered less.

The Jaguar cannot be considered a total failure since the most advanced feature installed, the variable-sweep wing, functioned entirely satisfactorily. The results of the Jaguar program were most valuable in designing the next generation of swing-wing aircraft.

Test pilot "Corky" Meyers takes the prototype for a taxi test at Grumman's Bethpage plant. Later the Jaguar was shipped to Edwards for flight tests.

Grumman

The Jaguar landing after its first flight, May 19, 1952, at Edwards AFB.   *Grumman*

The Jaguar after the F9F stabilizer was installed. The XF10F-1 landing gear was raised hydraulically but lowered solely by gravity.   *Richard DeMeis*

The first true "swing-wing" airplane was the Bell X-5. This plane was patterned after a captured German fixed-wing fighter, the Messerschmitt P1101.   *Air Force*

GRUMMAN
F11F-1 TIGER

The Tiger's four 20mm cannons are seen under the air intakes. Additional armament could be carried on the four underwing pylons.   *Wayne Morris*

Although its slim appearance belies its origin from the lines of the Grumman Cougar, the F11F Tiger was actually the offspring of this earlier swept-winged fighter. In fact, its first official designation was F9F-8; but with the Navy's acquisition of the refined Cougar, this was changed to F9F-9.

The lines of the Tiger were the result of an in-depth study of a means to achieve even greater performance from the Cougar. The study was focused on four specific areas that needed modification. The large wing fillets containing the engine air inlets had to be eliminated. To accomplish this, the intakes were built into the fuselage beside the cockpit. The wing cross-section was thinned, requiring relocation of the main gear in the fuselage. Next, the fuselage was recontoured in accordance with the new area-rule principle, and the high-mounted horizontal stabilizer was lowered and fastened directly to the fuselage.

All these refinements were carefully combined into the most compact airframe possible, then a single 7,500 lb. thrust Wright J65-W-7 engine was encased within. Grumman was so successful at compressing the overall design, that only the tips of the wing

needed folding for carrier stowage—and these hinged downward. The J65 could be fitted with an afterburner, but development of this unit trailed that of the new airplane so initial flights were made without the extra power. The first flight took place on July 30, 1954, and the need for an afterburner was clear; but it was six months before one could be obtained. The afterburner brought the available thrust up to 11,200 lbs. and encouraged the Navy to order forty-four more Tigers, redesignated F11F-1's due to the extensive remodeling of the Cougar contours.

Teething problems began to appear as the trials continued. The J65 was a source of trouble and pilots brought up the age-old complaint of poor visibility. Even the improved performance with the afterburner was not considered suitable for the Tiger's role as a day fighter. By February 1955, the third prototype was subjected to some redesigning to overcome these problems. The changes were incorporated into the production models and these planes were assigned to the development program to expedite the test schedule.

The sixth production F11F-1 was delivered to the Navy early in 1955 with a

Grumman F11F-1

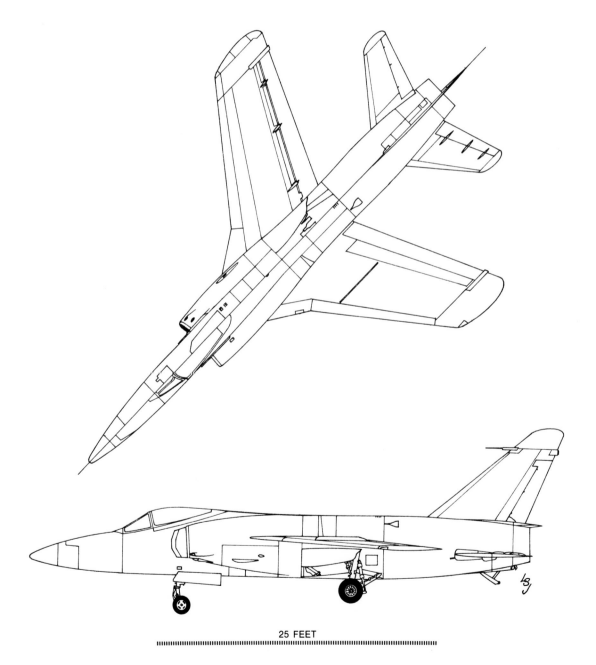

25 FEET

When the General Electric engine was installed in this Tiger, it became an F11F-1F and had a maximum speed of 1,220 mph. Only two were modified.   Grumman

slimmer fuselage and enlarged vertical tail. Their evaluation of the Tiger was discouraging. The J65 engine could not deliver adequate power to sustain supersonic speeds, one of the original contract requirements. The Navy had already ordered a second batch of F11F-1's, totaling 157 planes, in hopes of having the troubles ironed out.

The main problem was clearly in the powerplant, and two Tigers were experimentally fitted with 15,000 lb. General Electric J79-GE-3A engines. As F11F-1F's, their performance was phenomenal! During tests they reached 1,220 mph and soared upward to 79,939 feet. Unfortunately, the Tiger's small wings could not support the higher gross weight of the F11F-1F with combat gear at slow carrier approach speeds.

The Tiger passed its carrier qualification trials in April 1956, but an exceptionally high fuel consumption shortened its useful operational time. To overcome this, Grumman stuffed fuel tanks into the only remaining empty spaces—along the air intake ducts and in the vertical fin. That did the trick and the Tiger was finally accepted into the fleet on March 1957, but its marginal performance did not merit any additional contracts. The last Tigers were delivered in

December 1958. New planes with truly exceptional performance were already under test and the Tigers served on the front line until late 1959 when they were phased out to make room for the new supersonic generation. Many of the Tigers became advanced trainers before their eventual retirement. In 1962, the remaining Tigers became F-11A's.

Due to its innocuous record with the fleet, the Tiger is best known for its years of service with the Navy's Blue Angels flight demonstration team. Here, its subsonic performance was ideally suited to the team's requirements; and millions of spectators were delighted as the graceful blue Tigers flashed through the skies.

The Tiger did not have ailerons, but used large spanwise spoilers to achieve roll control. This freed the wing trailing edge for full-span flaps.

With the Wright J65-W-18 providing 7,450 lbs. of thrust (10,500 lbs. with afterburning) the F11F-1 had a maximum speed of 752 mph at sea level. Fuel capacity was 1,049 gallons for a range of 1,250 miles. Air-to-air refueling gear was eventually installed for extended ranges, actually making the earlier problem of fuel capacity academic. Service ceiling was 41,900 feet.

BuNo 138605, the second prototype Tiger. At this point the plane was designated F9F-9.   *Grumman*

The Tiger had a wingspan of 31 feet 7½ inches with 250 square feet. Length was 46 feet 11 inches and height was 13 feet 3 inches. Empty weight was 13,428 pounds, maximum gross was 24,078 pounds.

Four 20 mm cannons fired from beneath the air intakes and four air-to-air missiles could be attached to underwing hardpoints.

One of VF-33's Tigers, resplendent in yellow lightning bolts and black stars.   *Grumman*

Grumman's Tiger was the first Navy fighter to use the area-rule principle, giving the fuselage a coke-bottle shape and substantially reducing drag.
Navy

Wing up, flaps down, a Crusader crouches for a launch from the catapult of the USS Constellation CVA-64.
                                                                                        Vought

There was little doubt about the destiny of the sleek arrow-like silver fighter when it thundered across the dry desert lake called Muroc in 1955. The day was March 25, and that morning it was the center of attraction at Edwards Air Force Base in California. The Navy called it the XF8U-1, Vought called it a Crusader, and to both it was the embodiment of three-and-a-half years of design and development. At the end of its fifty-two minute test flight, it had given an indication of its superior abilities by slipping past Mach one without a quiver. The highly successful start of the Crusader's testing was a good indication of the fighter's future. It was the first carrier-based plane with a speed in excess of 1,000 mph to become operational. It earned the Collier Trophy for its design and development, won the Thompson Trophy for its speed, and was given the first Bureau of Aeronautics Certificate of Merit ever awarded.

In September 1952, the Bureau of Aeronautics chose the Vought proposal from among eight submitted for a carrier-based supersonic air-superiority fighter. It was particularly interested in Vought's at-

tention to the fighter's slow speed characteristics. Their plane used a tilting wing to increase the incidence for takeoff and landing, thus allowing the fuselage to remain level during the critical approach to the carrier deck. The prototype XF8U-1's were ordered on June 29, 1953.

Flight tests proceeded with remarkably few problems, and the first production F8U-1 flew less than six months after the prototype. The original contract authorized the assembly of 318 Crusaders and VF-32 began accepting the first ones in March 1957.

The F8U-1, later designated F-8A, used a Pratt & Whitney J57-P-4A offering 16,200 lbs. thrust with its afterburner. It carried four 20 mm cannons in its fuselage sides and thirty-two 2.75 inch missiles were concealed within a retractable launching tray in the belly.

To expand the Crusader's all-weather capabilities, a small radar scanner was located in the nose of the next 130 F8U-1E's (F-8B's). These were followed by the air superiority version F-8C's with 700 lbs. of added thrust. The 187 F-8C's are limited to

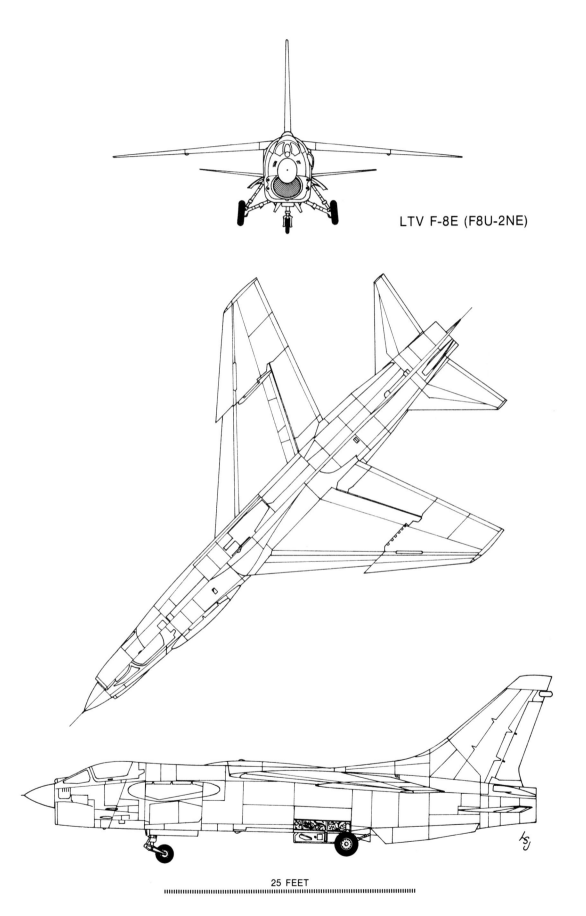

LTV F-8E (F8U-2NE)

25 FEET

Killer Crusader! This F-8E displays six kill markings on its ventral fin representing the enemy aircraft destroyed by VF-211 while deployed in Vietnam.   Vought

Mach 1.7 because of instability at higher Mach numbers, despite the addition of two ventral fins.

The F-8D traded its retractable rocket launcher for another fuel tank—152 models of this type were built. The final production version of the Crusader is the F-8E, formerly the F8U-2NE of which 286 were constructed, with the added capability of carrying external ordnance for ground-attack operations. An enlarged search and fire control radar is fitted into the nose of this Crusader, which also displays a streamlined electronics package on its back.

In September 1955, Crusaders were fitted with aerial refueling probes, but since these were retrofits, it was necessary to install the plumbing outside the fuselage and cover it with a sheet-metal fairing.

The combat effectiveness of the F-8 was put to the test in Vietnam, where it was pitted against the Russian MiG-17 and MiG-21 types. Through a combination of pilot skill and rugged construction, the Crusader emerged the superior weapon. Here, supersonic speed was not necessarily an advantage. The average speed at which combat was undertaken was 300 mph. The Crusader's 20 mm cannons and air-to-air missiles proved devastating to the lighter MiG's. By the end of the Vietnam War, 14 MiG-17's and 4 MiG-21's had been

destroyed by Crusader pilots. Credit for the final Crusader MiG kill is given to the airplane itself. Here, two Crusader pilots had chanced upon a MiG-17 near Haiphong. As the F-8's moved in for the battle, the enemy pilot donated his plane to the Allied cause and simply ejected before a shot was fired.

Total production of the Crusader came to 1,261. Four hundred forty-six of these were remanufactured and brought up to the latest F-8 configurations and redesignated F-8H, J, K and L.

The F8U-2N (F-8E) has a maximum speed of 1,120 mph (Mach 1.7) at 40,000 feet. Power comes from a Pratt & Whitney J57-P-20A with 10,700 lbs. normal thrust and 18,000 lbs. with afterburning. Service ceiling is 58,000 feet.

Wingspan and area are 35 feet 2 inches and 350 square feet. Overall length is 54 feet 6 inches, height is 15 feet 9 inches. Fully loaded, the F-8E weighs 34,000 pounds.

The excellent performance of the Crusader encouraged Vought to evolve the design further for a fighter to probe the elements at Mach 2. In 1957, the Navy awarded a development contract for three of the advanced F8U-3 "Crusader III's."

The Crusader III physically resembled the earlier F8U's, but it was actually a new aircraft. The F8U-3 was completed in April 1958. As with the XF8U-1, preliminary

The original XF8U-1 Crusader in bare metal with red trim. This plane is now part of the Smithsonian collection.   *Vought*

The F-8E is fitted with underwing racks permitting it to carry external weapons.   *Vought*

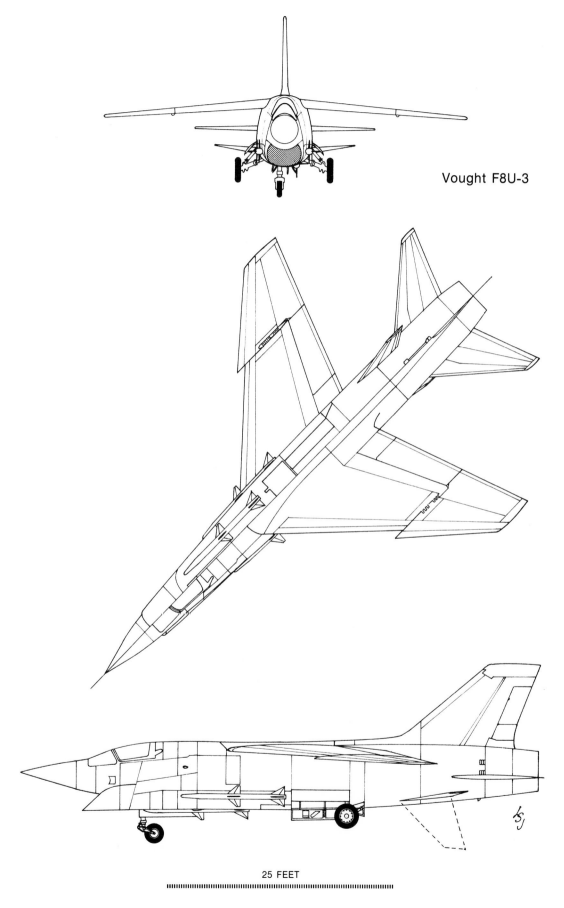

Vought F8U-3

25 FEET

flight testing was scheduled to take place at Edwards AFB, so the big fighter was airlifted in a C-124 Globemaster. That is, the fuselage was inside. The wings were bolted to the underside of the Globemaster's fuselage . . . shades of the biplane days!

The first flight (outside of the Globemaster) was made on June 2, 1958, when the Crusader III accelerated so rapidly it outdistanced the chase plane even before the gear was retracted. On June 11, the first supersonic run was made; and in August, the needle-nosed fighter pierced Mach 2. One flight took the Crusader III through a Mach 2 climb to 60,000 feet; then pulling up to a 30 degree flight angle, the F8U-3 zoomed upward. At 71,000 feet the compressor stalled and the engine shut down while the big fighter soared further upward to 75,960 feet. Unable to start the engine because of overheating from the compressor stall, pilot John Konrad glided the Crusader III back to a dead-stick landing at Edwards. The tendency for the engine to stall when the afterburner was operated was the only serious problem encountered in the test program.

The Crusader III was entered in the competition that produced the McDonnell Phantom II. Fifteen development F8U-3's were ordered, but only three were completed before the program was dropped. Two additional airframes were constructed but not assembled. All five machines were assigned to NASA for high-speed research.

The F8U-3 was termed a "push button" interceptor because of an advanced automatic flight control system. By using a "Mach Hold" button, a constant speed and climb angle could be maintained—similar to the cruise control on an automobile. Other buttons assured a constant heading, or kept the plane orbiting around a given point, as if riding on an invisible drafting compass.

The Crusader III weighed 24,928 pounds empty and had a gross of 38,772 pounds. Fuel capacity was 2,036 gallons (or 13,844 pounds). The F8U-3 had a supersonic combat ceiling of nearly 60,000 feet. Wingspan was 39 feet 11½ inches, length was 58 feet 9 inches, and height was 16 feet 4½ inches. Armament was three Sparrow III or Sidewinder missiles.

The F8U-3 powerplant was one Pratt & Whitney J75-P-4 of 17,500 lbs. thrust increasing to 23,500 lbs. with afterburning.

A Marine F-8A of VMF-232 with everything hangin' out, approaches for landing.   *Vought*

The housing over the inflight refueling gear can be seen in this view of a VMF-232 F-8A. The Red Devil emblem is visible under the wing.
                                                                                    Vought

The advanced Crusader III had a distinctive "sugar scoop" jet intake. This is similar to the scoop used on their Regulus guided missile. The folded ventral fin can be seen just behind the right main wheel. Like the F-8, the Crusader III used a hinged variable-incidence wing.
                                                                                    Vought

318

The Crusader III had several advance features and was called a "push button" interceptor. The ventral fins are lowered to improve lateral stability at high Mach numbers.   *Vought*

Three Sparrow AAM's were mounted in troughs on the F8U-3's fuselage. The nose gear is offset to the right to make room for the installation of the missile on the fuselage bottom.   *Vought*

319

McDONNELL F4H
(F-4) PHANTOM II

Family portrait. A prototype F4H-1 joins with a Demon and Banshee. Note the perforated air brakes on the Phantom wings. These were used only on the prototypes.   *McDonnell Douglas*

Seldom does one aircraft rise to such a degree of excellence that it dominates its class and crosses interservice boundaries— even on an international scale. North American's P-51 Mustang and F-86 Sabre were among this elite class; but the superlative McDonnell Phantom II has earned tributes far exceeding any other fighting plane in history. Since its appearance in 1957, it has performed in every important military action. And, more than two decades after its inception, the Phantom II is still the major first-line fighter-bomber in the ranks of the free world.

When first requested in a letter of intent, dated October 18, 1954, the new McDonnell craft was envisioned as a single-seat attack bomber and ground support machine. In this respect, it was designated AH-1 and two examples were ordered. Within a year, however, the mission was changed. Now the Navy wanted a far-ranging high-altitude interceptor relying solely on air-to-air missiles for armament. An advanced intercept radar to be included would require the addition of a second crewman. With the change in combat roles came the fighter designation,

F4H-1, and a contract for 23 service test vehicles. The DOD order later changed the Phantom II to the F-4—and the first machines became F-4A's.

Initially, the Phantom II had what could be considered an orthodox layout. It was a twin-jet two-place monoplane with swept wings and tail surfaces. First flown on May 27, 1958, the Phantom II soon underwent a dramatic metamorphosis that would lead to its phenomenal career. Preliminary testing indicated the need for an increase of three degrees of wing dihedral. To accomplish this would necessitate a complete redesign of the wing and landing gear retraction system. The designers determined that tilting the outer wing panels upward twelve degrees would give the same results. At the same time, the chord of these panels was increased to eliminate premature wingtip stalling. The vertical tail area was enlarged; and to place the horizontal stabilizers out of the wing downwash, they were angled downward 23 degrees. It was thus that the new Phantom took on a distinctive character of its own.

The first deliveries of the Phantom ab-

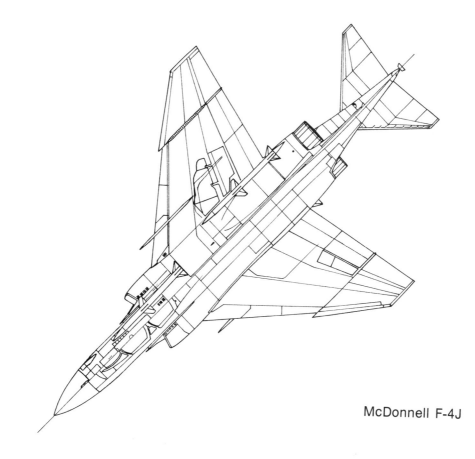

McDonnell F-4J

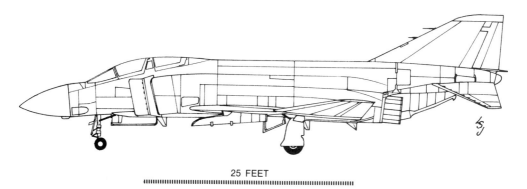

25 FEET

The early F4H-1 Phantoms had low canopies and small radomes, as shown by this example.

McDonnell Douglas

A reconniassance RF-4B peels away from a group of Marine F-4N's.

Harry Gann

F-4B Phantoms from Marine squadron VMF(AW)531.   *McDonnell Douglas*

sorbed the order for the original AH-1's, those becoming part of the first 23 F4H-1's. These aircraft were used in the development program and appeared with progressively enlarged nose radomes as larger radar antennas were mounted. By the nineteenth F4H-1, the antenna diameter had grown from 24 inches to 32 inches; and the cockpit canopy was raised for better visibility.

During its test phase, the Phantom began breaking records. It established two closed-course records of 1,390.21 mph for 100 km., and 1,216 mph for 200 km. And to show how high it could climb, a record altitude of 98,557 feet was reached. On November 22, 1961, the Phantom pushed the world's official absolute speed to 1,665.89 mph, thus becoming the second Navy fighter to hold that coveted record.

In February 1960, the Phantom became carrier qualified. Transitional crew training began with VF-121 a year later, followed soon by the first Marine squadron, VMF-314. By 1966, twenty-nine squadrons were flying the F-4B, the first major Navy version of the Phantom.

Since the performance of the Navy's new fighter had clearly outdistanced the equivalent Air Force types, the USAF undertook a direct comparison between the Phan-

tom and the Convair F-106, their own standard bearer. The results gave the F-4 higher points in load carrying, range, radar effectiveness, and ease of maintenance. These results proved conclusively the superiority of the Navy's fighter, and it was promptly ordered as the Air Force F-110 Spectre. On delivery, they were classed as F-4C Phantoms. The acquisition of the Phantom by the USAF also added another feature to all subsequent F-4's—wider main tires which necessitated bulging the wings at the roots.

The F-4B was the first major production model to reach the Navy. Several of these had extended noses carrying a battery of cameras and were classified as RF-4B's for use by the Marines. On a typical intercept mission, an F-4B with four heat-seeking Sidewinders can attain a speed of Mach 2.4. This version, with two General Electric J79-GE-8 engines of 17,000 lbs. of afterburning thrust can accelerate from Mach 0.92 to Mach 2.2 in 3.5 minutes. That amounts to some 1,450 mph. Over five hundred F-4B's were delivered to the Navy. They are guided by an APQ-72 fire control system which locates the target, tracks the prey, and sets up the attack. The system is jam-proof and also has a ground mapping mode. The F-4B has a combat altitude in excess of 60,000 feet.

The F-4B was the first major production version of the Phantom II. It can be distinguished by the infrared sensor under the nose radome.
Harry Gann

Just a small part of the Phantom's load-carrying ability is shown here. The Phantom can haul up to 16,000 pounds of ordnance.
McDonnell Douglas

VMFA 323, the Death Rattlers, trimmed their Phantoms in brown and yellow. This one is up-graded F-4N, a rebuilt F-4B.
Harry Gann

RF-4B Phantoms are used for aerial surveillance by the Marine Corps. These planes belong to VMFP-3 and VMCJ-1.
McDonnell Douglas

The second major production Phantom for the Navy is the F-4J. This is readily identifiable by the absence of the small infrared sensor under the radome. These Phantoms use J79-GE-10 engines and feature many refinements, some of which were offshoots of the Air Force types. The Navy has also received 178 F-4N's, reworked from F-4B's.

The Phantom's unequalled versatility in the role of fighter, bomber, interceptor, reconnaissance, and even research, has taken it to all parts of the globe. F-4's of one type or another are used as front-line equipment in Israel, England, Germany, Japan and Iran. The success of the Phantom is even more amazing when you consider it was originally designed under the very strict requirements for a carrier-operated fighter. The Phantom's performance would certain-

ly class it as one of the most significant fighting machines in aviation history.

The Navy's F-4J has a wingspan of 38 feet 5 inches; wing area is 530 square feet. Length is 58 feet 3 inches and height is 16 feet 5½ inches. Empty weight is 29,000 pounds, maximum takeoff weight reaches 59,000 pounds. Two General Electric afterburning J79-GE-10's give the F-4J 35,800 lbs. of total thrust for a speed of 1,584 mph (Mach 2.4) at 48,000 feet. Initial climb rate is 30,000 fpm. Service ceiling is 70,000 feet.

The F-4J is equipped to make automatic carrier landings, among its other talents. The Phantom was the first production Navy fighter to dispense with guns as part of its built-in armament. Troughs are designed into the F-4's fuselage to hold four Sparrow missiles, and under-wing pylons can carry a wide variety of rockets and bombs. These

This black-tailed F-4N is assigned to VF-51 on the USS Coral Sea.
Harry Gann

fixtures can carry up to 16,000 pounds of conventional or nuclear weapons.

The latest models of the F-4 are fitted with new automatic maneuvering, or combat, slats to increase its dogfighting capabilities. These flaps change the wing chamber to increase lift during tight turns, and are being retrofitted to earlier F-4's to increase their already potent capability.

Aside from the Blue Angels, this is probably the most photographed Phantom there is. Based at Pt. Mugu, the all-black Phantom is a featured performer at the annual Space Fair. It is shown here before it received a white "bunny" on its tail.   *Harry Gann*

The most famous of all, the renowned Blue Angels. The Blues flew these F-4J's several years before moving to the A-4 Skyhawk.   *Harry Gann*

A pair of VF-101's "Grim Reaper" F-4J's.   *Harry Gann*

DOUGLAS
F6D-1 MISSILEER

This painting depicts the Douglas F6D-1 Missileer with six AAM-N-10 Eagle missiles.   *Douglas*

In an age of sleek Mach 2+ aircraft, a proposal for a straight-winged blunt-nosed fighter seems anachronistic. But the proposal for which the **Douglas Missileer** was developed envisioned the aircraft as a flying launch pad instead of a combat machine. In fact, no defensive armament even appears to have been considered for the plane. Its sole purpose in being was to launch six Grumman Eagle long-range air-to-air missiles in the direction of a distant attacker. The missiles themselves were considered the interceptors.

Development contracts for the Eagle missile and its airborne control center were awarded by the Navy on December 5, 1958. Bendix was to develop a long-range interceptor missile for fleet defense, a type now known as "Stand-off" missiles. On July 21, 1961, Douglas won a lengthy competition to design an airframe around the Bendix system and build two prototypes as the XF6D-1.

The AAM-N-10 Eagle was developed by Bendix with the construction of the airframe to be carried out by Grumman. Six of these weapons were to be carried under the wings of the Missileer. On a typical operation, the F6D-1 would be launched from a carrier and fly out to a patrol zone about 150 miles distant. Here, it would loiter at an altitude of 35,000 feet for ten hours. Should it become necessary to launch an Eagle, the missile would accelerate to Mach 4 and climb to 100,000 feet seeking its prey. A lock-on cruise and homing radar guidance system would then direct the Eagle toward its goal—up to 100 miles from the launch point. The Eagle was 20 feet long and weighed approximately 2,000 pounds. It could carry either conventional or nuclear explosives.

The Douglas Company proceeded with the design and development of the Missileer and received an order for 120 F6D-1's—worth about six million dollars. But due to a reevaluation of the "Stand-off" concept, the contracts were withdrawn on April 25, 1961, before any prototype construction had begun.

The F6D-1 Missileer would have had a wingspan of 70 feet with an area of 630 square feet. Length would have been 53 feet and the height 18 feet 1 inch. The tip of the fin could be folded to reduce the height to 16 feet 3 inches for stowage below decks. Gross weight was to be 60,000 pounds. Two TF-30-T-2 turbofans by Pratt & Whitney were to power the Missileer with a total of 16,500 lbs. thrust. This would give a maximum speed of 543 mph. The F6D-1 was to be operated by a crew of two.

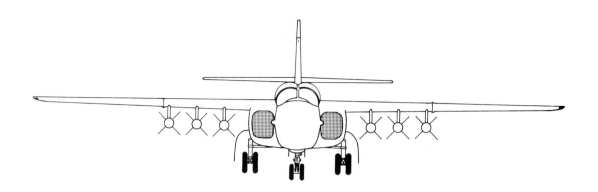

Douglas F6D-1

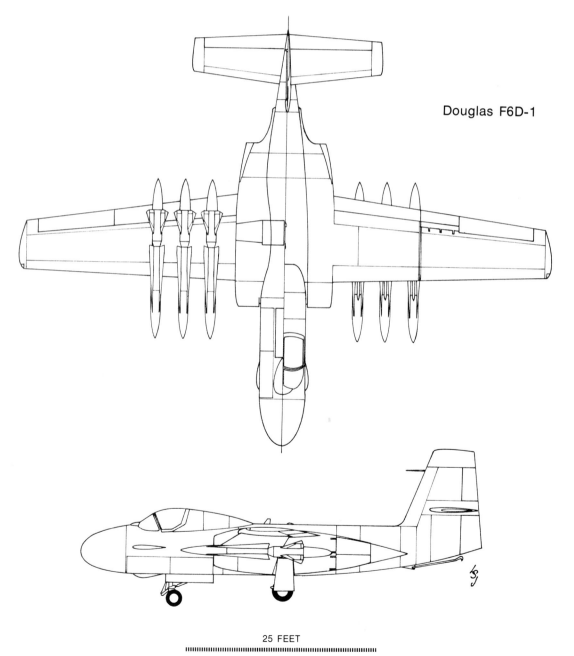

25 FEET

GENERAL DYNAMICS/GRUMMAN
F-111B

Two F-111B's showing the extemes of the wing positions.   **General Dynamics**

As we have seen, the criteria for a successful Navy carrier fighter is dependent upon a clearly defined set of qualifications revolving around its ability to operate from an aircraft carrier. Most assuredly, the development of the carrier is also influenced by airframe progress as well. As an example of the latter, the high gross weights of the jet fighters dictated the installation of steam catapults for safe launches. Also, the higher landing speeds brought about the angled carrier deck. But even these new features brought with them new and specific parameters for future aircraft development. Thus, the stage was set for the Navy's participation in the TFX program.

The TFX was unique in its original concept. It represented the first time a single airplane was to be designed from the outset for both the Navy and the Air Force. On the surface, it appeared to be practical and economically sound. But it overlooked the wide discrepancy between the operational requirements of the two services. When first presented with the commonality concept, both services rejected the plan. It was physically impossible to build an airplane

that was adequate for such diverse missions.

Despite the protests, the requirements for the TFX (Tactical Fighter-Experimental) were drawn up. It is interesting to note that it was the Air Force who was asked to develop the details; and they were told simply that the basic airplane must be able to operate from a carrier. General Dynamics and Grumman were declared winners of a heated competition.

The Navy plane, designated F-111B, would have long wings for slow carrier approaches, and a short nose to allow for a larger radar dish. The two planes would otherwise share 84 percent of the overall structure which featured variable-sweep wings. General Dynamics would build the Air Force's F-111A and Grumman would be responsible for the Navy plane.

The F-111B flew on May 18, 1965; and, although the Air Force machine had shown some promise, the compromises to which the Navy had yielded were to plague the Navy fighter throughout its test program. Seven F-111B's were constructed and their performance as carrier fighters was not acceptable. In 1968, the political furor over the F-

329

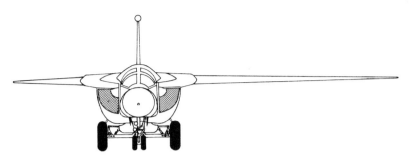

Grumman-General
Dynamics F-111B

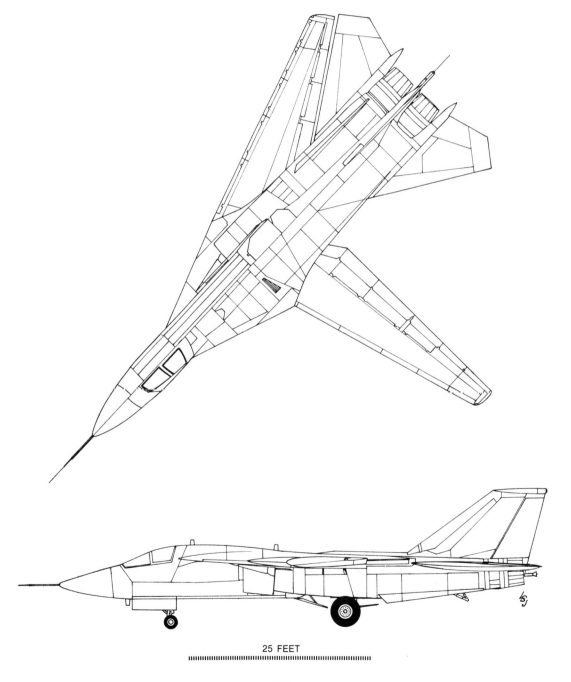

25 FEET

The F-111B compromised too much to the dual-service concept to be of value to the Navy. General Dynamics

The emblem on the tail of this F-111B signifies its use as a participant in the Phoenix Missile program.
General Dynamics

331

Four AIM-54A Phoenix missiles are fastened to swiveling pylons on this F-111B.   **General Dynamics**

111 program prompted Congress to refuse further funding for the Navy version of the fighter.

On the other hand, the F-111A and its derivatives have gone on to a successful operational life with the Air Force and they are now considered outstanding weapons.

The wings of the F-111B could move from a fully-forward leading edge sweep of 16 degrees back to 72.5 degrees giving the plane a delta planform. Since much of the wing trailing edge was inside the fuselage when swept back, there were no ailerons. Roll control was achieved by deploying spoilers on top of the wing. These were fully operational when the wing was forward, but as sweep-back increased, they were progressively locked out. When fully swept, roll function was handled by the stabilators working differentially.

The two crewmen were seated side by side in an ejectable cockpit capsule. The capsule was self-stabilizing and was lowered to earth by a parachute system.

Two 20,250 lb. thrust Pratt & Whitney TF-30-P-12A afterburning turbofans provided Mach 2 performance for the F-111B. It had an extended wingspan of 70 feet and swept span of 33 feet 10 inches. Length was 66 feet 8 inches and it was 16 feet 8 inches high. Empty weight was 47,278 pounds; maximum gross weight approached 70,000 pounds. It was this factor that contributed greatly to the unsuitability of the F-111B for carrier service. Armament was intended to be six AIM-54A Phoenix missiles.

In 1954, the Navy placed a letter of intent with McDonnell that was to lead to the creation of the F4H-1 Phantom II. Another company competing for the production of the twin-engine two-place interceptor was Grumman with their Model 118. Two Bureau Numbers, 143401 and 02 were assigned to the Grumman project, but the XF12F-1 did not proceed beyond the blueprint stage.

According to the proposal, the XF12F-1 had some interesting features. One of them concerned the crew accommodations. To permit entrance to the fighter, the two seats would be lowered and the crew would mount them to be elevated upward into the cockpit. In the event of an emergency requiring abandonment of the aircraft, the entire nose section forward of the wing would be jettisoned. The inboard segments of the wing leading edge were attached to this escape capsule and would serve as stabilizers as the capsule decelerated. The escape capsule would be lowered by parachute to earth and the crew would then exit through hatches over their seats.

The armament arrangement also was of interest. The XF12F-1 was to be armed solely with missiles, as was the original Phantom II. Troughs were designed into the lower fuselage sides which would permit the installation of three Sparrow AAM's. One was located on the center-line amidship, the other two fitted on either side of the center-line just behind the cockpit. Normally, the missiles were mounted flush with the horizontal fins against the fuselage bottom. For firing, the forward missiles would swing downward on a trapeze and allow a 10 inch clearance between the fins and the fuselage. The aft missile was to be installed in a retractable box which would also be lowered for firing. Alternatively, three Sidewinders could be carried within the box, replacing the centerline Sparrow. An APQ-50 fire control radar scanner was to be installed in the nose for target interception.

Power was to be obtained from a pair of General Electric J79-GE-3 units of 15,600 lbs. thrust with afterburners. This was to be supplemented by a 5,000 lb. thrust throttleable rocket engine. Production F12F-1's would use J79-GE-207 turbojets with 18,000 lbs. of afterburning thrust. Estimated performance was in excess of Mach 2 at a ceiling above 60,000 feet. For high-speed stability, two ventral fins were mounted to the aft fuselage. These folded inward against the fuselage bottom when the landing gear was extended.

The proposed F12F-1 was to weigh 26,355 pounds empty; combat weight is given as 37,300 pounds, and maximum takeoff weight would be 46,510 pounds. Wingspan was 43 feet 11 inches with an area of 595 square feet. Overall length was 58 feet 6 inches; height was 14 feet 10 inches.

No ailerons were used—their functions were to be performed by a pair of "flaperons" (spoilers) in the wing. Leading and trailing edge flaps were also incorporated into the design. The elevator functions were performed by a slab-type stabilator near the top of the vertical fin.

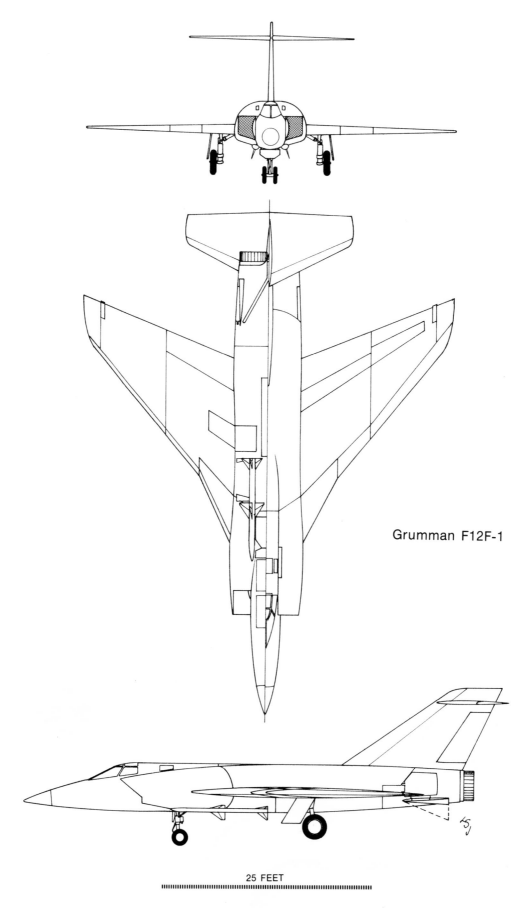

Grumman F12F-1

25 FEET

GRUMMAN F-14A
TOMCAT

VF-2 was one of the first squadrons to receive the Tomcat. The red, white and blue band under the cockpit is called the Langley stripe, and was applied to the first planes assigned to the USS Langley in the 1920's.

Grumman

Since the F-111B had failed to qualify as a carrier fighter, a new competition was begun to select its successor. The requirements did not specify variable-geometry wings, but Grumman's experience with the XF10F-1 Jaguar and ill-fated F-111B gave them considerable experience in this field. Taking advantage of this background, Grumman proposed the feature on their Model 303; and on January 15, 1969, six examples were ordered as the F-14A, the Navy's new air superiority fighter.

The prototype F-14A was completed by the end of 1970 and christened Tomcat—an appropriate appellation since it was intended to be a dogfighter. The F-14A made its first flight on December 21, 1970—a full month ahead of schedule. However, the program suffered a setback when the hydraulic system failed on the second flight and the first F-14 was lost. This flight did prove successful in one respect. The ejection system performed flawlessly!

The second Tomcat resumed the interrupted tests on May 24, 1971. Progress was so rapid that introduction to the fleet took place on October 12, 1972, when VF-1 and VF-2 received their first planes.

During comparative tests between the F-14A and the F-4 with combat slats, the Tomcat easily bested the Phantom. The smoothly curved fuselage back creates additional lift allowing the F-14 to be pulled into steep angles of attack. With the wings fully swept, the Tomcat's nose can be pulled up vertically, seemingly hovering on its jet thrust. It is virtually unstallable and resists any tendency to spin.

A pair of retractable vanes, mounted in the leading edge of the wing glove, extend outward for added stability as required. The action of the triangular vanes is controlled by computer, as is the wing positioning, and both operate in conjunction as determined by the operating conditions.

Combat experience in Vietnam clearly defined the need for cannon armament in a fighter involved in plane-to-plane combat. Although the need for missiles is undisputed, Vietnam brought the relative values of the two weapons into perspective. The result is the return to an internally-mounted cannon on the Tomcat. This, an M61A-1 20 mm rotary cannon, is located in the port side of the fuselage beneath the cockpit. Four Phoenix AIM-54A missiles

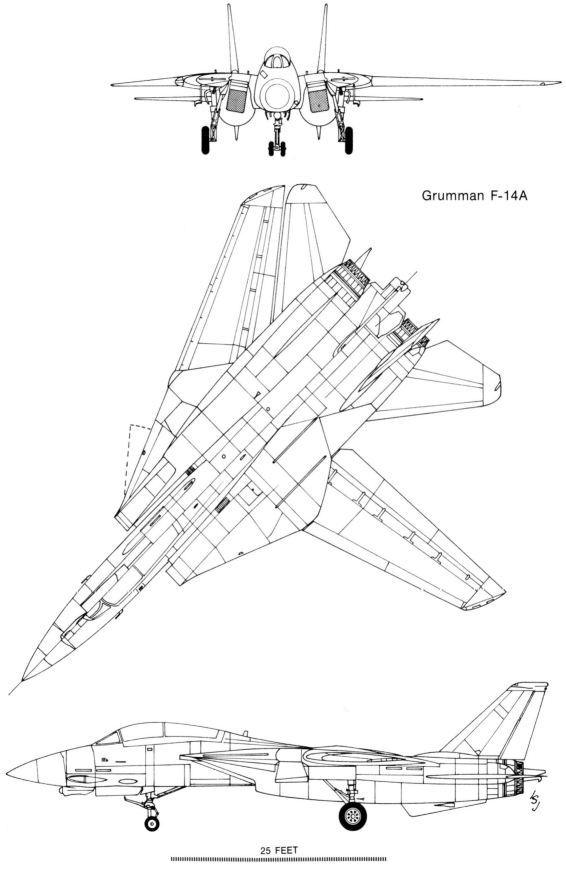

Grumman F-14A

25 FEET

The Tomcats flown by VF-1 bear bright red stripes and tail trim, denoting their membership in the "Wolf-pack."   *Grumman*

An F-14 of VF-124 in the high-speed configuration.   *Grumman*

can be mounted on pylons beneath the engines. These can be launched singly or simultaneously, each one directed to a different target. Since all the hard points are located on the fixed glove, no swiveling pylons are required.

The Tomcat's two Pratt & Whitney TF30-P-412 turbofans are housed in nacelles alongside the fuselage. These are rated at 20,900 lbs. with afterburning and push the F-14 to over 1,500 mph (Mach 2.34). Internal fuel capacity is 16,445 pounds of the Tomcat's 65,000 gross takeoff weight. Empty weight is 40,070 pounds.

The variable-sweep wing moves from 20 degrees to 68 degrees while in flight; but for carrier stowage, it can be overswept to 75 degrees. With the wing fully forward, stall speed is 90 mph. Flaps form the entire trailing edge of the wing. Roll control is obtained from spoilers working with the stabilators in the low-sweep mode, but with the wings fully aft, the stabilators handle the entire function.

In order to keep the overall height of the F-14 low enough for below deck storage yet retain sufficient keel area, two vertical stabilizers are used. The placement of these also counteract the unstable air flowing over the intake lips at high attack angles.

The maximum span of the F-14 is 64 feet 1½ inches with an area of 565 square feet. Normal sweep-back reduces the span to 38 feet 2 inches; but oversweep for deck handling gives the Tomcat a width of only 33 feet 3½ inches. Overall length is 61 feet 11½ inches and height is 16 feet.

Pratt & Whitney's 28,096 lb. F401-PW-400 turbofan engines were mounted in two Tomcats to become F-14B's. Although the Navy had ordered the F-14B as a follow-on to the F-14A, delays in the engine development led to their cancellation.

The F-14A Tomcat is the Navy's strong arm into the 1980's. It is the most sophisticated fighter ever to become a part of the Navy inventory. *Grumman*

Climbing away from the deck is an F-14A carrying a Phoenix missile on a pallet beneath the fuselage.
Grumman

McDONNELL DOUGLAS
F-18 HORNET

The McDonnell F-18 Hornet was developed from the Northrop contender in the USAF's lightweight fighter competition in 1975.
Northrop

With the McDonnell F-18 air combat fighter, the Navy is adding a new dimension to its combat capability. With the Phantom and Tomcat, the carrier force has the heaviest, most complex, and most expensive, albeit the fastest, fighters in its history. With the F-18, they will have a combat weapon that combines the attack capabilities of the LTV A-7 Corsair II with the dogfighting features of the F-4 Phantom II. This will be in a package sized between the two, and at a relatively low price. The F-18 has been developed to replace both of these aircraft by offering superior performance in both roles.

There are several advantages to this approach. The most obvious is a reduction of the number of aircraft on the carrier deck. But it also reduces the amount, and therefore cost, of spare parts, personnel training, and support equipment.

The F-18 is an adaptation of Northrop's YF-17 which came up second best in the Air Force's lightweight fighter competition held in 1975. The Navy felt a twin-engine plane was more suited to its needs, so they in turn rejected the winning single engine General Dynamics F-16.

To make the Northrop fighter conform to the Navy's specifications, the wing area was increased and the landing gear redesigned to absorb the impact of hard carrier landings. Further refinements in the airframe were made to improve the F-18's aerodynamic characteristics.

The F-18 program began on January 22, 1976, with an order for 11 test aircraft. The first flight has been scheduled for July, 1978. Production of 800 units is planned for completion by 1990.

Basically a derivative of the Northrop P-530 Cobra, the F-18 features a forward-sweeping fillet extending almost to the nose. This sets up a controlled vortex over the wing. Slots in this fillet allow the boundary air to bleed upward before reaching the engine inlets. Two vertical stabilizers, located on the upper edges of the fuselage, are canted outward into the free airstream.

The F-18 features a variable-camber wing to provide maximum lift during combat maneuvers and carrier landing approaches. The leading edge drops in conjunction with slotted trailing edge flaps and drooping ailerons. The positioning of the movable parts is determined by the aircraft's angle of

McDonnell F-18

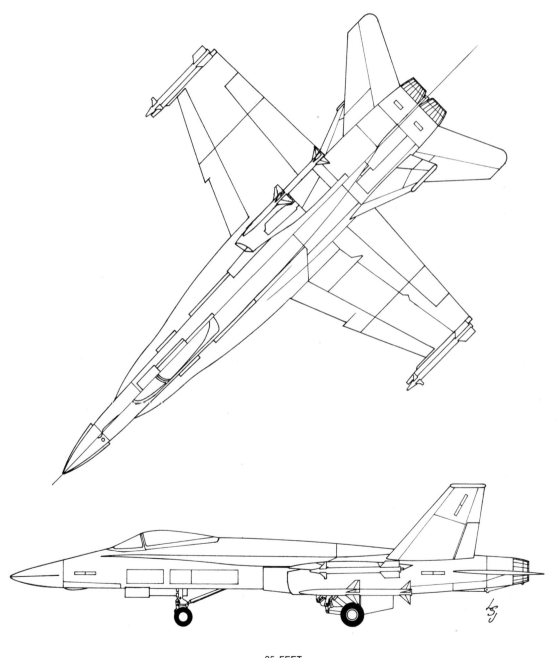

25 FEET

This rendering shows the F-18 Navy fighter of the 1980's.   *McDonnell Douglas*

The F-18 has been designed as a replacement for the Phantom and Corsair II, offering an improved performance in the fighter and attack categories.
McDonnell Douglas

attack and Mach number.

The F-18 and its avionics are designed for one-man operation. For air-to-air combat, the F-18 will carry two Sidewinders on wingtip rails, two Sparrows on the fuselage sides, and a 20 mm M61 six barrel rotary cannon in the nose. Ordnance for attack missions would be mounted on five hardpoints and the Sparrows would be replaced by FLIR and LST pods. Total ordnance capacity is 13,700 pounds.

Two General Electric F404-GE-400 low bypass turbofans of 16,000 lbs. thrust are employed to give the F-18 a 1-to-1 power to weight ratio during combat. Takeoff gross weight is 33,500 pounds. The F-18 has a wingspan of 40 feet 8 inches including the tip-mounted Sidewinders. Wing area is 448 square feet. Length is 56 feet and the fin tips are 15 feet 4 inches from the deck.

Delivery of the first F-18 is anticipated in 1980 with the new fighter entering both Navy and Marine squadrons by 1981. The contract for the F-18 provides for a two-seat training version. Two of these are to be delivered for every eleven single-seaters produced.

TYPICAL COLOR SCHEMES APPLIED
TO U.S. NAVY FIGHTERS

Marine Corps color schemes have paralleled those of the Navy. This Marine Boeing FB-1 has added embellishments of red and white tail stripes plus U.S. MARINES across the top of the yellow wing.
Boeing

As the overall design of Navy fighters has evolved through the years, so have the color schemes which have been applied to them. It is particularly important to know the colors for the accurate reproduction of these planes in model form or for illustrations depicting events in which these aircraft participated. Much information regarding color schemes has already been documented by such outstanding organizations as the American Aviation Historical Society (AAHS) and the International Plastic Modelers Society (IPMS). For more detailed information about specific aircraft, we would refer you to these organizations.

In the following material we have described, type by type, the most common exterior color schemes used on each aircraft during its service life. Interior colors are more difficult to trace on an individual basis. Generally, they were either silver or light gray during the biplane era, chromate green during World War II, and black or light gray in the postwar types.

The numbers following the colors are Federal Standard codes which identify each specific shade. Books containing chips of these official colors with their identifying code numbers can be obtained from the Government Printing Office for a nominal fee.

National insignia is well documented and the information is readily available to those interested. Therefore, unless a unique situation is noted, we have not discussed this facet of markings. The official colors are insignia red FS 11105, insignia white FS 17875 and insignia blue FS 15044.

Lettering is black on light colors and white on dark colors, unless otherwise specified.

From the mid 1930's, each aircraft carrier was assigned an identifying color. This color was painted on the tail surfaces of every plane based on the carrier. (Prior to this time, solid colors were used to identify planes in a given squadron regardless of the carrier assignment.) The carrier colors were:

CV-2 Lexington = Lemon yellow FS 13655
CV-3 Saratoga = White FS 17875
CV-4 Ranger = Willow green FS 14817
CV-5 Yorktown = Insignia red FS 11136
CV-6 Enterprise = True blue FS 15102
CV-7 Wasp = Black FS 17038

To further identify the position of each plane within the squadrons, these same shades were used by all the squadrons, (regardless of carrier assignment) on the engine cowlings, for wing formating chevrons and fuselage bands. Only the tail color indicated the carrier to which a plane was attached.

Planes tested at Anacostia were often highly polished like the XFF-1 shown here.   Gordon S. Williams

A Navy squadron was comprised of six sections of three planes each. Every plane carried its section color on the nose and wings and carrier color on its tail. Only the lead plane in each section carried a colored band entirely around the fuselage. All squadrons used the same color system.

Section colors were as follows:
1st Section = Insignia red
2nd Section = White
3rd Section = True blue

4th Section = Black
5th Section = Willow green
6th Section = Lemon yellow

The planes in the squadron were numbered 1 to 18. These numbers were preceded by the squadron number, and, in the case of fighters, the letter F. For example, the seventh fighter in VF-5 would carry the code 5-F-7 on the fuselage. Since it was the lead plane in the third section, 5-F-7 would have a true blue cowling, wing

This Curtiss BFC-2 displays the color scheme which was standard on Navy fighters through the 1930's. Propeller tips were red with yellow and blue stripes as seen here. Note the yellow of the top wing can barely be seen in this view, but often wrapped around the leading edge for a few inches.   Gordon S. Williams

chevron and fuselage band. The second plane in the section would have only the top half of the cowling painted and the third plane would have the bottom half of the cowling painted. Both of these planes would have the wing chevrons in the section color, in this case true blue.

In the early 1920's, Navy and Marine fighters were painted overall with silver lacquer. Later, as the use of aluminum paneling increased, metal parts were painted light gray. This period also saw the introduction of chrome yellow upper wing surfaces. The entire top surface of the upper wing, including the controls, was painted this shade as an aid to visibility. The yellow was carried over the leading edge of the wing and extended underneath the front edge about 6 inches.

With the outbreak of war, several types of camouflage paint schemes appeared, but only two types were used to any extent on Navy fighters. These were the two-color and three-color designs. The former consisted of matt blue-gray on the top surfaces with the undersides painted matt light gray. The tricolor pattern used matt sea blue on the upper surfaces with matt intermediate sea blue on the fuselage sides. The entire underside of the plane was finished in matt white.

With the end of World War II, Navy and Marine fighters appeared in a coat of glossy sea blue. Aircraft finished in this manner had the blue deleted from the U.S. national insignia since the insignia blue was so close in value it was virtually invisible anyway.

By the early 1950's some of the Navy's jet fighters were tested with a layer of clear paint over the bare metal. Aluminum has a tendency to corrode when exposed to salt water and spray so it was necessary to have some protection. The main advantage was in the lighter weight of the unpigmented paint. This experiment was short-lived, however, and by the mid 'fifties gull gray and white had become the standard Navy and Marine fighter finish. In this scheme, all upper surfaces, except the movable controls, were painted matt gull gray. The undersides were painted glossy white, as were the top surfaces of the movable controls, and usually both sides of the rudder.

Following are the Federal Standard numbers for the more common colors mentioned in the accompanying color descriptions for each aircraft.

Light gray	FS 16376
Chrome yellow	FS 13538
Insignia red	FS 11105
Matt light blue-gray	FS 36118
Matt sea blue	FS 35042

In this picture of an F9C-2 Sparrowhawk, the formating stripe is visible on the top wing. The stripes on the Sparrowhawk differed from those on most other Navy fighters in that the "V" converged at the trailing edge. Normally the "V" joined at the leading edge.   Lowell Dixon

Matt intermediate sea blue	FS 35164
Matt white	FS 37875
Glossy sea blue	FS 15042
Matt gull gray	FS 36440
Chromate green (interior)	FS 34151

Vought VE-7
  Fabric surfaces: Aluminum lacquer.
  Metal surfaces: Light gray.
Curtiss TS-1
  Fabric surfaces: Aluminum lacquer.
  Metal surfaces: Light gray.
Curtiss racers (R2C and R3C)
  Fuselage and struts: Royal blue similar to FS 16817.
  Wings and tail: Chrome yellow (R3C had blue fin).
  Radiators: Brass
  Floats: Gray, possibly FS 16817.
  Navy emblem: Gold disc with dark blue details.
Wright NW-1 and NW-2
  Overall: Aluminum lacquer, except metal cowl, landing gear struts and floats, which were gray, possibly FS 16817.
  Radiators: Brass
Wright F2W-1
  Fuselage: Insignia red.
  Radiators: Brass.
  Spinner: Natural aluminum.
  All other surfaces: Glossy White.

Wright F2W-2
  Radiators: Brass.
  Entire airplane: Medium blue similar to FS 15105, except rudder, which had not been painted and remained in natural linen.
  Spinner: Natural aluminum.
  Racing number: White with black outline.
Curtiss F4C-1
  Overall: Aluminum lacquer.
  Top of upper wing: Chrome yellow.
Boeing FB
  Metal surfaces: Light gray.
  Fabric surfaces: Aluminum lacquer.
  Top of upper wing: Chrome yellow.
Wright F3W
  Fuselage: Aluminum lacquer.
  Metal panels: Natural metal.
  Wing and tail surfaces: Aluminum lacquer.
  Top of upper wing: Chrome yellow.
  During the altitude record flights the wing and tail surfaces appeared to be white and no insignia was carried.
Curtiss F6C
  From 1925 the Navy color scheme was standardized through the end of the biplane era. The F6C and subsequent biplanes were decorated in this manner. Unless otherwise mentioned, the remaining biplane fighters were painted as follows:
  Fabric surfaces: Aluminum lacquer.

Here is an overall gray F2A-2 Buffalo. This scheme appeared just before World War II.

Gordon S. Williams

Here is a factory-fresh F4F-7 wearing matt blue-gray and light gray early in 1942. The red dot in the insignia was deleted after May 15, 1942.   *Grumman*

Metal surfaces: Light gray.
Top of upper wing: Chrome yellow.
Tail surfaces: Color of assigned carrier.
Cowling, fuselage strip and wing chevrons: Section color.

Eberhart XFG
Fabric surfaces: Aluminum lacquer.
Metal surfaces: Light gray.
Top of upper wing: Chrome yellow.
Comanche emblem: Red and black.

Boeing XF5B
Fuselage: Medium blue, similar to FS 15180.
Wings, struts and tail surfaces: Chrome yellow with medium blue trim around tail surfaces.

Seversky NF-1
Overall bare metal.

Brewster F2A
Initially, the F2A received the standard scheme of light gray overall with chrome yellow upper wing surfaces. Shortly before World War II an overall light gray, FS 36493, was adopted. Some F2A's were painted matt blue-gray, FS 36118, on the upper surfaces while the undersides remained light gray.

Grumman F4F
The prototype, and early production Wildcats received the standard scheme. However, before the F4F went into combat this scheme had been abandoned, and Wildcats were painted overall light gray FS 36493. By early 1942 the top surfaces were being painted matt blue-gray with the light gray remaining on the undersides. Wildcats in service in 1943 were subject to the tri-color scheme of matt sea blue on top, intermediate blue on the fuselage sides fore and aft of the wings and on the vertical surfaces, and matt white on the undersides. Any F4F's in use after the war were colored glossy sea blue overall.

Bell XFL
Overall aluminum lacquer except chrome yellow wing top surface.

Grumman XF5F
Originally aluminum lacquer overall with chrome yellow wing tops. This scheme remained until sometime after the modifications were made when the camouflage blue-gray and light gray colors were applied.

Vought F4U
Prototype: Overall aluminum lacquer with chrome yellow wing tops. First production models: Matt light blue-gray upper sides, matt light gray on the bottom. The undersides of the folding wing panels were light blue-gray. Later models received the three-color camouflage with the top surfaces matt sea blue, sides and lower folding wing panels in intermediate sea blue with the remainder of the bottom matt white. On night fighter F4U-2's the fuselage sides were matt black. By the end of the war the F4U's were painted glossy sea blue overall.

Curtiss XF14C
Overall matt grayish-white similar to FS 37722.
Diving figure on cowling: Insignia red.

Grumman F6F

Prototype: Bare metal.

Most of the production Hellcats were finished in the tri-color camouflage. After the war, an overall coat of glossy sea blue became standard. Remote-controlled drone Hellcats were painted glossy chrome yellow or insignia red overall.

Grumman F7F

Prototype: Bare metal.

Production Tigercats were painted glossy sea blue overall.

Boeing F8B

First airframe: Glossy sea blue.

Second and third F8B's were bare metal.

Grumman F8F

Overall glossy sea blue.

Vought V173

Aluminum lacquer on all surfaces except top of circular wing, which was chrome yellow.

Vought XF5U

Overall glossy sea blue.

Bugs Bunny emblem: Gray bunny with white cheeks and stomach. Orange carpet with yellow fringe. Pale blue sky with white clouds. Carrot in bunny's hand was orange with green top. The entire design was detailed in black. A red ring encircled the background.

Propellers were natural wood finished in clear gloss.

Lockheed FO-1 (P-38)

Reportedly natural metal with Bureau

This close-up view of an F4U-1C shows the application of the tri-color scheme. The top is sea blue, the area behind the number is medium blue and the undersides are white. Note the sea blue under the folding wing sections. This area was sometimes intermediate blue.   *Vought*

Numbers painted in black on outside of vertical stabilizers.

Bell F2L (Airacobra)
No information regarding colors has been found.

Lockheed P-80
Overall glossy pearl gray, slightly lighter than FS 16492.

Northrop F2T

Overall glossy black, somewhat dulled by age.

Ryan FR-1
Overall glossy sea blue.

Ryan XF2R
Overall glossy black.

Curtiss XF15C
Overall glossy sea blue.
The name "Stingaree" was painted on the

Lt. Donald Balch grins at his good fortune after an encounter with the Japanese. His F4U-1 is blue-gray and gray, but repairs and the corrosive effects of the weather have given the paint a blotchy look.   *Vought*

cowling in yellow on the first prototype.

McDonnell FH-1
Overall glossy sea blue.

Vought F6U
Overall glossy sea blue.
Pirates with afterburners had bare metal skin on the aft fuselage.

No. American FJ-1
Overall sea blue.
Planes used by reserve squadrons had a band of orange FS 12197 around the fuselage.

McDonnell F2H
Overall glossy sea blue.
For a short while a clear finish was

applied over the natural metal of some F2H-3's. By the end of their careers, however, they were painted matt gull gray on the top and glossy white underneath and on both sides of the control surfaces.

Grumman F9F Panther
Prototypes: Bare metal with a black panther silhouette on each side of the nose. Production Panthers were overall glossy sea blue. Drones were overall glossy insignia red. Drone controllers had the fuselage painted glossy seaplane gray FS 16081, with wings and tail surfaces chrome yellow. Insignia red was applied

The effectiveness of the overall dark blue scheme is apparent as this photo of an F7F-2N Tigercat shows how it blends into the background.
Grumman

to the rudder and a band encircling the outer wing panels.

Vought F7U
Prototypes: Glossy sea blue.
The first F7U-3's were natural metal with a clear protective coating. Eventually the Cutlass received the new matt gull gray and white scheme.

Douglas F3D
Production of the Skyknight began during the era of glossy sea blue finishes. Ultimately, the F3D's were given the gull gray and white treatment.

Douglas F4D
The original Skyray was delivered in the standard glossy sea blue color. Skyray's used for the world speed record runs were glossy white with insignia red trim. Operational F4D's were gull gray and white.

McDonnell F3H
The first Demon was flown in bare metal. Production F3H-1's were finished in glossy sea blue but the redesigned F3H-2's wore the gull gray and white finish.

Grumman F9F Cougar
Glossy sea blue was the initial color of the Cougar. Wing and tail leading edges were bare metal. This was done because the high speeds attained by jets could cause the paint to chip and peel away with detrimental effect on the aerodynamics of the plane. This feature is typical of modern high-performance aircraft. Most Cougars received the gull gray and white camouflage, but some were used as drones and painted bright gloss insignia red overall.

No. American FJ-2/4 (Sweptwing Furys)
The FJ-2's were delivered in glossy sea blue.
FJ-3's had both natural metal finish and gull gray and white schemes. The standard scheme for the FJ-4 was gull gray and white.

Douglas F5D
All four Skylancers bore glossy white paint jobs with insignia red trim. Anti-glare panels were dark gull gray.

Lockheed XFV
Overall bare metal finish.
Spinner: Medium gray FS 36373.
Bands around tip tanks: Black.

Convair XFY
Overall bare metal.
Convair emblem: Red, white and blue.
Spinner and fin tips: Black.

Convair F2Y
Overall glossy sea blue. Visibility stripes were white or chrome yellow, depending on the airplane.

Grumman F10F
Overall glossy sea blue. The Jaguar emblem was tan, similar to FS 10371, with dark brown spots. Chest and muzzle were white.

350

Grumman F11F

The original Tiger appeared in bare metal but was soon painted overall gloss white. During tests, large areas were painted Day-glo red FS 28913. Production Tigers were finished in the now-standard matt gull gray and white.

Vought F8U

The prototype first flew in bare metal. A red arrow, thinly edged in white, appeared on the fuselage sides. The second F8U was also bare metal but had a different scheme of red areas applied behind the cockpit and along the leading edge of the fin. Production Crusaders carried the gull gray and white scheme. The F8U-3 was bare metal with Day-glo red FS 28913 outer wing panels, vertical stabilizer (except the rudder), outer stabilizer tips and the leading edges of the ventral fins. Two Day-glo bands circled the radome.

McDonnell F-4

The most widely used scheme is the standard matt gull gray and glossy white. Recently the matt gray has been replaced with a glossy gull gray.

Grumman/GD F-111

Matt gull gray and glossy white.

Grumman F-14

The first models of the Tomcat were matt gull gray and glossy white, but this is giving way to the smoother glossy gull gray and glossy white surfaces.

A clear protective finish was applied to some Navy and Marine fighters for a short time. It gave the appearance of bare metal, as seen on this F2H-3 Banshee.
McDonnell

This photo of an RF-4B shows the glossy white control surfaces typical of the gull gray and white scheme. The entire underside of the plane is glossy white.
McDonnell

A gray and white Tiger loses itself in the background clutter in this view. This scheme blends well with sky, land and water and is virtually invisible from a distance of a few miles.
U.S. Navy

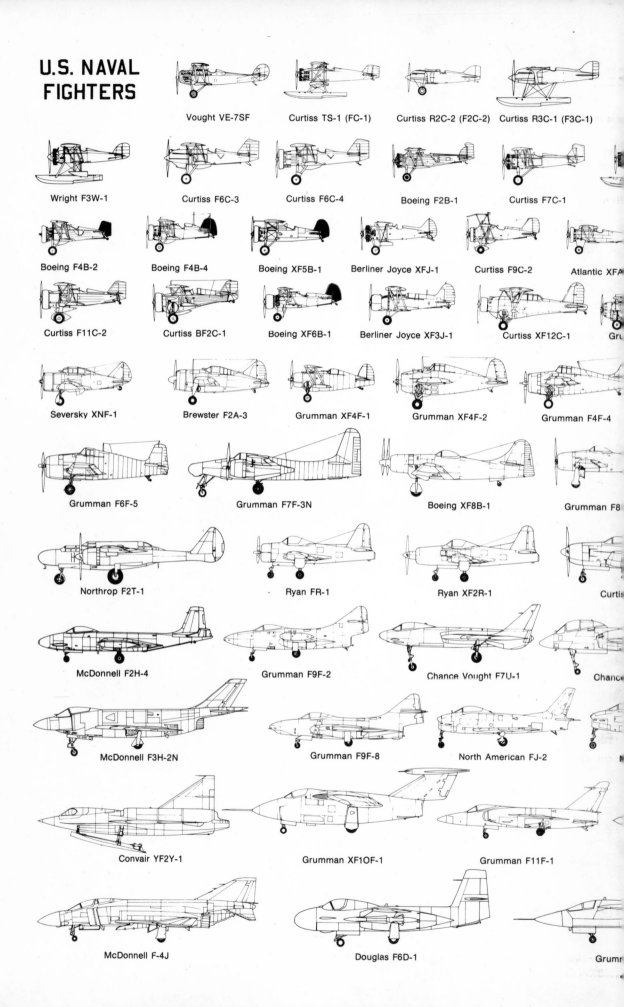

U.S. NAVAL FIGHTERS

Vought VE-7SF Curtiss TS-1 (FC-1) Curtiss R2C-2 (F2C-2) Curtiss R3C-1 (F3C-1)

Wright F3W-1 Curtiss F6C-3 Curtiss F6C-4 Boeing F2B-1 Curtiss F7C-1

Boeing F4B-2 Boeing F4B-4 Boeing XF5B-1 Berliner Joyce XFJ-1 Curtiss F9C-2 Atlantic XFA

Curtiss F11C-2 Curtiss BF2C-1 Boeing XF6B-1 Berliner Joyce XF3J-1 Curtiss XF12C-1 Gru

Seversky XNF-1 Brewster F2A-3 Grumman XF4F-1 Grumman XF4F-2 Grumman F4F-4

Grumman F6F-5 Grumman F7F-3N Boeing XF8B-1 Grumman F8

Northrop F2T-1 Ryan FR-1 Ryan XF2R-1 Curtis

McDonnell F2H-4 Grumman F9F-2 Chance Vought F7U-1 Chance

McDonnell F3H-2N Grumman F9F-8 North American FJ-2

Convair YF2Y-1 Grumman XF1OF-1 Grumman F11F-1

McDonnell F-4J Douglas F6D-1 Grumm